Pete Browning and Patrick Walsh-Atkins

Series editor: Patrick Walsh-Atkins

Cambridge International AS Level

History of the USA 1840–1941

CAMBRIDGE
UNIVERSITY PRESS

CAMBRIDGE
UNIVERSITY PRESS

University Printing House, Cambridge CB2 8BS, United Kingdom

One Liberty Plaza, 20th Floor, New York, NY 10006, USA

477 Williamstown Road, Port Melbourne, VIC 3207, Australia

4843/24, 2nd Floor, Ansari Road, Daryaganj, Delhi – 110002, India

79 Anson Road, #06–04/06, Singapore 079906

Cambridge University Press is part of the University of Cambridge.

It furthers the University's mission by disseminating knowledge in the pursuit of education, learning and research at the highest international levels of excellence.

www.cambridge.org
Information on this title: www.cambridge.org/9781107679603

First published 2013
20 19 18 17 16 15 14 13 12 11

Printed in the United Kingdom by Latimer Trend

A catalogue record for this publication is available from the British Library

ISBN 978-1-107-67960-3 Paperback

Contents

Introduction

Cambridge International AS Level History is a new series of three books that offer complete and thorough coverage of the Cambridge International AS Level History (syllabus code 9389). Each book is aimed at one of the AS History syllabuses issued by Cambridge International Examinations for first examination in 2014. These books may also prove useful for students following other A Level courses covering similar topics. Written in clear and accessible language, *Cambridge International AS Level History – History of the USA 1840–1941* enables students to gain the knowledge, understanding and skills to succeed in their AS Level course (and ultimately in further study and examination).

Syllabus and examination

Students wishing to take just the AS Level take two separate papers at the end of a one-year course. If they wish to take the full A Level there are two possible routes. The first is to take the two AS papers at the end of the first year and a further two A Level papers at the end of the following year. The second is to take the two AS papers as well as the two A Level papers at the end of a two-year course. For the full A Level, all four papers must be taken. The two AS papers are outlined below.

Paper 1 lasts for one hour and is based on *The Origins of the Civil War 1846–61*. The paper will contain at least three different sources, and candidates will have answer two questions on them. Students are not expected to have extensive historical knowledge to deal with these questions, but they are expected to be able to understand, evaluate and utilise the sources in their answers, and to have sound background knowledge of the period. In the first question (a) candidates are required to consider the sources and answer a question on one aspect of them. In the second question (b) candidates must use the sources and their own knowledge and understanding to address how far the sources support a given statement. Chapter 1 provides the appropriate level of historical knowledge to deal with Paper 1.

Paper 2 lasts for an hour and a half. This paper contains four questions, and candidates must answer two of them. Each question has two parts: part (a) requires a causal explanation; and part (b) requires consideration of significance and weighing of the relative importance of factors. A question on each of the four topics outlined in the Cambridge syllabus (for example, *The Great Crash, the Great Depression and the New Deal 1929–41*) will appear in every examination paper.

Examination skills

Chapter 6, which is entirely dedicated to helping students with examination skills and techniques, gives guidance on answering all the different types of exam questions in detail. Students should read the relevant section of the exam skills chapter *before* addressing practice questions, to remind themselves of the principles of answering each type of question. Remember that facts alone are not enough; they must be accompanied by a clear understanding of the question and must employ a range of skills such as focused writing, evaluation and analysis.

All chapters have a similar structure. The key features are as follows:

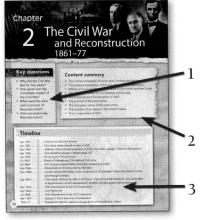

1 **Key questions** pose thought-provoking pointers to the key issues being dealt with in the chapter.

2 **Content summary** explains the essence of a chapter.

3 **Timeline** offers an overview of significant events of the period.

4 **Notes** highlight significant points from within the text.

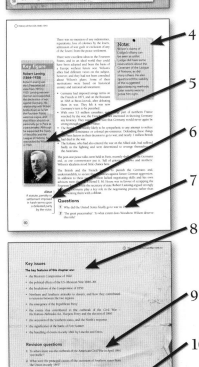

5 **Key figures** offer a detailed profile of key personalities.

6 **Definitions** of key terms enhance students' understanding of the text.

7 **Questions** interspersed within the chapters help to consolidate learning.

8 **Key issues** outline the key aspects of the content that might be significant for exam preparation.

9 **Revision questions** help students assess their own understanding and skills.

10 **Further reading** provides a list of extra resources that will help with gaining a wider perspective of the topic.

Chapter

1

The origins of the
Civil War 1846–61

Key questions

- How and why did the outcomes of the war with Mexico in 1846–48 add to sectional difficulties?
- Why did the Compromise of 1850 break down so quickly?
- Why did the Republicans win the 1860 presidential election?
- Why did the Civil War begin in April 1861?

Content summary

- The Missouri Compromise of 1820 and the Wilmot Proviso of 1846.
- The outcome of the US–Mexican War 1846–48 and the Treaty of Guadalupe Hidalgo in 1848.
- The Compromise of 1850 and the reasons for its breakdown.
- The Fugitive Slave Act and the Kansas–Nebraska Act.
- The political effect of *Uncle Tom's Cabin*.
- The formation of the Republican Party and the Republican victory in the 1860 presidential election.
- The secession of the Southern states and the outbreak of war.
- The leadership of Lincoln and Jefferson.

Timeline

Jan 1820	Missouri Compromise
Dec 1845	Texas annexed by the USA
Apr 1846	War with Mexico begins
Jun 1846	USA settles dispute with Britain over Oregon
Feb 1848	Treaty of Guadalupe Hidalgo ends US–Mexican War
Sep 1850	Compromise of 1850
May 1854	Kansas–Nebraska Act; Bleeding Kansas (to 1861)
1854–56	Formation of the Republican Party
Mar 1857	*Dred Scott* judgment
Oct 1859	Raid on Harpers Ferry
Nov 1860	Abraham Lincoln elected as president
Dec 1860	South Carolina secedes from the USA
Jan–Feb 1861	Six other states secede from the USA; the Confederacy established
Mar 1861	Lincoln inaugurated as president
Apr–May 1861	Four more states join the Confederacy

Introduction

The United States was formed in 1776–83 as the result of 13 colonies winning a revolutionary war against their British rulers. The USA was different to the monarchies and empires of the time, in that it was based on the revolutionary ideas of democratic government and liberty of the individual. Furthermore, the USA was the first nation with an official constitution – that is, a single document containing the rules by which the country was to be governed. By agreeing this constitution, the 13 states (then all located on what is now the east coast of the USA) achieved a careful compromise between their different interests. There were several points of tension between different regions of the United States, particularly between the Northern and Southern states, and these conflicts became greater over the next 70 years. Issues such as cultural and industrial differences between North and South, the ownership of slaves and the extent of state rights versus federal rights eventually led to a four-year civil war. Political attempts to resolve the conflict repeatedly failed, and more than 600,000 people died as a result of the war.

Figure 1.1 The signing of the US Constitution in 1787

Sectional tensions in the United States

In 1789, the USA consisted of 13 states based on the east coast of North America and stretching across to the Mississippi River. The rest of North America was governed – very loosely – by other European powers: Britain, Spain and Russia and, from 1800 to 1803, France. There were tensions between the new, revolutionary United States and the European powers. The colony of Louisiana, taken by France from Spain in 1800, was sold to the USA three years later for just $15 million, or 3 cents per acre. The Louisiana Purchase, as it was called, more than doubled the size of the USA.

federal
If something is described as federal, it relates to the central government of a union of states.

The USA expanded westwards and gained new lands. Those lands had to be organised into **federal** territories before being allowed to become states. This westward expansion raised an issue that would trouble US development for the next 80 years – the issue of slavery.

The two main sections of the early USA became known as the North and the South. The 13 original states were split roughly half and half, with three main differences between the sections:

- slavery
- economic differences
- cultural differences.

Note:
The difference between federal territories and states was that although both territories and states were under federal government, states had much greater freedom from federal control.

Slavery and the Missouri Compromise

In 1860, slavery was legal in the South of the USA, but was illegal in the North. The US Constitution had allowed slavery, and it was a fundamental feature of the Southern economy and society. However, by the 1820s all Northern states had banned slavery.

	White	Black and mixed race	
		Free	Slave
North	18.42 million	0.23 million	–
South	6.29 million	0.26 million	3.95 million

Table 1.1 US population by racial groups in 1860 (1860 Census, page xii)

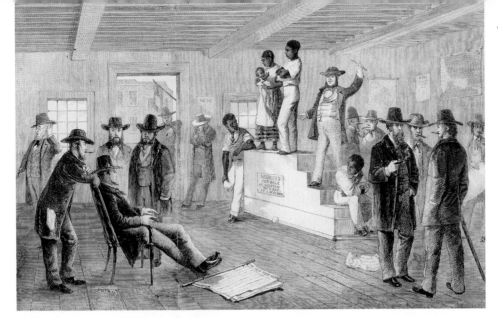

Figure 1.2 A slave auction in Virginia, 1861

More than one-third of the people in the South were slaves, and white Southerners found themselves having to try and justify slavery in various ways: economic, political and moral. As new states joined the USA, a key issue was whether they did or did not allow slavery – whether they were 'slave' states or 'free' states. The United States relied on a careful balance between these two. If that balance was disturbed, then the political stability of the nation was at risk. In 1820, plans to admit Missouri as a slave state caused problems because it upset the equal numbers of slave and free states. There were a growing number of Northerners who thought slavery was morally wrong and wanted to abolish it throughout the USA. These people were known as abolitionists.

Note:
The abolitionists became an increasingly important political force from the 1830s onwards. They came from a wide variety of groups and classes. Some were liberal humanitarians and some had deeply religious reasons for opposing slavery. They received a lot of support in the popular press of the day. Some abolitionists were prepared to support direct action and joined the 'Underground Railroad' (see page 19), helping slaves to escape to the North.

An early compromise between North and South, known as the Missouri Compromise, was eventually agreed by **Congress** in 1820. Missouri could join the United States as a slave state if Maine, in the north-east, joined as a free state. A second feature of the Compromise proved to be of great importance in the following 40 years: Congress agreed that in the Louisiana Territory bought from France in 1803, there would be no slavery in lands north of latitude 36° 30' that were still awaiting statehood. The only exception to this was the state of Missouri itself.

Congress
The legislative (law-making) branch of the US government is made up of elected members and divided into two chambers – the Senate and the House of Representatives. There must be a majority agreement in both houses in order for legislation to be passed.

Figure 1.3 A map of the 1820 Missouri Compromise, showing free and slave states

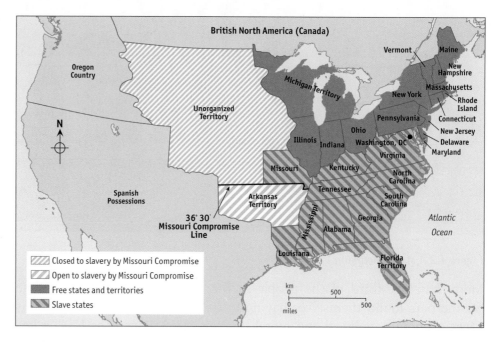

Economic differences

Economic and social differences between the North and South became more apparent over time, especially after the Northern states abolished slavery in the early 19th century. Population growth was one major difference between North and South. By 1860, the original 13 states of the USA had grown to 18 free states and 15 slave states. The North's population was 18.65 million, the South's 10.5 million. A higher standard of living was primarily responsible for the North's population growth, but another important factor was that the North was the destination for the majority of immigrants to the USA.

Another major difference between North and South was the growth of industry in the North. Increasing internal and foreign trade, helped by transport changes (canals, roads and river use), led to the growth of a range of industries such as engineering and textiles. With great support for business and enterprise from state governments, and the growth of a mobile society that respected wealth and business skills, a very different socio-economic system emerged in the North than existed in the South.

Not everyone saw industrialisation as either desirable or inevitable. The South didn't welcome industrialisation, and largely retained its agrarian (farming-based) economy with much less industrial production – in 1860, only 8% of US factories were located in the South. A large part of the Southern workforce was involved in the production of cotton, with some tobacco and rice, and slaves were vital to the harvesting of those crops. Foreign competition had led to the lowering of cotton prices on the world market, and many of the larger farmers and slave owners were falling into debt. There was growing feeling in the South that its economic interests were being sacrificed in order to increase the profits of Northern industrialists.

Note:

As production on the plantations was very labour-intensive, the plantation owners used slaves to grow and harvest the cotton and also to work in the mills to produce the raw cotton cloth. This free labour was essential to the plantation owners' profits.

Figure 1.4 A cotton gin (machine for extracting cotton fibres from their seeds) in the Southern United States

By the 1850s, more than half of US exports consisted of raw cotton, largely sent to the Lancashire cotton mills in Britain. The economic interests of the South and North began to come into conflict. The South supported **free trade** in order to encourage greater trade with Britain. The North wanted **tariffs** to protect the new industries being formed in the Northern region against competition with Britain. Some historians argue that these economic differences were more important than slavery in causing the Civil War.

Cultural differences

North and South were divided not only socially and economically, but also culturally. Although Americans from the North and South came from the same European emigrants, by the middle of the 19th century different social values were emerging in the two regions. In particular, the importance of 'honour' was still central to Southern life, while it was disappearing from the North. Honour is a code of duties imposed by a social group on its members. If your honour was questioned, you had to defend it – to the death if necessary. Therefore violence was part of this 'honour' code, usually taking the form of duels. In the North, states began passing laws that suppressed duelling, and a formal legal code started to replace an informal social code.

Some historians argue that the cultural distinctiveness of the South was so great that it is possible to speak of an independent Southern nationalism, based on slavery, chivalry and a strong Christian faith. The North's own regional identity was based on free labour, liberty and a more puritanical Christianity.

free trade
This describes international trade that is left to run its course according to market forces rather than being manipulated through tariffs, quotas or other restrictions.

tariffs
Tariffs are taxes or duties paid on certain imported and exported goods. Tariffs mean that particular imported products or materials are more expensive to consumers. By selectively restricting foreign trade in this way, governments can encourage consumers to buy from alternate sources – often from inside the country itself.

From all quarters of South Carolina have come to my ears the echoes of the same voice; it may be feigned but it sounds in wonderful strength all over the country, 'nothing on earth shall ever induce us to submit to any union with the brutal, bigoted blackguards of the New England states, who neither comprehend nor regard the feelings of gentlemen! Man, woman and child, we'll die first.'

Imagine these and an infinite variety of similar sentiments uttered by courtly, well-educated men, who set great store on a nice observance of the usages of society and who are only moved to extreme bitterness and anger when they speak of the North and you will fail to conceive the intensity of the dislike of the South Carolinians for the free states. There is nothing in the dark caves of human passion so cruel and deadly as the hatred the South Carolinians profess for the Yankees.

From *Pictures of Southern Life* by British author William Howard Russell, 1861.

The North is prosperous and the South is not. The one increases and multiplies by a process which freedom and civilization constantly accelerates. The South goes far backward by a process which ignorance and slavery inaugurate. The wealth, the power, the intelligence, the religion and advanced civilization are with the first. The last is secondary and retrograde. It is the infirmity of semi-barbarous men to hate what they cannot imitate; hence the bitterness which marks the utterances and emphasizes the actions of the rebels. Dislike of what is above and beyond them is at the bottom of this.

From the *Chicago Tribune*, February 1861.

Political issues

Understanding the political tensions that began to develop in the 19th century requires an initial awareness of the US political system, which was founded on the 1787 Constitution:

- The USA is a republic, the head of state being an elected president.
- The USA is a federal state, with powers shared between the national government – known as the federal government – in Washington, DC, and the various states.

- The US system of government is based on a system of **checks and balances** to ensure that no one part of government becomes too powerful.
- The US government is built on the idea of the **separation of powers**. The elected national assembly, Congress (see page 9), makes the laws. The separately elected president is in office for four years, and recommends national policies. The Supreme Court decides whether the politicians' laws and policies are within the rules of the Constitution.
- Amending the Constitution is very difficult. To do so, two-thirds of both houses of Congress and three-quarters of the states have to agree.

checks and balances
Each branch of government is able to veto (prevent) or amend acts or decisions made by other branches.

separation of powers
Separate branches of government are given separate powers that other branches have no control over (apart from overseeing fair practice with checks and balances).

Although the creators of the US Constitution had hoped to create a system of government that would prevent political parties ever being formed, this did not happen. National political parties began to emerge immediately after independence, and initially they proved to be important unifying factors in the United States. There were plenty of issues, such as expansion, on which people in both the North and the South could agree. Issues that might prove divisive, such as slavery, tended to be left to local politicians to deal with, rather than being raised at a national level. However, once slavery became a national issue, political parties became forces for disunity.

Note:
By the 1840s, two political parties had emerged: the Democrats and the Whigs. Both were national parties that attracted support across the USA. In broad terms, the Democrats identified more with rural, agricultural America and were very suspicious of the federal government taking too much power from the states. The Whigs were more concerned with the growing industrial towns and cities. They wanted to use the powers of federal government to protect and develop a more integrated national economy.

Another issue that divided the North and South and further split the national parties was the nature and extent of the powers of the president and Congress. Many Southern states and Democrats from the South were anxious to prevent a president or Congress from harming their interests – particularly in the case of slavery. They wanted to ensure that a state could retain the right to legislate for itself and not be dictated to by a president or Congress in Washington, DC. Northern Democrats were less hostile to growth in the power of federal government, so 'states' rights' (the right of a state to decide its own destiny) became an issue that divided parties, as well as North and South.

Questions

1 What picture do Sources A, B and C below paint of Southern society?

2 What arguments do Sources B and C give for and against slavery?

3 Read through all three sources. Which source is more useful for a historian? Which is more reliable? Explain your answers.

Source A

Each bank [of the Ohio River] forms the frontier of a vast state: the one on the left is called Kentucky, the other [on the right] takes its name from the river itself. The two states differ in only one respect: Kentucky has accepted slaves but Ohio has rejected them.

On the left bank of the river, the population is sparse; occasionally a troop of slaves can be seen loitering in half-deserted fields; society seems to be asleep; man looks idle while nature looks active and alive.

On the right bank, a confused hum announces from a long way off the presence of industrial activity; the fields are covered by abundant harvests; elegant dwellings proclaim the taste and industry of the workers; in every direction there is evidence of comfort; men appear wealthy and content; they are at work.

Alexis de Tocqueville (a French writer), Democracy in America, 1835.

Source B

I appeal to facts. The black race of central Africa came to us in a low, degraded and savage condition. In the course of a few generations it has grown up under the fostering care of our institutions to its present comparatively civilized condition. This, with the rapid increase of numbers, is conclusive proof of the general happiness of the black race, in spite of all the exaggerated tales to the contrary.

In the meantime, the white race [in the South] has not degenerated. It has kept pace with its brethren in other parts of the Union where slavery does not exist. Have we not contributed our full share of talents and political wisdom in forming and sustaining this political system? Have we not constantly inclined more strongly to the side of liberty and been the first to resist the encroachments of power?

An extract from a speech to the US Senate by the senator for South Carolina, John Calhoun, 1837.

Source C

The question of slavery is undeniably, for this country at least, the great question of the age. On the right decision of it depend interests too vast to be fitly set forth in words. Here are three millions of slaves in a land calling itself free; three millions of human beings robbed of every right, and, by statute and custom, among a people self-styled Christian, held as brutes.

Knowledge is forbidden, and religious worship, if allowed, is clogged with fetters; the sanctity of marriage is denied; and home and family and all the sacred names of kindred, which form the dialect of domestic love, are made unmeaning words. The soul is crushed, that the body may be safely coined into dollars.

Charles Burleigh, 'Slavery and the North' (an abolitionist tract), 1855.

The outcomes of the war with Mexico

> *Up until the Mexican war, there were committed abolitionists, men who carried their hostility to slavery into all elections. They were noisy but not numerous … Opposition was not a creed of either political party. In some sections, more anti-slavery men belonged to the Democratic Party and in others to the Whigs. But with the inauguration of the Mexican war, in fact with the annexation of Texas, the 'inevitable' conflict commenced.*
>
> Ulysses S. Grant, *Personal Memoirs*, 1885–86.

The extract above is from a book by **Ulysses S. Grant**, military leader of the Union (Northern) armies in 1864–65 and US president between 1869 and 1877. Grant's perception of when the Civil War commenced provides a useful starting point for explaining how events unfolded from the annexation of Texas in 1845 to the outbreak of the war 16 years later.

Figure 1.5 The attack over Chapultepec (1846) during the US–Mexican War

Key figure

Ulysses S. Grant (1822–85)

Grant was a career soldier who, despite a difficult start at his military academy, was an excellent horseman and a keen fighter. Not content with his responsibilities as a quartermaster in the US–Mexican War, he went to the frontlines to engage in combat. He had much success as a general during the Civil War, and went on to become US president in 1869.

The Wilmot Proviso and the Treaty of Guadalupe Hidalgo

Tensions between Mexico and the USA over Texas

Until it declared independence in 1836, Texas was part of Mexico. In the decades leading up to 1836, American settlers had moved to Texas, many of them with slaves. Slavery, however, was illegal in Mexico. The Mexican government tried to assert its authority and the settlers resisted, eventually declaring Texas's independence from Mexico. Some Texans wanted to join with the USA, others to keep complete independence. Eventually, in 1845, the United States offered to **annex** Texas. A year later, an agreement was reached and Texas became a state in the USA.

annex
Annexing a territory means incorporating it into an existing political entity such as a country, state or city.

Mexico refused to accept the loss of Texas without a fight. Conflict between the USA and Mexico grew much more likely when **James Polk** became president in 1845. He was a keen expansionist, a strong believer in 'manifest destiny' and in his election campaign he had promised to annex Texas if elected.

Note:
Manifest destiny was the belief that the continued expansion of the United States across the North American continent was a pre-ordained, entirely positive development.

Key figure

James Polk (1795–1849)

Polk was president of the USA from 1845 to 1849. He was a Democrat and a committed expansionist, and hoped to acquire much of Mexico, California and Oregon. He believed the USA should have a strong and assertive presidency. Polk died as a result of overwork after serving a single term in the White House.

Polk proved to be the major cause of the war with Mexico. He had offered to buy the two northernmost territories of Mexico for $25 million, but the Mexicans turned him down. He then sent US troops beyond the Nueces River, the recognised border between Texas and Mexico, to the Rio Grande, 240 km (150 miles) further south, which the Mexicans did not accept as the border. Here, US troops provoked a clash with Mexican forces and war followed. Mexico was invaded and the capital taken by US troops, who remained there until a peace treaty was signed.

The Treaty of Guadalupe Hidalgo

On 2 February 1848 at Guadalupe Hidalgo, close to Mexico City, the United States agreed a treaty that reflected the scale of the American victory. The USA gained two territories, Upper California and New Mexico, as well as establishing the Rio Grande as the new boundary between Texas and Mexico. In return for this huge territory gain, which reduced the size of Mexico by half, the USA paid Mexico $15 million. The name of the region that thus became part of the USA was The Mexican Cession.

How the Cession was to be included in the USA posed major political problems. Much of it lay to the south of the dividing line between free and slave states laid down by the Missouri Compromise, now 25 years old and broadly accepted by North and South. Some Northerners felt that

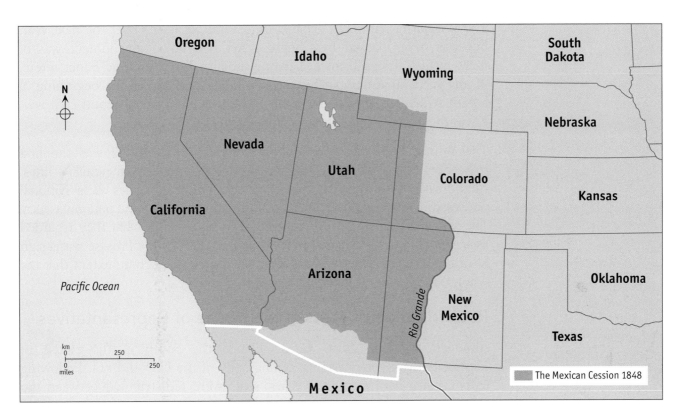

Figure 1.6 A map showing The Mexican Cession, the territory gained by the USA in the Treaty of Guadalupe Hidalgo

the informal division of power between the two regions was tilting in the direction of the South, because it seemed likely that if new territories became states they would be slave states. The North began to talk of 'Slave Power', the excessive political power of slave owners in the South.

Another factor causing a split between North and South was the way in which the Constitution allocated members to the popularly elected part of Congress, the House of Representatives. This was decided based on the population of a state, with a certain number of people per representative. However, although slaves could not vote, they still counted as three-fifths of a 'person'. With slaves only existing in the Southern states, this meant in practice that the South had 17 more members in the House of Representatives than the North felt it should have.

The Wilmot Proviso

The North attempted to limit what it perceived as the South's growing power by introducing the Wilmot Proviso. In August 1846, a Democratic congressman, David Wilmot, from the Northern state of Pennsylvania, introduced an amendment to a congressional bill that would provide President Polk with $2 million to assist in peace talks with Mexico. Many believed that the money would be used to buy territory from Mexico. Wilmot's brief amendment simply stated that slavery was not to be permitted in any land gained from Mexico, whether it was purchased or won in war.

The Wilmot Proviso was debated on several occasions over the next year, but was never passed by Congress. Yet this failed amendment was of great historical significance. Leading modern historian Eric Foner wrote: 'If any event in American history can be singled out as the beginning of a path which led almost inevitably to sectional controversy and civil war, it was the introduction of the Wilmot Proviso.'

The Wilmot Proviso's rejection by Congress in 1846–47 was the first indication of politicians voting on sectional – that is, regional – lines. In the early 19th century, the USA's two political parties were national parties, drawing support from both North and South around national issues. The political parties did not concern themselves with what they regarded as sectional issues, such as slavery. However, the Wilmot Proviso was a sign of things to come: the divisions it revealed grew to such an extent that the whole party system underwent a profound change.

Redistribution of seats in the House of Representatives

Although the three-fifths clause helped the South in the House of Representatives, the changing demography of the USA did not. Following each census, held every ten years, seats were redistributed between the various states.

Date	Total no. of seats	North		South	
		No. of seats	Percentage of seats	No. of seats	Percentage of seats
1827	213	123	57.7	90	42.3
1845	224	135	60.3	89	39.7
1861	237	147	62.0	90	38.0

Table 1.2 US House of Representatives: number and distribution of seats 1827–61

The table above shows the gradual decline in the proportion of Southern members of the House of Representatives. This, coupled with the increase in free states that each sent two senators to the Senate, led Southerners to fear that with a minority in Congress they would not be able to prevent the North from imposing its will on the South.

The Compromise of 1850 and its breakdown

The Wilmot Proviso, and its failed outcome, aroused anxieties in both the North and the South. This in turn raised other national issues concerning slavery, of which two proved particularly important:

- **The continuing slave trade in Washington, DC:** the US capital was not a state and therefore slavery in the district was a responsibility of the US federal government. Abolitionists wanted an end to this slave trade, while slave owners and traders believed that this would set a precedent for abolishing the slave trade between states.
- **The flight of fugitive slaves from slave states to free states:** slave owners had a constitutional right to regain escaped slaves if they were discovered. The Fugitive Slave Act of 1793 stated that federal officials had a duty to help return fugitive slaves, and that slave owners could receive compensation money from people who helped the slaves escape.

Note:
Washington, DC (the 'DC' stands for District of Columbia) is the capital of the USA but is officially not part of any state. It is administered directly by Congress.

By 1848, 12 Northern states had passed more than 40 personal liberty laws that aimed to counter the 1793 Fugitive Slave Act and to help fugitive slaves in their escape. In addition, since the early 19th century abolitionists had developed what became known as the 'Underground Railroad': a secret network of people who helped fugitives escape from the South and reach the North. Southern slave owners argued that their constitutional rights were being undermined by the North, and demanded a new Fugitive Slave Act.

Figure 1.7 A portrait of a slave named Anthony Burns, surrounded by illustrations of his escape from slavery, his trial and his return to slavery

Federal politicians faced a great challenge in settling all of the political issues related to slavery. Throughout 1850 there was a lot of complex bargaining, which in itself signified the growing difficulty of reaching agreement on this sensitive issue. An official compromise was eventually reached in September of that year, and it is simply known as the Compromise of 1850. This development was made easier by the death of President Zachary Taylor in July 1850. Taylor had proved not to be as enthusiastic a supporter of the South as the Southern states had hoped; he wanted to avoid any discussion on slavery. The appointment of Taylor's more flexible vice president, Millard Fillmore, in his place, led to an agreement over some of these issues.

Elements of the Compromise of 1850

The Compromise of 1850 was a set of agreements that consisted of four separate elements:

- California joined the USA as a free state, even though some of California was below the 1820 Missouri Compromise line (see page 9). The people of California wanted it to be a free state.
- New Mexico and Utah, the two remaining parts of The Mexican Cession, became US territories with no specified slave status. The people of the territories would decide later whether the territories would be free or slave.
- The slave trade was abolished in Washington, DC.
- A new Fugitive Slave Act was passed. It imposed criminal penalties on anyone interfering with a slave owner's rights to his slaves, and restricted the legal rights of fugitive slaves to a fair trial.

The Compromise of 1850 was an example of Congress working to resolve national tensions. All sides compromised, and although no one was entirely happy with the result, it did temporarily reduce the risk of civil war.

Implementing the Fugitive Slave Act of 1850

The new Fugitive Slave Act, passed in 1850, included the following key elements:

- Any federal marshal or other official who did not arrest a known fugitive slave was liable for a heavy fine. Officials who arrested a fugitive slave were entitled to a bonus.
- A slave owner's claim that a slave was a fugitive was sufficient cause for arrest.
- If arrested, fugitive slaves could not claim trial by jury nor legally represent themselves. This meant that many free African-Americans were actually arrested and became slaves, as they could not defend themselves.

The South felt that it was making territorial concessions – none of the new states and territories were slave – in return for the North's support in upholding the Fugitive Slave provision of the Constitution.

However, if agreeing the Compromise of 1850 had proved hard work, implementing the Fugitive Slave Act was even harder. Abolitionists now had to decide whether to uphold or defy the law, and many prominent Northern abolitionists chose to publicly resist the Fugitive Slave Act.

Uncle Tom's Cabin

The publication of a novel called *Uncle Tom's Cabin* in 1852 compounded difficulties for the federal government. This anti-slavery book, written by **Harriet Beecher Stowe**, centred on the character of African-American slave 'Uncle Tom' and exposed the cruel realities of slavery.

Figure 1.8 A first edition of Uncle Tom's Cabin, *1852*

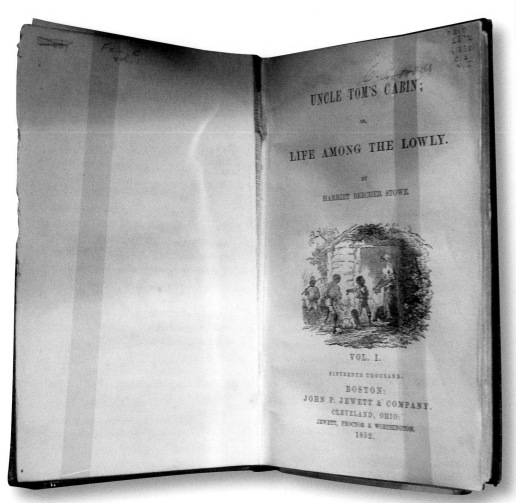

Key figure

Harriet Beecher Stowe (1811–96)

Stowe was a staunch abolitionist who wrote *Uncle Tom's Cabin* partly in response to what she saw as the injustices of the Fugitive Slave Act. She took up writing to help support her large family and was genuinely surprised at her national and international success, and at the impact her work had. When Lincoln met Stowe he said, 'So you are the little woman who wrote the book that started this great war?'

The book was an instant bestseller: 300,000 copies were sold in the first year, and it became the most successful novel of the 19th century. It was also turned into a play, and was therefore seen by many who did not read books. Its sentimental story had a great impact on public life in the USA, weakening the perceived case for slavery and fuelling the abolitionist cause. Southern authors wrote books, both factual and fictional, to try to counter the impact of *Uncle Tom's Cabin*, but to no avail.

36° 30' line
This is a circle of latitude: an imaginary line running around the Earth, connecting all the places whose position is along that line.

Key figure

Stephen Douglas (1813–61)

Douglas was the Democratic Party nominee for president in 1860. Despite winning several debates against the Republican candidate Abraham Lincoln, Douglas lost out to him in the presidential elections. A supporter of the Union who was married to a slave owner, Douglas was an advocate of popular sovereignty in the states as a solution to all problems. He ended up being strongly disliked in both the North and the South.

It is difficult to appreciate the impact the book had at the time, not least because the novel's two-dimensional, stereotypical characterisation of African-American people has been heavily criticised in more recent times. 'Uncle Tom' has become a term of abuse used to describe a black person who is subservient to white people and their culture.

The Kansas–Nebraska Act of 1854

There was a widespread hope that the Compromise of 1850 had settled the territorial dimension of slavery in the USA for the foreseeable future. However, within a few years the issue of the slave/free status of new territories and states returned. The focus was now on the parts of the Louisiana Purchase of 1803 (see page 8) that were north of the **36° 30' line** accepted as the division between slave and free states.

In 1820, the Missouri Compromise had established Missouri as a slave state located west of the Mississippi and east of the Missouri River. According to that 1820 Compromise, Missouri was the only slave state or territory that could be established within the Louisiana Purchase north of the specified 36° 30' line.

In 1852, the remaining Purchase lands had still not been organised into territories. Leading Northern Democrat senator **Stephen Douglas** of Illinois, among others, decided it was time that these territories were created. Settlers wanted to move into the region and needed effective government to do so. In addition, territorial status would allow the building of a transcontinental railway across the central USA.

Douglas realised that he needed the support of Southern congressmen and senators to pass a bill to create these territories. His plan was that the people of the new territory, Nebraska, would be able to decide for themselves whether this would be a slave or a free state. In January 1854, Douglas persuaded a reluctant President Franklin Pierce, another Democrat, to support the bill. It would apply popular sovereignty to what would now be two territories: Nebraska, the northern of the two, to the west of the free state of Iowa; and Kansas, west of the slave state of Missouri.

The Kansas–Nebraska Bill caused a great political storm. Southern Democrats used it as a test of party loyalty for Northern Democrats. Many failed the test, and the Democratic Party was split. Much the same happened to the Whigs. The national party system of the past 30 years was broken by the power of sectional rivalry.

The Kansas–Nebraska Act effectively repealed the Missouri Compromise of 1820, as the states had the option of choosing to be slave states rather than their free status being assured by federal law due to their geographic position. This was supported in the South and heavily opposed in the North.

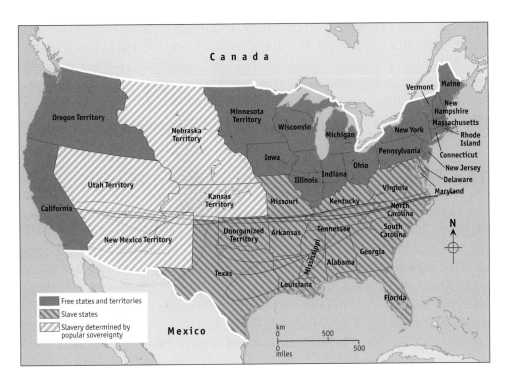

Figure 1.9 A map showing the outcome of the Kansas–Nebraska Act of 1854

'Bleeding Kansas'

In 1854, according to one estimate, just 1400 people lived in Kansas (Native Americans were not counted). If the free/slave status of this new territory was to be decided by its people, as the Kansas–Nebraska Act stated, supporters of slavery and abolitionism both quickly realised it was important to fill Kansas with as many of their own sympathisers as possible.

People moved into the territory with great speed, and an accurate population count a year later listed 8501 people living in Kansas. In the rush to gain control, the South had a great advantage. On the eastern border of Kansas was Missouri, a slave state, with a population of nearly 600,000 whites and 87,000 slaves.

The first territorial election in Kansas was planned for the spring of 1855. Rumours spread that anti-slavery groups from the north-east were planning to send 20,000 supporters to dominate the election. Around 5000 men from Missouri, known as the 'border ruffians', were sent to 'persuade' voters to support Kansas becoming a slave territory.

The election resulted in a pro-slavery vote of 5427 and a free-state vote of 791. The pro-slave winners threw out the few anti-slavers who had been elected to the legislature, and put through a law that made it a hanging offence to help a slave escape.

> **Note:**
> The border ruffians were some 5000 men, many of them armed, who crossed from Missouri and controlled the Kansas election by methods such as intimidation and illegal ballot papers. They continued to cause havoc across Kansas over the next few years.

Those opposed to slavery then held their own illegal election, wrote their own constitution that banned slavery in the territory, and elected a new governor and legislature. The result was a local civil war between the two 'governments', in which over 200 people died. This was a warning of things to come: the struggle over slavery was becoming increasingly violent. Furthermore, the events of the early 1850s – the Compromise of 1850 and the Kansas–Nebraska Act – caused many in the North to realise it was time to form a new party.

The formation of the Republican Party

The 1850s saw a major reorganisation of US political parties. Slavery, traditionally a sectional issue, had started to significantly affect national politics. Northern Whigs, Northern Democrats and the Free Soil Party came together between 1854 and 1856, united by their support for abolitionism, and formed the Republican Party. The Free Soil Party had been formed in 1848 by those strongly opposed to slavery, although few Free Soilers wanted immediate abolition. The party's full slogan was 'Free Soil, Free Speech, Free Labour and Free Men'. It had little political impact. However, when the Free Soilers joined with many Northern Whigs and Democrats, first of all in states such as Wisconsin and then across the North, they became a much greater political force. What kept these groups together was opposition to government policies towards Kansas and a desire to prevent any expansion of slavery.

For the 1856 presidential election, these groups combined in the Republican Party to become the main challenger to the increasingly 'Southern' Democrats. The Republican presidential candidate was John Frémont (see page 71), a well-known and popular explorer from California who had minimal political experience. Opposing him was the Democrats' candidate, James Buchanan, who strongly sympathised with Southern aspirations.

The North was a two-horse race between Buchanan and Frémont. Buchanan was victorious, winning five Northern states and 14 Southern states. Although Buchanan was the only candidate to win states in both North and South, his strength was clearly in the South. The electorate, and therefore the parties, were dividing along sectional lines. Mutual misunderstandings grew about the aims and intentions of both sides. There was much talk of **secession**, mainly in the South. The USA needed some calm and effective leadership in the next four years to avoid the eruption of conflict. Within three days of Buchanan's inauguration, however, the next milestone on the road to civil war came into sight.

secession
The act of withdrawing from an organisation, union or political entity. In the context of the USA, it typically refers to the withdrawal of a state from the United States.

Questions

1 To what extent did the Kansas–Nebraska Act reveal the inability of the US government to solve the problems caused by slavery?

2 How did the formation of the Republican Party increase the danger of civil war in the United States?

3 How would you define the North's position on slavery? Is the division of North = abolitionist and South = pro-slavery too simplistic?

4 Read the information below about the cartoon in Source A. What does the cartoon tell you about the nature of US politics during this troubled period?

Source A

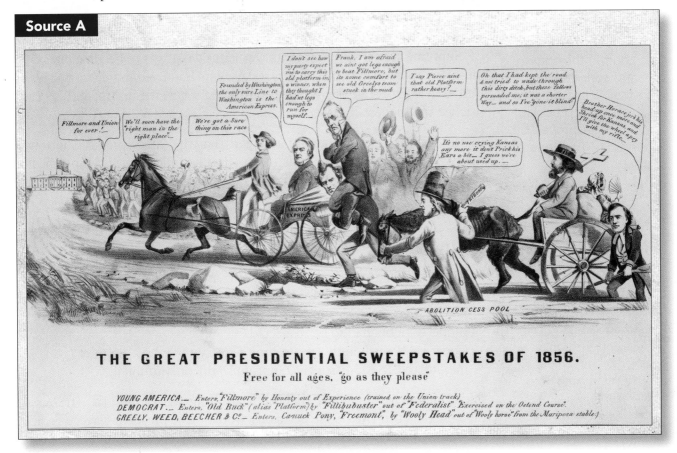

THE GREAT PRESIDENTIAL SWEEPSTAKES OF 1856.

Free for all ages, "go as they please"

The cartoon above, published some time before the 1856 presidential election, puts Millard Fillmore (see page 20) in the lead in the race for the White House. At the bottom of the page we are told that he is entered by Young America, bred by Honesty out of Experience. Next comes Buchanan, who is being carried by the current president, Franklin Pierce. Last comes Freemont [sic], entered by Horace Greeley (editor of the *New York Tribune*), Thurlow Weed and Henry Ward Beecher (Harriet Beecher Stowe's brother), all leading abolitionists. Frémont's carriage is being pulled by an old horse, which symbolises abolitionism. The horse is stuck in the cesspool of abolitionism. Frémont's jockey, carrying a cross that symbolises Catholicism, regrets his decision to go down the abolitionist route. Henry Ward Beecher tries to pull his carriage out of the pool by using a rifle as a lever.

The 1860 presidential election

Key figure

Abraham Lincoln (1809–65)

Lincoln was born to a poor farming family. A largely self-taught lawyer, he went on to serve for one term as a Whig in the House of Representatives. In 1856, he helped form the Republican Party. Lincoln stood for the Senate in 1858. In 1860, he won the presidential election as a Republican with just 39% of the vote. He remained president until he was assassinated in April 1865.

The *Dred Scott* case

Two days after Buchanan was inaugurated as president in March 1857, the US **Supreme Court** announced its verdict in what was to become one of its most famous cases. Dred Scott was a slave who had lived in free territories as well as in a slave state. He went to court to gain US citizenship, and his case reached the highest court in the nation.

By the 1850s, it was generally accepted that the US Supreme Court had the right of judicial review. This means that it could review the policies of the president and the laws of Congress to decide if they were constitutional or not.

In March 1857, in the case of *Dred Scott* v *Sandford*, the Supreme Court made three rulings:

- Dred Scott had no right to be a US citizen.
- Dred Scott was bound by the laws of the slave state he had left, and not the free territories in which he had lived; the original slave owner's property rights had to be respected.
- Congress had no authority to limit slavery to certain parts of the USA, making the 1820 Missouri Compromise unconstitutional.

These judgments delighted the South and angered the North. The South thought that the *Dred Scott* decisions would help preserve slavery against increasing abolitionist pressure from the Northern-based Republican Party. The North saw the judgments as evidence of the Supreme Court's bias – five of the judges were from slave states. There was talk of a conspiracy between Southern Democrats in Congress, the presidency and the Supreme Court.

The Lincoln–Douglas debates

The judgment in *Dred Scott* raised the question of the place of slavery within the USA. What had been confined to the South for a generation could now expand across the USA, as the judgment affirmed that every state government in the country should be able to decide on slavery without federal government intervention. The national debate on the subject became personified by two politicians: Stephen Douglas and **Abraham Lincoln**, Democrat and Republican respectively.

Abraham Lincoln helped found the Republican Party in 1856, and aimed to be a US senator for Illinois in 1858. Stephen Douglas – known as the 'Little Giant' – was a leading Democrat and a member of the US Senate since 1843, who was up for re-election for Illinois. Douglas had been a leading proponent of the popular sovereignty doctrine and proposed the controversial Kansas–Nebraska Act of 1854 (see page 22). Lincoln and Douglas took opposing views on slavery, a topic that they argued in a series of debates during the 1858 election campaign. Before the debates even began, however, Lincoln set out his position in what became known as the 'House Divided' speech.

'A house divided against itself cannot stand.' I believe this government cannot endure permanently half slave and half free. I do not expect the Union to be dissolved – I do not expect the house to fall – but I do expect it will cease to be divided. It will become all one thing or all the other. Either the opponents of slavery will arrest the further spread of it … or its advocates will push it forward till it shall become alike lawful in all the states, old as well as new, North as well as South.

Abraham Lincoln, June 1858. To read the entire speech, go to quod.lib.umich.edu/l/lincoln/lincoln2/1:508.1?rgn=div2;view=fulltext

Lincoln's pessimistic analysis of the *Dred Scott* judgment argued that it was part of the Democratic strategy to expand slavery. Yet while the Republicans were united in their opposition to the Supreme Court ruling, the Democrats were divided. Some, mainly in the South, supported the judgment. Stephen Douglas found himself in a very difficult position. As the author of the Kansas–Nebraska Act, he was a keen advocate of popular sovereignty – the right of the people (although only a selected electorate) of a territory to choose whether to live in a free or slave state. Douglas could not reject *Dred Scott* and yet he could not fully support it because of its pro-slavery implications. The compromise he came up with during the debates with Lincoln was the Freeport Doctrine. This stated that the people of a state or territory should have the right to vote for its slave or free status, and that they should subsequently be able to refuse any legislation that went against this decision.

Douglas was put in another difficult position by developments in Kansas. The pro-slavery assembly in the territory had agreed on its constitution, the Lecompton Constitution. After a complex and very dubious series of elections and referendums to legitimise the constitution, it was submitted to the US Congress with a request for statehood. Needing to maintain his support among Southern Democrats, President Buchanan decided to support their request. Stephen Douglas, believing in popular sovereignty and trying to develop his support among Northern Democrats, had to oppose it. In December 1857, the two men had a face-to-face row in the White House. Relations were never repaired. The Democratic Party was now divided firmly into Northern and Southern Democrats. Some Northern Democrats had already left the party to join the Republicans.

The row over the Lecompton Constitution for Kansas had long-lasting consequences. The majority in the Senate refused to agree to Kansas's request for statehood and it served to divide North and South still further. In January 1861, Kansas did at last join the USA – as a free state.

Lincoln and Douglas had seven long debates in the summer of 1858, almost entirely focused on the issue of slavery. The debates gave huge publicity to the issue and helped Lincoln to become a national figure. Douglas won the election to the Senate, although Lincoln went on to win the presidential election against Douglas in 1860. In the time between these two elections, another event was to bring civil war closer for the USA.

> **Note:**
> Only one Senate seat per state is up for re-election at a time. The election for the other Senate seat comes either two or four years later.

Key figure

Robert E. Lee (1807–70)

Lee was general of the Confederate army during the Civil War, and was Jefferson Davis's senior military advisor. He was an able general who hoped to bring victory to the South by destroying the North's army in battle. He came close to achieving this at the Battle of Gettysburg (see page 42), but the North's victory in this battle led to the South's defeat in the Civil War.

The raid on Harpers Ferry 1859

On 16 October 1859, a group of 22 men – 17 white and five black – attacked the US army's munitions depot in the town of Harpers Ferry, Virginia. Their leader was John Brown, who had been involved in fighting in the Kansas–Nebraska conflict. Brown was an abolitionist who often resorted to violence. He hoped that the seizure of weapons would encourage African-Americans in the area to rise in support. No uprising occurred. The local militia regained control of the town, killing eight of the rebels in the process. US troops, led by Colonel **Robert E. Lee**, quickly recaptured the fire-engine house in which the rebels made their last stand. Brown was caught alive but wounded. The surviving rebels were tried and punished. This disorganised, short-lived attempt to provoke rebellion became significant not for the events of the raid, but for the responses to it.

Figure 1.10 The raid on Harpers Ferry, with militia firing on the rebels from the railway bridge and trapping John Brown's group in the fire-engine house

John Brown's behaviour in the aftermath of the raid won him considerable public sympathy. In the last few weeks of his life, he showed great dignity and courage. In court, having been sentenced to death, he made a five-minute speech that people have compared to Lincoln's Gettysburg Address. Almost a century later, in 1950, the historian Allen Nevins wrote: 'In his last weeks John Brown rose to a height of moral grandeur which went far to redeeming his name from the terrible blots which he had placed upon it.' Brown was hanged on 2 December 1859.

The American people, especially in the North and West, displayed a strong emotional reaction to Brown's execution. In Lawrence, Kansas, the editor of the *Republican* wrote: 'The death of no man in America has ever produced so profound a sensation. A feeling of deep and sorrowful indignation seems to possess the masses.'

Victor Hugo, the French novelist, wrote an open letter on the day of Brown's hanging, pleading that he be spared. Henry Ward Beecher said that people should not pray for Brown's release: 'Let Virginia make him a martyr … His soul was noble, his work miserable. But a cord and a gibbet would redeem all that and round up Brown's failure with heroic success.' Although many disagreed with Brown's actions, they also argued that slavery itself was wrong. He became a hero – a martyr to those opposed to slavery.

In the South, however, the raid on Harpers Ferry confirmed people's worst fears about the Northern abolitionist threat to slavery. Rumours and suspicions only added to these fears. Visitors to the South who were thought to be abolitionists risked being whipped, **tarred and feathered** or hanged. The contrasting responses of the North and South to the death of John Brown shows how divided the USA had become by the end of the 1850s. A presidential election was due in November 1860. Buchanan's presidency had widened sectional divisions; the president elected in 1860 could be decisive in deciding the future of the United States.

tarred and feathered
Being covered with boiling hot tar and then a large number of downy feathers, so that the tar burns the skin and sticks the feathers to the body.

The election of Abraham Lincoln

Lincoln was the surprise winner of the 1860 election, but he had also been an unexpected victor in the nomination process of the Republican Party. He was not even one of the leading candidates before the nomination process began, let alone the favourite. Most people seemed to be backing William Seward, from New York, a strongly anti-slavery candidate who was vastly experienced – he had been governor and then senator for New York since 1839.

The Republican convention (where a party decides on its presidential candidate) was held in Chicago, Illinois – a fact that almost certainly helped Lincoln. Coming from the Midwest, Lincoln came to be seen as more of a vote-winner in the borderline states such as Illinois and Ohio. New York and the East would vote Republican no matter who the candidate was. Lincoln was also known for his 1858 debates with Stephen Douglas, a leading Democratic candidate, in which he had been very effective. Lincoln won the Republican Party's nomination for presidential candidate.

The Democratic Party had already held its convention – this time in Charleston, South Carolina, arguably the most pro-slavery state in the whole of the South – in April 1860. Stephen Douglas was the favourite to win. After no less than 57 ballots, however, he still had not gained the two-thirds majority needed to win the nomination. The convention agreed to meet in Baltimore in June. This time Douglas was elected, though many delegates from the South stayed away. They organised a separate convention, at which they chose their own candidate, John C. Breckinridge, the current vice president. The Democratic Party remained critically divided.

There was a fourth party in 1860, the Constitutional Party, formed by some ex-Whigs. John Bell, a wealthy slave owner from Tennessee, was its candidate. This party had no **platform**, only a commitment to 'recognise no political principle other than the Constitution … the Union … and the enforcement of law'. In practice, the party wanted to defend the interests of the South, but it wanted to do so without mentioning the issue of slavery.

platform
A 'platform' is what a political party or candidate promises to do if elected to office.

The cartoon below, which shows three of the four political parties, makes the point that the Democratic Party was greatly weakened by the division between its Northern and Southern wings. In 1856, it was the one party that could claim to be national and to draw support from both sections, but by 1860 it had become as sectional as the Republican Party.

Figure 1.11 A political cartoon from 1860

As in 1856, the 1860 presidential election involved two sectional contests: Lincoln versus Douglas in the North, Breckinridge versus Bell in the South. Lincoln only gained 39% of the popular vote, but it proved enough to win. He earned few votes in the South, and thus became a president chosen by one section of the nation. Lincoln was known across the USA as a leading abolitionist, and the dedicated anti-abolitionists in the South believed he would certainly outlaw slavery when he took office. They decided to act immediately, rather than waiting five months for his inauguration to see what he would do. The last milestone on the path to civil war was in sight.

The beginning of the Civil War in April 1861

The secession of the South 1860–61

Lincoln's election in 1860 sent a worrying signal to the South. It was clear that the region's influence at a national level was waning. Many of the Southern states decided that the only option was to secede from the United States and rule themselves. However, the fact is that Lincoln's election did not necessarily pose a direct threat to the Southern way of life:

- Lincoln explicitly stated that he did not intend to act against the institution of slavery in the Southern states; in fact, the political limitations of his office meant that it was unlikely that he could abolish it, as the Republican Party did not have control of Congress or the Supreme Court.
- In early 1861, the 'South' did not present a unified political entity opposed to the 'North'; instead, the South had numerous different factions and interests, and internal state loyalties there were stronger than those to a theoretical 'Southern country'.

None of this stopped Southern secessionists from reacting strongly against Lincoln's election. South Carolina was the first state to act decisively. On 20 December 1860, a convention (special assembly) decided to dissolve the union between South Carolina and all the other states of the USA. Six other states followed by February 1861: Mississippi, Florida, Alabama, Georgia, Louisiana and Texas.

Figure 1.12 A map showing the secession of the Southern states

The people of Georgia having dissolved their political connection with the Government of the United States of America present to their confederates and the world the causes which have led to the separation. For the last ten years we have had numerous and serious causes of complaint against our non-slave-holding confederate States with reference to the subject of African slavery. They have endeavored to weaken our security, to disturb our domestic peace and tranquillity, and persistently refused to comply with their express constitutional obligations to us in reference to that property, and by the use of their power in the Federal Government have striven to deprive us of an equal enjoyment of the common Territories of the Republic. This hostile policy of our confederates has been pursued with every circumstance of aggravation which could arouse the passions and excite the hatred of our people, and has placed the two sections of the Union for many years past in the condition of virtual civil war. Our people, still attached to the Union from habit and national traditions, and averse to change, hoped that time, reason, and argument would bring, if not redress, at least exemption from further insults, injuries, and dangers.

The state of Georgia's declaration of secession, approved 29 January 1861.

state legislatures
Elected bodies of people that have the power to make, change or repeal state laws.

referendum
A public vote held on a specific issue.

The average vote on secession in the **state legislatures** resulted in 80% in favour. Texas was the only state that put its convention's decision to the people – it held a **referendum** in which secession was approved by 44,317 votes to 13,020. Another four states – Arkansas, Tennessee, North Carolina and Virginia – left the Union once the fighting started in the spring. Importantly, the four slave states closest to the North – Missouri, Kentucky, Maryland and Delaware – stayed in the Union. The fact that not all slave states had broken away from the USA was to prove significant. The northern half of Virginia, refusing to follow the rest of the state, broke away to form West Virginia.

I have no purpose, directly or indirectly, to interfere with the institution of slavery in the states where it exists. I believe I have no lawful right to do so, and I have no inclination to do so.

From President Lincoln's first inaugural address, March 1861.

On the occasion corresponding to these four years ago, all thoughts were anxiously directed to an impending civil war. All dreaded it – all sought to avert it. While the inaugural address was being delivered from this place, devoted altogether to saving the Union without war, insurgent agents were in the city seeking to destroy it without war – seeking to dissolve the Union, and divide effects, by negotiation. Both parties deprecated war; but one of them would make war rather than let the nation survive; and the other would accept war rather than let it perish. And the war came.

From President Lincoln's second inaugural address, March 1865.

Forming a confederacy

In February 1861, delegates from the rebel Southern states met in Montgomery, Alabama, to form a new union: the Confederate States of America. They established their own 'Southern' legislature, made up of politically or economically influential men, and they quickly got down to business:

- On 9 February, **Jefferson Davis** was appointed provisional president of the Confederacy.
- On 11 March 1861, a Constitution of the Confederate States was ratified, mirroring the US Constitution but protecting rights such as slavery.
- The Confederate states set about creating their own army.
- The Confederacy adopted its own flag, sharpening the South's sense of separate identity.

During this dramatic period, the president was still Buchanan, a Democrat who avoided hasty action. Lincoln was heading from Illinois to Washington, DC, to be inaugurated on 4 March 1861. As soon as he took office, Lincoln was faced with the problem of Fort Sumter, a federal fort in Charleston Harbor, South Carolina. The commander of the fort, Major Robert Anderson, was a former slave owner who nevertheless remained loyal to the Union. When the state of South Carolina seceded, local forces demanded that the US troops abandon their positions and surrender the fort. Fort Sumter thus became a flashpoint for conflict. Lincoln could not be seen to give up federal property to secessionists, but for the secessionists Fort Sumter now virtually amounted to a 'foreign' occupation in the midst of its territory. As the Sumter garrison found itself under siege, Lincoln and his advisors debated the right course of action.

After some delay, Lincoln decided that he would send an unarmed naval force to resupply Fort Sumter, as the garrison was running out of food. In response, on 9 April, Davis ordered that Sumter either surrender, or be taken by force. On 11 April the Charleston military commander, General Beauregard, issued Major Anderson with a demand for surrender. Anderson refused, and in response Confederate forces began to pound Sumter with artillery fire on the morning of 12 April. The outcome was inevitable. Anderson surrendered Fort Sumter the following day, and the outraged North was provoked into action. On 15 April, with hostilities now open, Lincoln issued a call to arms, asking for 75,000 men to defend the Union. Four days later, he announced a **naval blockade** of the Confederate states. Tens of thousands of men rushed to join both the Union and Confederate armies. The American Civil War had begun.

Key figure

Jefferson Davis (1808–89)

Davis was born in Kentucky and was a soldier and slave owner. He became a Democratic member of the House of Representatives and then the Senate, and also served as US secretary of war between 1853 and 1857. A senator again in 1857, he was chosen as president of the Confederate States of America in 1861. Davis retained this position throughout the Civil War, until the CSA's defeat in 1865. At the end of the war he was charged with treason and imprisoned, but he was later released without trial.

naval blockade
Preventing ships from entering or leaving a certain area.

Historical debate

The true causes of the American Civil War remain hotly debated to this day. There are two main schools of thought: the 'irrepressibilists' and the 'blunderers'. The arguments of the irrepressiblists are summarised in William Seward's 1858 speech (below), which describes the Civil War as an 'irrepressible conflict'. The blunderers are those who believe that the Civil War was caused by a blundering generation of politicians who sleepwalked into war.

Shall I tell you what this collision between North and South means? They who think that it is accidental, unnecessary, the work of interested or fanatical agitators and therefore ephemeral, mistake the case altogether. It is an irrepressible conflict between opposing and enduring forces and it means that the United States must and will, sooner or later, become either entirely a slaveholding nation or entirely a free labor nation …

It is the failure to apprehend this great truth that induces so many unsuccessful attempts at a final compromise between the slave and free states and it is the existence of this great fact that renders all pretended compromises, when made, vain and ephemeral.

From a speech by William Seward made in October 1858.

The idea of a fundamental clash between enduring forces was further developed in the 20th century by Marxist historians. Marxists believed that the prime driving forces of history were economic and social, and that the 'great men' of history were less important than they seemed. Historians on the Progressive wing of US politics, who were not declared Marxists, thought much the same. The best known of this group – and the most influential American historian of his time – was Charles Beard. Writing with his wife, Mary, he labelled the Civil War as 'the second American Revolution'. Louis Hacker, a fellow Progressive, later developed Beard's ideas, writing in 1940 that 'the American Civil War turned out to be a revolution indeed. But its striking achievement was the triumph of industrial capitalism.' The withdrawal of Southern states from the USA allowed the Northern Republicans to establish an economy that suited the needs of Northern industry.

The leading 'blunderer' was J. G. Randall, a mid 20th-century historian.

Note:
American Progressivism was a movement that advocated political, cultural and economic reform to encourage the development of an increasingly industrialised USA.

> *None of the 'explanations of war' make sense, if fully analyzed. The war has been 'explained' by the choice of a Republican president, by grievances, by sectional economics, by the cultural wish for Southern independence, by slavery or by events at Fort Sumter. But these explanations crack when carefully examined … If one word were selected to account for the war, that word would not be slavery, or state-rights, or diverse civilizations. It would have to be such a word as fanaticism on both sides or misunderstanding or perhaps politics.*
>
> J. G. Randall, *The Civil War and Reconstruction*, 1937.

According to the blundering generation theory, the war occurred because the politicians on both sides made mistakes. They did not intend a civil war but their actions incited one nonetheless.

The debate continues in varying forms some 70 years later. Some historians believe in the importance of fundamental social and economic causes of the war; other are convinced that it was an accidental war. The objectives of the North and South in the Civil War are perhaps clearer than the war's causes: the two sides and their leaders certainly stated what they were fighting for. Lincoln sought to preserve the United States of America. In his inaugural address on 4 March, he clearly stated his belief that 'no State upon its own mere motion can lawfully get out of the Union; that resolves and ordinances to that effect are legally void, and that acts of violence within any State or States against the authority of the United States are insurrectionary or revolutionary, according to circumstances'.

This is not to say that Lincoln was committed to war as a matter of course, as he also stated that 'there needs to be no bloodshed or violence, and there shall be none unless it be forced upon the national authority. The power confided to me will be used to hold, occupy, and possess the property and places belonging to the government and to collect the duties and imposts; but beyond what may be necessary for these objects, there will be no invasion, no using of force against or among the people anywhere'.

In late 1860 and early 1861, Buchanan and Lincoln exercised caution, keen not to inflame Southern opinion (particularly amongst the states of the upper South) by ill-advised military action. In February 1861, for example, a Peace Conference was held in Virginia, although the Confederacy did not send any delegates. The conference reinforced a message that the North was quite prepared not to interfere with the institution of slavery. Where Lincoln was very clear, however, was on the integrity of the Union and on his conviction that secession was both illegal and unjustifiable. This point is important – Lincoln was prepared to go to war to preserve the Union, not to abolish slavery. As for racial equality, only a few radical abolitionists gave it much thought.

Lincoln showed political skill during 1861. As we have seen, four slave states stayed with the North: Delaware, Kentucky, Maryland and Missouri. Known as the Border States, these states all adjoined Northern states and were the least committed to slavery. The relative lack of slaves in these states was one reason why they looked North rather than South. Lincoln's policies were another reason. In Missouri, Lincoln sacked his military commander, Frémont, when the latter gave Missourian slaves their freedom. This reassured the Border States that they could keep their slaves, and thus kept them on the Union's side. It also showed that Lincoln did really intend to maintain the Union rather than free the slaves.

The decision of the four Border States to stay in the Union would go on to have a significant effect on the outcome of the Civil War. Instead of the South having 13 states and the North 19, the balance in terms of political geography was very much in favour of the North. Maryland, in particular, made a big difference, as three of the four borders of Washington, DC, were in Maryland. Although there was a certain level of support for Lincoln and the North in the Border States, the only way that the new president could make sure that Maryland did not join the Confederacy in the spring of 1861 was by imposing **martial law** there. This meant Lincoln could take all the decisions in the state. The inclusion of these slave states in the North, however, also affected the politics of the USA. The four Border States, so crucial in the conduct of the war, carried great weight in policy debates. Within the USA, they counter-balanced the power of the abolitionists in the Northeast.

martial law
In emergency situations, leaders can sometimes impose martial law in designated areas. This means that the military authorities rule over the area in accordance with military law.

For Jefferson Davis, the prime objective was to preserve the Southern way of life, built around slavery – which meant secession. Davis also argued that secession was about a state's right to exercise self-determination as much as it was about the perceived threat to slavery. He stated this in his farewell speech to the Senate.

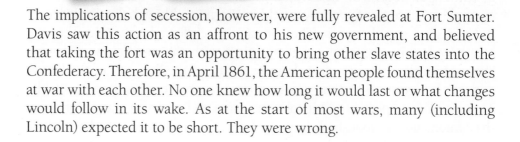

Secession belongs to a different class of remedies. It is to be justified upon the basis that the States are sovereign. There was a time when none denied it. I hope the time may come again, when a better comprehension of the theory of our Government, and the inalienable rights of the people of the States, will prevent any one from denying that each State is a sovereign, and thus may reclaim the grants which it has made to any agent whomsoever.

From the US Senate farewell speech by Jefferson Davis, 21 January 1861.

The implications of secession, however, were fully revealed at Fort Sumter. Davis saw this action as an affront to his new government, and believed that taking the fort was an opportunity to bring other slave states into the Confederacy. Therefore, in April 1861, the American people found themselves at war with each other. No one knew how long it would last or what changes would follow in its wake. As at the start of most wars, many (including Lincoln) expected it to be short. They were wrong.

Key issues

The key features of this chapter are:

- the Missouri Compromise of 1820

- the political effects of the US–Mexican War 1846–48

- the breakdown of the Compromise of 1850

- Northern and Southern attitudes to slavery, and how they contributed to tensions between the two regions

- the emergence of the Republican Party

- the events that contributed to the outbreak of the Civil War – the Kansas–Nebraska Act, Harpers Ferry and the election of 1860

- the secession of the Southern states, and the North's response

- the significance of the battle of Fort Sumter

- the handling of events in early 1861 by Lincoln and Davis.

Revision questions

1 To what extent was the outbreak of the American Civil War in April 1861 'inevitable'?

2 What were the principal causes of the secession of Southern states from the Union in early 1861?

3 Read the quotes in the historical debate section on pages 34–36. To what extent do they argue that the outbreak of civil war in 1861 was purely about the issue of slavery? How convincing are these arguments?

Further reading

Chadwick, F. E. *The Causes of the US Civil War*. Lightning Source. 2011.

Farmer, A. *The Origins of the American Civil War*. London, UK. Hodder. 1996.

Reid, B. H. *The Origins of the American Civil War*. (Origins of Modern War). Prentice Hall. 1996.

Stampp, K. *The Causes of the Civil War*. London, UK. Touchstone. 1992.

Chapter

2 The Civil War and Reconstruction 1861–77

Key questions

- Why did the Civil War last for four years?
- How great was the immediate impact of the Civil War?
- What were the aims and outcomes of Reconstruction?
- How successful was Reconstruction?

Content summary

- The military strategies of Union and Confederate forces.
- The political leadership of the two sides, and key decisions.
- Military and social resources available to the North and the South.
- The effect of the war on civil liberties and society.
- The Emancipation Proclamation of 1863.
- The policies of Reconstruction.
- The changing nature of Reconstruction.
- The position of ex-slaves in the United States.
- The Compromise of 1877.

Timeline

Apr 1861	CSA forces take Fort Sumter
Jun 1861	Four slave states decide to stay in USA
Nov 1861	Jefferson Davis elected president of CSA; Trent affair, danger of British intervention
Apr 1862	USA abolishes slavery in Washington, DC
Jan 1863	Emancipation Proclamation
Jul 1863	Battle of Gettysburg; USA defeats CSA army
Jul 1864	US Congress passes Wade–Davis Bill; vetoed by Lincoln
Sep 1864	Atlanta falls to US forces led by Sherman
Nov 1864	Lincoln defeats McClellan to be re-elected as US president; Sherman's March to the Sea through Georgia
Apr 1865	CSA capital, Richmond, falls to US forces; CSA commander Robert E. Lee surrenders at Appomattox; Lincoln assassinated; Andrew Johnson appointed president
Dec 1865	13th Amendment to the US Constitution
Apr 1866	Civil Rights Act
Jul 1868	14th Amendment to the US Constitution
Mar 1869	Ulysses S. Grant becomes US president
1876–77	Presidential election leads to inauguration of Rutherford B. Hayes

Introduction

The American Civil War was one of the most destructive events in US history. The four years of the war (1861–65) saw the deaths of 620,000 Americans – more than the total losses the USA has suffered in all its wars since then. By the end of the war, a president had been assassinated and large areas of the nation were ruined. The conflict ended in 1865, with a Union victory, and the Confederate states were reabsorbed into the USA.

Then came peace and the time known as Reconstruction, when the USA rebuilt itself. The Constitution was reformed by the passage of major amendments, and slavery was abolished. African-American men both voted for, and were elected to, the US Congress. The forces of progress seemed dominant superficially, but the Reconstruction era was both politically and socially complex. During this period, one president was impeached, the racist Ku Klux Klan was formed, and lynchings (executions without legal process) became a feature of life in the South. Military rule was imposed on some Southern states.

In addition to this, in 1877 a president was elected in what is perhaps the most outrageous of the four **misfired elections** in US history. The Republican candidate, Rutherford Hayes, won because the Democrat and Republican party leaderships made a private deal. The Democrats agreed that the Republicans could have the presidency if they withdrew the federal government from the South. The Republicans thus retained the presidency for most of the next 50 years, while the Democrats controlled the South for the next 90 years.

misfired elections
Elections in which the candidate who wins the all-important Electoral College vote does not win the popular vote. In other words, more voters voted for the candidate who came second. The three other misfired elections occurred in 1824, 1888 and 2000.

Figure 2.1 This picture depicts freed slaves travelling to Kansas to start their new lives

Four years of civil war

At the start of the Civil War, the odds of victory seemed heavily stacked in the North's favour. The North had more men, more manufacturing industry and more railways. It also had the more skilful political leader in Abraham Lincoln. So why did the Civil War last for four years?

Figure 2.2 A map showing the position of the two sides in 1861

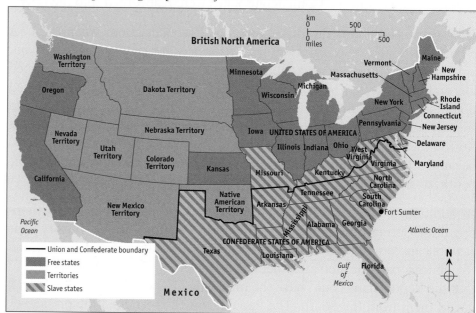

Political aims

There were several reasons why the South actually posed a serious challenge to the North in the Civil War, despite the North's apparant advantages:

- **The two sides' aims in the war:** all the South had to do was get the North to accept the existence of the CSA. The South did not have to occupy the North or force it to surrender. It was the North that had to be more ambitious. It had to make the South surrender and admit defeat. The longer the war went on, the greater the likelihood of pressure in the North for a negotiated peace.
- **The culture of the white South:** the majority of Southern whites saw the South as culturally and morally worthy, particularly in contrast with the North. They believed the North was inferior and dominated by immigrants. The South therefore thought it could recruit effective fighting forces more easily than the North, and better retain purpose and unity.
- **The geography of the war:** defending the South, the CSA had the benefit of interior lines of communications, as well as the support of the local population.
- **The leadership of the CSA:** the South's political leader was Jefferson Davis, who had moved between the army and politics through his career. Davis appointed Robert E. Lee to command the Southern armies, and Lee quickly proved to be a talented military leader. Northern military leaders,

by comparison, were much less skilful. This enabled the CSA to score some significant victories in 1861–62.

- **Support from Britain:** the CSA expected the support of Britain and its powerful navy, as the country was a major importer of the South's cotton.

Ultimately, the North was able to defeat the South. However, it took a great deal longer than anyone expected.

Military strategies and leadership

From April 1861, both sides began to prepare for battle. Neither was well organised and neither had a large army. In the North, Lincoln was formally commander-in-chief of the federal army as well as head of government. Although he was a lawyer, with no formal military experience, Lincoln began to study the history of war. After Southern forces shelled Fort Sumter, Lincoln immediately called for a blockade of the coastline of the seceded states and requested 75,000 volunteer soldiers to enlist for three months. The naval blockade continued for the duration of the war.

Initially, Lincoln appointed Winfield Scott, hero of the War of 1812 and the US–Mexican War, as his general-in-chief. Scott, one of the few who expected a long war, started to create a formidable Union army and designed the long-term plan that would ultimately win the war for the North. However, in 1861 Scott was 74 years old and he soon retired, handing over command to General George McClellan. In the South, Davis was also both president and commander-in-chief. As he had led forces in battle, Davis could justify his role as a military leader more readily than Lincoln could. Several hundred officers of the US army joined the CSA forces, which helped strengthen the Confederacy's military leadership. In March 1861, the CSA had an army of 100,000, which rose to over 350,000 by January 1862 and reached a peak of just over 480,000 in January 1864 before dropping to 445,000 in January 1865. Northern army figures were 576,000 for January 1862 and 959,000 for January 1865.

size of military

The generals on both sides had been educated at the same military college, West Point, where they had learnt the same outdated principles and strategies of warfare. However, the two sides' military tactics began to vary as their respective leaders faced very different situations.

The South

If the South was to defeat the North in the war, then there were three strategies it could use:

South's strategies to win

- The first might be called passive defence – simply protecting the South's borders.
- The second was strategic withdrawal, drawing Northern forces into the South, where they could be isolated and defeated.

- The third was what became known as offensive-defensive – attacking the North in certain areas, withdrawing Southern forces in other areas, and then fighting a defensive battle that the South expected to win.

The first was impossible in practice, as the Southern people needed basic goods from outside the region. The second was politically unacceptable, as the people of the South would not willingly concede any territory. This left only the third strategy. The advantage of interior communication lines enabled the South to bring together troops scattered over a wide area. Southern generals were able to make good use of the new technologies of telegraph and railway, pulling in soldiers from several hundred kilometres away.

The master of these strategies was Robert E. Lee (see page 28), the greatest of the Southern generals. He believed that the only way to achieve victory was to defeat the enemy in direct battle. In both 1862 and 1863, therefore, he concentrated Southern forces on the eastern front and marched them into Northern territory. There was also an important logistical benefit to such moves, in that the troops lived off Northern farms and therefore used up Northern food resources. Southern farmers were able to harvest their crops, leaving more food for the Southern people.

The 1862 attack into the North led to the Battle of Antietam, the first Northern victory on the eastern front and the bloodiest single-day battle of the war. The 1863 incursion ended in the Northern victory at Gettysburg in Pennsylvania, the furthest the South advanced into the North. There were terrible casualities on both sides (over 20,000 on each side at Gettysburg). However, the North, with its larger population, could absorb these losses more easily.

> ## Note:
> The Battle of Gettysburg was fought over 1–3 July 1863, and was the largest single Civil War battle. The South came very close to victory, but Lee's inability to give precise orders led to Confederate defeat and the loss of a third of the side's men. The Confederate army was unable to win the war after this battle.

Figure 2.3 Confederate prisoners after the Battle of Gettysburg in July 1863

After Gettysburg, despite Lee's best efforts, the South was forced onto the defensive. The Confederates rarely risked large-scale battles, mainly because they lacked the necessary arms and men. At this stage of the Civil War the North also avoided direct conflict, though for completely different reasons.

The North

The North faced problems when it won battles and thus advanced its armies, as this meant that it had to maintain ever-lengthening lines of communication through hostile Southern territory. The high number of casualties that resulted from such battles also created tension amongst the anti-war sections of the North. Lincoln had to be wary of public opinion as he needed public support for continuing the war and winning re-election.

Therefore the initial Northern strategy, which Scott devised with the support of Lincoln, aimed to strangle the South by surrounding it on all sides. Union forces provided a barrier in the north, and a naval blockade was set up to the east and south. The coastline of the CSA stretched 4830 km (3000 miles) from Virginia to Texas. At the start of the war, the North gained the greater part of the US navy – 90 vessels out of a total 120. The naval blockade, often overlooked by historians, became more effective as the war went on. The final part of Scott's plan was to gain control of the Mississippi River, which would split the South in two and complete the Northern stranglehold on the South. The strategy became known as the Anaconda Plan (or 'Scott's Great Snake'), because of the way in which the North would coil around the South and squeeze it until it could struggle no more.

Figure 2.4 Scott's Anaconda Plan, 1861

Note:

The Anaconda Plan was an unorthodox strategy in that it required the dispersal of forces, thus contradicting the conventional wisdom that the concentration of forces is the best way to win a war. It was cautious in approach, aiming to wear down the South without inflicting painful military defeats. This would make post-war reconciliation a lot easier – another important consideration.

By the summer of 1862, it was clear that Scott had adopted the right strategy. A year of conventional, limited war had brought little success. The South was dominant on the eastern front and providing determined opposition on the western front. Thus, the North decided it would wage war on the Southern people rather than their armies. It would wear down resistance by occupying more and more Southern land, controlling the CSA's economy and undermining its will to resist. This, the North believed, would win the war without having to risk fighting too many major battles.

Therefore, after the summer of 1862, the North began fighting a different type of war. It refined its military strategy by prioritising its main campaigns. Resources went to the campaign to gain control of the Mississippi River, and troops on the Virginian front to the east were instructed only to hold their position rather than advancing any further. The North's main priority was the western front. There were two reasons for this: Lee's dominance of the eastern front, and the relative success achieved by Northern forces west of the Appalachian Mountains under the leadership of Ulysses S. Grant and William T. Sherman in 1862–63.

Lincoln appointed Grant as the commander of the federal forces in March 1864. Grant made sure that the Northern military effort was unrelenting, keeping Southern forces fully stretched. Sherman, a close colleague of Grant, took his place as leader on the western front and also proved an effective military leader. Together, Grant and Sherman developed a new type of warfare regarded by many as unconventional and much more ruthless. After the battles of Chickamauga and Chattanooga in late 1863, the North further refined its tactics. It began to make infantry raids into enemy territory in order to destroy civilian property and supply lines, especially railways, and isolate Southern armies.

Sherman's advance towards Atlanta in the spring of 1864 was co-ordinated with Grant's offensive on the eastern front. Here, Grant decided on continuous warfare against Lee's army. For 44 days in the summer of 1864, the armies of Grant and Lee engaged in a series of non-stop battles, after which both sides settled for **trench warfare** around Petersburg, south of Richmond. The constant fighting of the summer resulted in many casualties. In less than seven weeks, the North's Army of the Potomac (the major Union force in the east) suffered 65,000 casualties, which roughly equalled the size of Lee's army. Such figures caused Grant to be seen as a callous leader, indifferent to the wellbeing of his men.

Throughout the autumn of 1864, the South experienced a rapid decline. Food was running short. By December, Sherman had taken both Savannah and Atlanta and cut the Confederacy in two. On Sherman's infamous 'March through Georgia' his men destroyed buildings and crops, and the terror the Union troops inspired demoralised the South. A few months later, after some final attempts to break the Northern stranglehold, Lee surrendered to Grant at Appomattox. His capital, Richmond, had been abandoned – and torched – a few days before. The war was over.

trench warfare
This is a type of fighting in which troops construct and then occupy long, narrow ditches that face the enemy.

Resources

After the secession by the Confederate states, the North initially contained 23 states: 19 free states and four slave states. Its population totalled 23 million, and it contained most of the USA's industry. The primarily agricultural South had 9 million people, around 5.5 million free people and 3.5 million slaves.

In 1861, both sides faced major problems in preparing to fight. The American people had no experience of raising mass armies. In a country with a very strong tradition of individual liberty, recruiting and retaining troops was a major problem. Soldiers also needed adequate supplies of munitions and food. They had to be moved around a very large country as quickly as possible. Before fighting, they needed feeding; after a battle, many needed nursing care.

Troops

In both the North and the South, the initial enthusiasm to sign up and fight soon faded; many who volunteered at the start of the war did not re-enlist. The South was the first side to introduce **conscription** as a way to gather sufficiently large numbers of troops. In April 1862, all able-bodied white males aged between 18 and 35 were required to serve in the army for three years.

> **conscription**
> Making joining the army compulsory for certain people.

However, individuals could hire substitutes – and many wealthier men did so. This caused many in the South to summarise their side's war effort as 'a rich man's war but a poor man's fight'. Conscription was extremely unpopular. 'Draft dodging' became common. Some men in the South argued that they were fighting to defend their rights, not to have them taken away. Despite this internal opposition, conscription expanded the army by more than one-third, to 450,000 men. However, even that growth was not enough and the Southern need for manpower became more desperate. In December 1863, the practice of substitution had to be abolished.

The North delayed introducing conscription until March 1863, almost a year after the South. It had a much larger population on which to draw, and had used several tactics to raise troops without having to conscript them. By the end of 1862, the Northern armies numbered just over 900,000 men. However, in 1863 all male citizens aged between 20 and 45 had to enrol in the army. Those who were eventually called to serve could hire a substitute. They could also pay a fee of $300 to gain exemption. Conscription was just as unpopular in the North as in the South. It is estimated that only 7% of those who were chosen for the draft (itself a minority of those eligible) actually joined the Northern army. The North always had a much larger reserve of manpower than the South.

Figure 2.5 Two Union soldiers

Railways

Helped transport goods / troops much faster

Helped the North more.

In many respects, the American Civil War was the first railway war. By 1860, before the war began, the USA had built 48,280 km (30,000 miles) of railway track. All but 14,480 km (9000 miles) of this was in Northern states. During the war, the railways enabled troops and supplies to be transported more quickly than ever before, especially over longer distances. Railways were used tactically. In September 1863, the North moved 23,000 troops and their equipment from the eastern front to Alabama, a distance of 1930 km (1200 miles), in seven days. This eventually allowed Grant to win the Battle of Chattanooga in November 1863. At the First Battle of Bull Run on 21 July 1861, the South moved in 2500 troops by train and thus helped tilt the battle in its favour.

railhead
A point on a railway system where military supplies are loaded, unloaded and transferred to different modes of transport.

The railways could be used to deliver supplies to armies – or at least to the nearest **railhead** – and also to carry the injured away from the battlefield. They had a great impact on the conduct of the war, even if this was often limited by shortages of railway vehicles and damage to the track. Petersburg, south of Richmond, became very important in 1864–65 because it was the centre of the remaining rail links between Richmond and Confederate lands to the west. The Confederacy had only two main lines connecting Richmond with the rest of the South. After the Battle of Chattanooga in November 1863, the South lost control of one of those lines, which further isolated Richmond.

guerrillas
Members of a small independent group that takes part in irregular fighting, usually against larger, professional forces.

However, the benefits of the railways made them targets for enemy attacks. Train routes were easily disrupted, as lines and bridges could be destroyed by small groups of cavalry or **guerrillas**. Such attacks had the effect of widening the zone of warfare, as the railways were usually some distance from the battlefields.

Questions

1 Why were railways so important in the Civil War?

2 To what extent was military leadership the decisive factor in the outcome of the Civil War?

The impact of the Civil War

The Civil War brought about a variety of unexpected changes, many of which had a lasting effect. Government took up more powers in order to wage war effectively. Economies had to adapt to supply and equip large armies. Political parties changed, and society had to respond to the demands of war. Devastation caused by death and injuries had to be absorbed. Slavery was abolished, and a way of life in the South that had existed for generations went with it. Few anticipated at the start of the war just how great its impact would be.

Civil liberties

Loss of civil liberties in the North

To win wars, governments often take away many of the rights that citizens usually enjoy. The American Civil War was no exception. The rights and freedoms of Americans are laid out in the Bill of Rights, the first ten Amendments to the Constitution. One of these rights is the freedom from arrest and imprisonment without good reason. If a prisoner feels he has been arrested and detained without good reason, then he can ask the courts to release him by issuing what is known as a 'writ of **habeas corpus**'. However, the Constitution maintains that if there is a 'rebellion or invasion' the courts should not issue these writs.

The Merryman case

The Merryman case is an example of a writ of habeas corpus being ignored by the courts. John Merryman was a Maryland politician who had been involved in the Baltimore riots of April 1861, at the very start of the Civil War. In these riots, thousands of Southern sympathisers stopped US troops from getting to Washington, DC. For a week, the city was cut off from the rest of the USA. As a result, Lincoln suspended habeas corpus along a key railway line in the state of Maryland. John Merryman was placed under military arrest for his role in organising resistance to US forces by committing acts such as cutting telegraph wires. Merryman appealed to Judge Roger B. Taney to issue a writ of habeas corpus and get him released. Taney did so, and waited for the local army general, George Cadwalader, to bring Merryman to him. The general sent one of his colonels instead, who explained that Cadwalader had been authorised by the president to suspend habeas corpus. Taney ordered a court official to bring the general to him the next day, but Cadwalader did not appear. Taney then ruled that the president was acting unconstitutionally.

Lincoln simply ignored Judge Taney, and Congress supported the president. Taney could do nothing. Merryman was soon charged and released on bail, but he was never tried. The suspension of habeas corpus was itself later suspended, but was then introduced again in August 1862. This time, the suspension applied to the whole of the USA. Thousands of people were detained without trial, often for the flimsiest of reasons. In 1863, Congress supported this nationwide suspension. With no means of enforcing his decision, Judge Taney was powerless.

> **Note:**
> The Bill of Rights, made up of the first ten Amendments to the US Constitution, lists the rights of all US citizens. These include the right to free speech, the right of assembly and the right to due process of law. The Bill of Rights guarantees more freedom to its citizens than in any other country in the world.

habeas corpus
The right of any person under arrest to appeal to a court of law before being detained; this ensures that no one is held without sufficient legal evidence.

The Vallandigham case

With popular support for his use of emergency powers during the war, Lincoln was able to restrict opponents' liberties when he felt it necessary. An example of this was the case of Clement Vallandigham, a politician from Ohio and, until the 1862 elections, a US congressman. Vallandigham became a leading opponent of the conduct of the Civil War. He was the unofficial leader of the **Copperheads**, the name given to Northern Democrats who wanted an early peace with the South.

On 1 May 1863, Vallandigham addressed a crowd of 10,000 in Ohio. He spoke for about two hours in what Lincoln described in a letter as 'words of burning eloquence of the arbitrary measures and monarchical usurpations of the Administration, the disgraceful surrender of the rights and liberties by the last, infamous Congress and the conversion of the government into a despotism'. Five days later, Vallandigham was arrested, accused of breaking a military order prohibiting speeches sympathetic to the South. Soon after, the army also closed down the *Chicago Times* for supporting Vallandigham, using its emergency powers to control the press.

Vallandigham was tried by a military court, which did not have to follow usual legal processes. He applied for a writ of habeas corpus but was refused, as habeas corpus was suspended. The court found Vallandigham guilty and sentenced him to imprisonment until the war was over. A political storm broke out in both Ohio and Washington, DC, where Lincoln's Cabinet ministers opposed the use of the military to limit freedom of speech. Under pressure, Lincoln responded in the following ways:

- He backed the army.
- He exiled Vallandigham to the South rather than put him in prison.
- He overturned the ban on the *Chicago Times*.
- He wrote an open letter to a group that had criticised his actions, in which he defended himself by asking, 'Must I shoot a simple-minded soldier boy who deserts while I must not touch the hair of an agitator who induces him to desert?'

Vallandigham escaped to Canada. In February 1864, the US Supreme Court refused to issue a writ of habeas corpus on Vallandigham's behalf, saying that it had no authority over military commissions. In June 1864 Vallandigham, heavily disguised, returned to the USA. This time, however, the authorities left him alone. He played an important part in the Democratic Party Convention in the autumn of 1864, by which time the Union was clearly winning the war and Lincoln did not feel he was much of a threat.

The Milligan case

Another example of the government removing conventional US civil liberties can be found in the Milligan case. Lamdin P. Milligan was a lawyer and a Peace Democrat. In October 1864, in the Northern state of Indiana, Milligan and four others were arrested and charged with treason. They were alleged

Copperheads
Also known as Peace Democrats, the Copperheads were a group of Democrats who were outspoken in their opposition to the Civil War; their name was a derogatory label given to them by the Republicans, likening these dissidents to the venomous copperhead snake.

to have planned to liberate Southern prisoners of war, thereby undermining the North's war effort. The five men were tried by a military court, and in December 1864 they were sentenced to death by hanging. The execution was to take place in May 1865.

However, by that time the Civil War was over and Lincoln had been assassinated. Two days before the men were due to be executed, the new president, Andrew Johnson, commuted their sentence to life imprisonment. While in prison, Milligan petitioned the US Supreme Court for a writ of habeas corpus. This was granted on the grounds that the civil courts in Indiana were in operation during the war and so could have heard Milligan's case. Milligan was freed and later pardoned by President Johnson.

Although the cases detailed above are the best-known examples concerning the suspension of civil liberties during the war, many others faced either detention without trial or trial by military commissions. One source estimates that over 10,000 people were incarcerated with a 'prompt trial' and that over 4000 military trials took place during the war.

Loss of civil liberties in the South

In the CSA, the issue of civil liberties was even more delicate, for several reasons. Firstly, most of the war was fought in the South, which meant that military requirements took priority over civilians' rights. Secondly, the individual Southern states were reluctant to put the CSA's rights before their own. Thirdly, the South was far from united, so it was difficult to universally define rights.

In addition, Davis was reluctant to take the lead in suspending habeas corpus as Lincoln did. He preferred to ask the CSA Congress to pass the relevant law, and often it was hesitant about doing so. Congress granted Davis the power of suspension for only limited periods, as it felt obligated to represent the states' strong opposition to these moves. People's principle objection was that the suspensions gave too much power to the military. Nevertheless, the CSA paralleled the USA in its suspension of habeas corpus and its inclination towards military courts. However, the South's use of these measures receives less attention than the North's because only the latter had a lasting impact on the USA.

The Emancipation Proclamation

In the mid 19th century, the majority of African-Americans lived in the South and most of them were slaves. At the start of the war, Lincoln was fighting to maintain the Union, not to end slavery. It was the needs of war that slowly pushed him towards **emancipation** of the slaves, if only in rebel states. In 1861, the North had been prepared to accept the continuation of slavery in existing slave states. In August 1862, in response to an open letter from Horace Greeley, a leading abolitionist and the editor of the *New York Tribune*, Lincoln had replied with his own open letter (see page 50).

emancipation
This means to liberate, or give freedom to, certain groups who are not allocated the same rights as other people.

My paramount object in this struggle is to save the Union and is not either to save or to destroy slavery. If I could save the Union without freeing any slave I would do it and if I could save the Union by freeing all slaves I would do it and if I could save it by freeing some and leaving others alone, I would do it. What I do about slavery and the colored race, I do because I believe it helps to save the Union.

Abraham Lincoln, in an open letter to Horace Greeley, August 1862.

The Emancipation Proclamation was issued on 22 September 1862. It contained two key measures:

- Slavery would be allowed to continue in all states that returned to the Union before 1 January 1863.
- From 1 January 1863, the Union would set free any slaves in territories taken by the Union's armed forces.

In order to grant full emancipation, freeing all slaves in both rebel and Union states, Lincoln would have had to pass an amendment to the Constitution. Even if he could persuade Congress to vote in favour of this, the amendment would take too long to implement. However, as commander-in-chief of the army Lincoln could issue the Emancipation Proclamation, freeing slaves only in the rebel states, without congressional approval.

Figure 2.6 The Emancipation Proclamation

The main reason that Lincoln wanted some type of emancipation, however limited, was because he believed that it would greatly weaken the CSA's war effort. The South was proving difficult to defeat and it would be undermined if the foundation of its way of life – that is, slavery – was weakened. Emancipation might also strengthen the USA by increasing recruitment into its army. It might have a diplomatic benefit, too, in that Britain was more likely to support the North if it came out against slavery.

Davis issued a blunt response in a message to the CSA Congress. He called the Emancipation Proclamation 'the most execrable measure recorded in the history of guilty men'. The slaves of the South had a different response, even if it was not immediately apparent. The proclamation encouraged them to take more steps to support the North. The Confederate states could not rely on the loyalty of their slaves, which weakened their war effort. In the next three years, around 180,000 African-Americans joined the Northern armies. This increased the North's already superior manpower, and tipped the military advantage even further towards the USA.

Life in the Confederate states

By 1864, the enthusiasm with which most white Southerners had welcomed the war was long gone. Life in the South had become hard for many, especially for those who sat directly in the path of Union armies. In November and December 1864, for example, Sherman's forces marched through Georgia, inflicting death and destruction on both civilian and military targets. On 6 December 1864, the city of Milledgeville's *Confederate Union* wrote: 'If an army of Devils, just let loose from the bottomless pit, were to invade the country, they could not be much worse that Sherman's army.' Yet even for those communities not directly involved in the fighting, the Civil War affected every aspect of life in the South.

Economic hardship

The people of the South soon experienced economic hardship. The naval blockade by the North had a devastating effect, as the South's cash crop of raw cotton could not be exported to Britain. Basic foodstuffs such as salt, essential as a preservative, were soon in short supply. By December 1861, a few months into the war, the price of salt in one city in Georgia had risen from 50 cents per sack to $10.

Not everyone in the South suffered from inflation and food shortages straight away. One diary entry for a Christmas Day of 1863 spent in Richmond read: 'We had for dinner oyster soup besides roast mutton, ham, boned turkey, wild partridge, plum pudding, sauterne, burgundy, sherry and Madeira. There is life in the old land yet!' The introduction of a 10% tax on all farm products in 1863 did not seem to greatly affect the lifestyles of the well-to-do. Conversely, poor farmers struggled as they found themselves being forced to hand over 10% of their produce.

However, by the end of the war even the rich Southerners were negatively affected. The diary entry of one wealthy Southerner, writing on 23 April 1865, gives an example of this. The family concerned lost its 1000 slaves.

> *My silver wedding day and I am sure the unhappiest day of my life. One year ago we left Richmond. The Confederacy has double-quicked downhill since then. Now we have burned towns, deserted plantations, deserted villages … poverty with no future and no hope.*

Mary Boykin Chesnut, *A Diary from Dixie*, 23 April 1865.

Social divisions

At the start of the war, most white Southerners supported the move to independence from the USA. The plantation owners were probably keenest to break away in order to maintain the slavery on which their wealth was based. Most whites were not plantation owners, however, even if they sometimes had one or two slaves. Many whites had no slaves, and farmed alone or in small rural communities. They began to resent the ability of the better-off to escape the deprivations of war.

Conscription caused particular resentment amongst the poorer majority of people, because of the system of substitution that existed until late 1863 (see page 45). It is estimated that at least 50,000 wealthy white Southerners avoided the draft. Class resentments increased as the fighting went on, particularly because the war lasted much longer than anyone expected.

Political divisions

Not all white Southerners supported the Confederacy. Many left the South and joined the Northern army. One estimate puts the figure at 100,000 or more. Every Southern state except South Carolina raised at least one unit in the US Northern army. Many Union supporters remained in the South, their presence dividing and weakening the CSA's war effort.

The slaves

The presence of some 3 million slaves in a population totalling 9 million caused major problems in the South. At the start of the war, the whites refused to accept slaves into their army. While fearful of a slave rebellion, the whites expected their slaves to replace white men away at war on the plantations and farms. There was no rebellion, but historians talk of slaves undertaking what they call a **general strike**, which did much to weaken the Confederacy.

general strike
This occurs when the majority of the labour force refuses to work, often until their demands are met or a compromise is agreed.

The slaves also helped the Northern armies succeed. Once Union armies entered Southern states, the slaves became more open in their support for the enemy. They worked as scouts and informers, giving the North a significant advantage as it advanced deep into enemy territory. Around 180,000 African-American soldiers served in the Northern army, making up 10% of the total troops. Around half of these soldiers came from the South. Some slaves (an estimated 65,000) stayed and joined the Southern army.

Democratic politics: North and South

midterm elections
All members of the House of Representatives and one-third of the Senate are up for re-election every two years.

The war between North and South was a new type of conflict. It was a civil war fought within a democratic state. Elections were still held by both sides, and party politics continued in the North throughout the fighting. In the North, the Democrats still contested elections against the governing Republicans. In the 1862 **midterm elections**, with the war not going well for the North, the Democrats gained many seats in the House of Representatives. The Republicans kept control only because they allied with a smaller party composed mainly of **War Democrats**. This was one reason for the continual fighting on the eastern front in the spring of 1864. Lee hoped that the heavy casualties inflicted on the North would harm Lincoln's chances of being re-elected as president.

Lincoln's re-election was by no means certain in 1864. The war was not going well for the North, and its fortunes only began to change with the fall of Atlanta on 3 September, just two months before the election. In July 1864, CSA troops were within 8 km (5 miles) of Washington, DC, catching sight of the White House in the distance. There were groups calling for peace negotiations: the Peace Democrats and a splinter group of Republicans. Relations between Lincoln and the Republican Congress were strained, especially when the president vetoed a bill that would have imposed harsher terms on the CSA at the end of the war.

In the 1864 election, Lincoln stood as the candidate for the National Union Party, a temporary name taken on by the Republicans in order to attract War Democrats who would not vote for the Republican Party. Lincoln won the Electoral College vote by 212 to 21, a clear victory. Just as significant for the future was the Republican triumph in the congressional elections, where 136 of the 193 congressmen were now Republicans. These representatives would play a great part in addressing the problems of transition to peace. Re-elected and successfully inaugurated, Lincoln saw in the end of the war. Lee, with his capital taken and his army surrounded, surrendered to General Grant at Appomattox Court House in April 1865. Tragically, Lincoln had little time to enjoy his victory and plan for post-war peace, as he was assassinated within days.

> **War Democrats**
> War Democrats supported the war, but disliked Republican economic policies and Lincoln's violation of civil rights in wartime. In the 1864 presidential election, they joined with the Republicans in forming the National Union Party, which renominated Lincoln for president.

Figure 2.7 A victory parade in Washington, DC, in 1865

Questions

1. What effects did the Civil War have on civil liberties?

2. 'Wars invariably bring about major social and political change.' How far does an analysis of the American Civil War support this view?

The aims and outcomes of Reconstruction

The era of Reconstruction

Reconstruction was the term applied to the process of reintegrating the Southern states into the USA and building new social structures in the South to replace the old slavery-based ones. The process of Reconstruction began long before the end of the Civil War. The partial emancipation of slaves in 1863 was followed by a policy aimed to encourage an end to the war and to 'reconstruct' the rebel states into the Union. This was summarised as the Ten Percent Plan. States could be readmitted if:

- 10% of their electorate from 1860 took an oath of future loyalty to the USA – in other words, they did not have to have been loyal to the USA in the past
- they supported all existing acts of Congress relating to slavery
- they allowed some African-Americans to vote (but no legal or civil status beyond personal liberty).

Louisiana was the first slave state under Northern control that met Lincoln's requirements. Congress wanted to adopt a much tougher line, however, and refused to admit Louisiana. In June 1864, it passed the Wade–Davis Bill, which was designed to make full re-admission to the Union more difficult:

- The bill required 50% of the 1860 electorate to take a far tougher 'ironclad oath' of past and future loyalty to the Union, stating that they had never given any voluntary help to Confederate forces.
- It excluded all those involved in the Confederacy from any role in future government.
- It demanded that the state constitution be changed to abolish slavery.

Lincoln vetoed the Wade–Davis Bill. He felt that his suggestions would encourage the South to consider ending the war, and that the Wade–Davis Bill would not only never work in practice, but would also prolong the war. The result was that although Lincoln recognised Louisiana's government and continued to administer the state, it was not allowed to take up its seats in Congress. In the months before Lincoln's death, there was a growing gulf between the president and Congress over how best to treat the South once the war was over.

As early as 1863, Lincoln had made it clear that he had two major objectives for the South. The first was to abolish slavery and give African-Americans the vote, and the second was to get the South back into the Union and restore normal government in the region. Lincoln made good progress on the first objective, but the second was largely left to his successor **Andrew Johnson**.

Key figure

Andrew Johnson (1808–75)

Johnson was a Democrat from Tennessee, a slave state that joined the Confederacy in 1861. He believed in the Union and thus stayed in the US Senate when his state seceded in 1861. He was keen on leniency for the South after the war. A brilliant speaker and a genuine believer in democracy, his crudeness, bad temper and drinking habits often alienated people.

The 13th Amendment

The 13th Amendment to the US Constitution, adopted on 6 December 1865, radically changed the federal position on slavery. There was now full emancipation across the USA, assured by a fundamental law embodied in the Constitution. The text of the Amendment read:

Section 1 *Neither slavery nor involuntary servitude, except as a punishment for crime whereof the party shall have been duly convicted, shall exist within the United States, or any place subject to their jurisdiction.*

Section 2 *Congress shall have power to enforce this article by appropriate legislation.*

US Congress, 13th Amendment to the US Constitution, 31 January 1865.

The Republican electoral success in November 1864 had encouraged Lincoln to pass the 13th Amendment, the first of three major amendments confirmed in the 1860s. Congress approved the Amendment in January 1865, a few months before the end of the war. By the end of 1865, enough states had approved the Amendment for it to become law.

In March 1865, Lincoln and Congress also introduced the Freedmen's Bureau, a US agency in place for just one year in order to help former slaves in a variety of ways.

Figure 2.8 This 1868 political cartoon depicts General Oliver O. Howard, head of the Freedmen's Bureau, mediating between angry groups

Note:
The Freedmen's Bureau provided advice on education and employment for former slaves, and help in establishing schools for African-American children in the South. One historian evaluates the Bureau as follows: 'The Freedmen's Bureau was the first, and in some ways the most important of all the great agencies for social welfare created by federal government. Though imperfect, it was a fitting addition to the massive enlargement of government functions that resulted from the civil war.' Another historian assesses the Freedmen's Bureau as 'totally without precedent'.

> **Note:**
> Lincoln was assassinated by John Wilkes Booth, a mentally unstable man and self-appointed Southern patriot, in a Washington, DC, theatre. Lincoln's visit had been widely advertised and he had no effective security to protect him.

In the complex political circumstances surrounding the end of the Civil War, Lincoln tried to address the various issues surrounding the emancipation of the slaves and the reintegration of CSA states into the USA. If the problems of reintegration were great, they were made many times worse by Lincoln's assassination on 14 April 1865. Johnson struggled to move the country from war to peace efficiently or effectively.

Lincoln: an assessment

Abraham Lincoln was US president for just over four years. He came to office with little political experience and at the very difficult time of the Civil War's beginning. Lincoln fought to preserve the Union, and eventually achieved this when the North won the war and the former Confederate states were reintegrated into the USA. Although he was initially prepared to accept the survival of slavery in existing slave states, by the end of the war he put through measures to ensure the total abolition of slavery in all states of the USA.

Due to his key role in preserving the Union and ending slavery, Lincoln is widely regarded as one of the USA's greatest presidents. Since his early death, he has been the subject of many biographical books and, later, movies. Some biographers have taken a critical view, arguing that Lincoln was a white supremacist and an autocrat. The majority, however, point to the humanity and skill with which Lincoln led the USA through extremely challenging times. Many today still wonder what Lincoln may have gone on to do if he had not been assassinated.

Johnson's Reconstruction

Andrew Johnson had been chosen as vice president in 1864 in order to help broaden the appeal of the National Union candidacy (see page 53) both in terms of party and region. Johnson had plenty of administrative experience by the time he became president in April 1865, and he was keen to push ahead with Reconstruction. He knew that in December 1865 Congress would meet, and he would have to deal with those Republicans who distrusted the ex-Confederate states and would make the reintegration of the South difficult. Lincoln's assassination had made Northern Republicans more determined to be harder on the South.

Johnson wanted to restore orderly government in the South as quickly as possible. Given the dislocation caused by the war, the sooner stable government was re-established the better. While accepting the Wade–Davis Bill's (see page 54) 50% minimum for the oath of loyalty, Johnson agreed that when each former Confederate state held a convention to revise its own constitution, those attending the convention would be elected by the 1860 white electorate. These conventions repealed secession and abolished slavery.

However, the new state legislatures then passed a series of laws known as the Black Codes. For example:

- African-Americans who were deemed to be unemployed could be forced into work (of white employers' choosing).
- African-American children could be forced into work on plantations as 'apprentices'.
- African-Americans could be stopped from renting or buying land.
- The legal system was impossibly stacked against African-Americans who took their grievances to court.
- African-Americans could be prevented from receiving an education.

These laws were obviously intended to minimise the impact of the abolition of slavery on the former slave owners, and to keep African-Americans as second-class citizens.

News of the Black Codes angered Northern Republicans. By the time Congress met in December 1865, it was determined to do more to help African-Americans in the South, and so it passed a bill that strengthened the powers of the Freedmen's Bureau. Johnson vetoed the bill because he knew it would anger the South and make Reconstruction more difficult. Congress then introduced a civil rights bill that aimed to give citizenship to ex-slaves, i.e. freed men in the South. Johnson vetoed this bill. However, for the first time in US history, Congress overturned the presidential veto. This required a supermajority of two-thirds in both houses, which the Republicans could provide, and the bill became law. This was the 1866 Civil Rights Act. However, Congress went even further. It introduced the 14th Amendment to the Constitution.

The 14th Amendment

The 14th Amendment was a complex series of proposals, the most important of which stated that people who were born in the USA or who were naturalised (granted the rights of a US-born person although they originally came from another country) were US citizens.

> *Section 1 All persons born or naturalized in the United States, and subject to the jurisdiction thereof, are citizens of the United States and of the State wherein they reside. No State shall make or enforce any law which shall abridge the privileges or immunities of citizens of the United States; nor shall any State deprive any person of life, liberty, or property, without due process of law; nor deny to any person within its jurisdiction the equal protection of the laws.*
>
> US Congress, 14th Amendment to the US Constitution, 9 July 1868.

The 14th Amendment also gave the federal authorities the right to intervene if states contravened its rules. The Amendment was primarily intended as an attack on the South. It merged several separate proposals aimed particularly at injuring the position and sensibilities of the white ruling class in the South.

All men, regardless of colour, would have citizenship as a right, and this meant the right to vote and hold office. In order to get the 14th Amendment accepted in the South, Congress started to put real pressure on the region with a series of plans known collectively as the 'Radical Reconstruction'.

Radical Reconstruction

Firstly, and most importantly, came the Reconstruction Acts of 1867–68. These imposed military rule across the South – with the exception of Tennessee, which had already been re-admitted to the Union. The ten remaining states were grouped into five military districts. Around 20,000 US troops were deployed to help establish the new constitutional order and thus allow representatives from the rebel states to re-enter Congress. In effect, the South experienced martial law for around ten years from 1867. The Reconstruction Acts also required all states to introduce votes for all men and to approve the 14th Amendment.

This move to a more authoritarian treatment of the South was assisted by the election in 1868 of the Republican Ulysses S. Grant as president. Having a Republican president reduced the likelihood of conflict with a Republican Congress. Grant was in favour of firm treatment of the South in the Reconstruction process.

Figure 2.9 Landmarks in Reconstruction

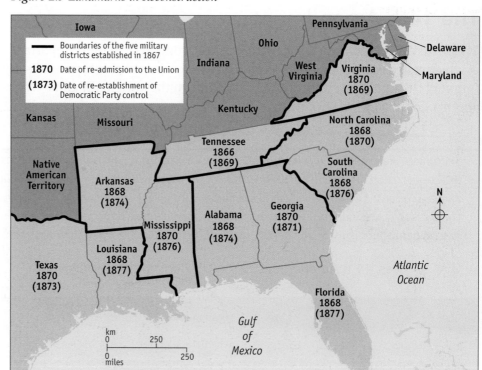

As a result of the Republicans imposing military districts, the South was subject to a kind of invasion from the North. New state governments were established, but they often proved to be both corrupt and inefficient. The majority of the new officials were Northerners (called 'carpetbaggers' after the type of suitcase they carried) seeking power and money, with a few renegade Southern whites (called 'scalawags') to assist. Although African-Americans in theory made up the majority of the Southern electorate, real power lay with the white carpetbaggers supported by the US army. Amongst these men there were some able idealists aiming to improve the South, but they were outnumbered by a dishonest majority.

Most Southern whites detested the Republican newcomers who wanted to destroy the Southern way of life. They rapidly organised themselves to defeat this Northern invasion and also to ensure that African-Americans were returned to a position as close to slavery as possible.

The 15th Amendment

Following the Reconstruction Acts, a further constitutional amendment was introduced in 1869. The 15th Amendment should also be seen as part of the Reconstruction process.

Section 1 *The right of citizens of the United States to vote shall not be denied or abridged by the United States or by any State on account of race, color, or previous condition of servitude.*

Section 2 *The Congress shall have power to enforce this article by appropriate legislation.*

US Congress, 15th Amendment to the US Constitution, 3 February 1870.

Figure 2.10 President Grant signing the 15th Amendment

Although the 15th Amendment was not aimed exclusively at the South, it was intended to have its greatest impact there. In 1860, the ability of African-American people to vote was restricted even in the North. This Amendment ensured that citizens of any colour or race could vote, wherever they lived. Collectively, the three Constitutional Amendments can be seen as one of the most significant outcomes of the Civil War. However, ensuring that they achieved what their supporters intended would take decades.

By 1870, all the Southern states had accepted the terms imposed by the US Congress and were readmitted to federal government. A key part of Reconstruction had been accomplished.

The 1876 presidential election

The results of the 1876 presidential election show the dilemma facing leaders of both the Democrat and Republican parties. The Democratic candidate, Samuel Tilden, won the popular vote – the majority of the votes cast; however, the Republican candidate, Rutherford B. Hayes, won the crucial Electoral College vote – by just one ballot. The contest was even more dramatic because 20 of Hayes's Electoral College votes, in three Southern states and Oregon, were initially disputed. Both parties accused the other of electoral fraud.

Candidate	Party	Electoral College vote		Popular vote	
		By number	By states	By number	By percentage
Rutherford B. Hayes	Republican	185	21	4,036,572	47.9
Samuel Tilden	Democratic	184	17	4,284,020	51.0

Table 2.1 A table showing the 1876 presidential election result

More than any other 'misfired' presidential election (see page 39), this one resulted in a long, complex and controversial process to try and resolve the crisis. A special commission was set up to allocate the Electoral College votes from the disputed states. Just two days before inauguration, the disputed votes were allocated to Hayes.

Questions

1 Why was the military so important to the process of Reconstruction?

2 'The Constitutional Amendments were the most important elements of Reconstruction.' How far do you agree with this assertion?

How successful was Reconstruction?

In one sense, Reconstruction can be seen as a success, as the former Confederate states rejoined the Union, adhering to the 'rules' required for membership and accepting the Constitutional Amendments. However, many of the aims of Reconstruction were not attained at all. African-Americans in the South were denied the vote and education, and were often terrified into accepting low economic status. This came about in a variety of ways. One vital cause was the political 'deal' between the Northern Republicans and the Southern Democrats, known as the Compromise of 1877.

The Compromise of 1877

The Compromise of 1877 was a secret deal between the largely Northern-based Republicans and the emerging Democratic Party of the South. The agreement was that if the Republicans could have the presidency, the Democrats, determined to deny African-Americans their newly acquired rights, would be allowed to control the Southern states. Federal troops would be withdrawn and the carpetbaggers would leave. In effect, this would bring an end to Reconstruction, the Republican attempt to modernise the politics, government and racial attitudes of the South.

By 1877, Reconstruction had been going on for more than ten years and there was still clear evidence of resistance to the North's efforts to achieve legal equality for African-Americans. Reconstruction had set up a series of reforms, not least the 13th, 14th and 15th Amendments to the Constitution, that aimed to encourage progress towards political equality in the South. However, the Republicans had done very badly in the 1874 midterm elections for Congress, mainly as a result of an economic depression that hit in 1873. As a result, they no longer enjoyed a supermajority in both houses. Also, by the mid 1870s the conditions for African-Americans in the South were no longer considered as important by the Republicans as they once had been. Other issues, such as the condition of the economy, began to take priority. Hoping that the Democrats of the South would obey both the letter and the spirit of the new constitutional rules, they turned their attention elsewhere. As it turned out, the situation for African-Americans in the South would be neglected by Congress and the presidency for decades.

The changing position of African-Americans and the responses of the white South

The Civil War had led to the emancipation of around 4 million slaves, and this fact radically changed the basis of Southern society. The efforts of African-American slaves had underpinned the lifestyle of the white community in the South for more than 100 years.

Lincoln's Emancipation Proclamation, and the subsequent Constitutional Amendments, showed how important African-Americans were in the new society. Yet there remained a huge gulf between the theory of equality and its practice. To begin with, ex-slaves entered the post-war era with little or no land of their own. In the summer of 1865, Johnson had ordered that all land that had been confiscated by the Union must be returned to those Southerners who had been 'pardoned' – those who swore an oath of allegiance to the Union and who consented to the emancipation of the slaves. In addition, the general lack of education and investment in the African-American community put its members at a further economic disadvantage.

In this vulnerable situation, most African-Americans, although now technically free, were still trapped by great poverty and the entrenched racism that persisted in both North and South. Many African-Americans in the South found themselves working as **sharecroppers.** Although this was something of an improvement, it was still a life of unrelenting labour for little reward. Without their own land to farm, many moved about in their search for work, going into the cities to find employment.

sharecroppers
Tenant farmers; sharecropping is an agricultural and economic system whereby a landlord allows a tenant to use an area of land in return for a portion of the crop produced on that land.

New problems arose in the South as white Southerners reasserted their social and political dominance. Some organised themselves into secret societies to attack African-Americans. The best known of these, notorious to the present day, was the Ku Klux Klan. Formed in 1866, the Ku Klux Klan was active across several states, intimidating African-Americans into not voting. Beatings and lynchings were their preferred methods. Neither President Grant nor the Republican Congress was prepared to accept this lawlessness. In 1870–75, Congress passed three enforcement acts, one actually called the Ku Klux Klan Act. This enabled Grant to suspend habeas corpus (see page 47) in parts of the South and use the army to stop KKK violence. The White League, another white supremacist organisation, was formed after the Colfax massacre of 1873.

Note:
At Colfax, Louisiana, white men armed with rifles and a cannon opened fire on a crowd of both black and white people, killing between 60 and 100 men – the vast majority of whom were black. The leaders of the massacre were arrested and charged, but were later released as the Supreme Court ruled that the law they had broken was unconstitutional.

Figure 2.11 An 1874 cartoon by Thomas Nast, entitled 'Worse than Slavery'

Reconstruction largely failed to bring African-Americans onto an equal footing with whites. Indeed, **racial segregation** (formalised by the so-called 'Jim Crow' laws of the 1890s) persisted in many parts of the South until the 1960s. Furthermore, sheer intimidation by local whites, often with the open endorsement of the police and judiciary, served to keep many African-Americans in the same inferior and oppressed position.

However, there were some successes. During the 1870s and 1880s, African-Americans voted in elections in significant numbers and so reshaped the political map of the post-war United States. Those African-Americans who had some money took the opportunity to invest in themselves, building their own schools and public buildings. A small African-American middle class began to grow.

racial segregation
The separation of different ethnic groups in terms of where they live and how and where they perform basic social activities.

Note:
The Jim Crow laws were local and state laws that enforced racial segregation. Black and white people had separate schools, drinking fountains and public toilets, and were allocated different areas of restaurants and public transport vehicles. Although conditions were supposedly 'separate but equal', in practice the laws discriminated against African-Americans.

Figure 2.12 The Skidmore Guard, an African-American military organisation, held its first annual ball at the Seventh Avenue Germania assembly rooms, New York City, in 1872

Economic and political changes

The Civil War and Reconstruction had profound effects on the economic and political life of the United States, but little actually changed in the South. It remained an economically depressed region with considerable poverty, in which white supremacists used their power to repress and otherwise harm African-Americans. The Constitution had certainly been radically reformed, but this had a limited impact on the lives of most of African-American people. The institution of slavery had been removed, but the issue of race relations was far from resolved, and African-Americans were a long way from enjoying full civil rights. That would not come for nearly another 100 years.

Politics became national, as opposed to local, to a far greater extent. The power of federal government had grown at the expense of individual states, as seen in the passage of Constitutional Amendments and the implementation of Radical Reconstruction (see page 58). It could also be said that a sense of American nationalism had grown at the expense of sectional identities. Yet, in balance, state rights and identity remained extremely powerful in the United States, arguably more powerful than any allegiance to a national identity. This can be seen partly in the government's general lack of willingness to enforce the 14th and 15th Amendments at a practical level – that job would fall to a much later generation. Many Southern communities still felt very distant from the government in Washington, DC, both culturally and politically. One interesting point to note is that, following the end of the Civil War, it was 100 years before a citizen of a former Confederate state was elected president. Northerners also dominated the most important governmental and Supreme Court positions until the beginning of the 20th century.

Another change brought about by Reconstruction was that the USA began developing into a true industrial power. The resources had always been there, and industrialisation had proceeded at speed in the North in order to help it win the Civil War. Now that the unity of the USA had been sustained in the 1860s, the rest of the 19th century saw the even more rapid industrialisation of America. The West, important in the 1840s and 1850s but forgotten in the wars of the 1860s, once more became a focus of growth and expansion. While Southern Democrats had turned their backs on the federal government, Republicans had taken the opportunity to impose their model of economic development. However, many historians point out that the economic rise of the United States actually began before the Civil War, and that the Reconstruction era was just a continuation of trends that had already been established.

The Civil War proved to be a vital step in the USA's progress from a former colony of the United Kingdom to a major world power. It shaped the direction the nation took both politically and economically. It ensured the ultimate dominance of the federal government over the wishes of individual states, and it stimulated massive economic forces that would lead to the United States becoming the largest economy in the world. The Reconstruction process, initially well intentioned, largely failed in its aim to bring social justice to the former slaves. However, it did ensure the restoration of the Union and it enabled the United States as a whole to move forward.

Key issues

The key features of this chapter are:

- the strengths and weaknesses of the military and political leadership of the two sides in the Civil War

- the nature and extent of change for the civilian populations and economies of the North and the South during and after the war

- the impact of the Civil War on political processes

- the theory behind, and the practice of, Reconstruction

- perceptions of Reconstruction – success or failure?

Revision questions

1 Why did racial segregation become established in the South?

2 'Ultimately, Reconstruction failed.' How far does an analysis of the period to 1877 support this view?

Further reading

Farmer, A. *The American Civil War (Access to History)*. London, UK. Hodder. 2008.

Farmer, A. *Reconstruction and the Results of the American Civil War*. London, UK. Hodder. 1997.

Foner, E. *Reconstruction: America's Unfinished Revolution*. London, UK. HarperCollins. 1988.

Glatthaar, J. 'Black Glory: The African-American Role in Union Victory' in Borritt, G. *Why the Confederacy Lost*. Oxford, UK. Oxford University Press. 1992. pp. 133–62.

McPherson, J. *Battle Cry of Freedom*. London, UK. Penguin. 1990.

Chapter

3 The expansion of US power in the 19th and 20th centuries

Key questions

- Why, and with what consequences, did the USA expand in North America from the 1840s to the 1890s?
- Why, and with what consequences, did US relations with the states of Central America and the Caribbean change between the 1840s and the 1930s?
- Why, and with what consequences, did US relations with Europe change between the 1840s and the 1930s?
- Why, and with what consequences, did US relations with Asia change between the 1840s and the 1930s?

Content summary

- Manifest destiny, westward expansion and the Indian Wars.
- The US–Mexican War of 1846–48 and US expansion to the Southwest.
- Oregon and Alaska and the expansion to the North and Northwest.
- US–Cuban relations in the 19th century and early 20th century.
- The USA, the Caribbean and Central America in the 19th century and early 20th century.
- The USA and Europe in the 19th century and early 20th century.
- US–Chinese and US–Japanese relations in the 19th century and early 20th century.
- The growth of the US Pacific empire – Hawaii and the Philippines.

Timeline

Apr 1846– Feb 1848	US–Mexican War
Dec 1853	The Gadsden Purchase
Jun 1858	Treaty of Tianjin with China
May 1862	The Homestead Act
1876–77	The Great Sioux War
1887	The Dawes Act
Apr–Aug 1898	Spanish–American War; acquisition of Cuba, Hawaii and the Philippines
Jul 1902	The Philippine Organic Act
1904	President Roosevelt issues the Monroe Corollary
Jul 1914	First World War breaks out in Europe
Apr 1917	USA enters the First World War
Jan 1918	President Wilson issues the Fourteen Points
Jun 1919	Treaty of Versailles

Introduction

The 19th and early 20th centuries were a period of great expansion for the United States. At the dawn of the 19th century, the USA was a small, new nation confined by the Appalachian Mountains to the west, the Atlantic to the east, Canada to the north and Spanish colonies to the south. By 1920, it had expanded its frontier to the Pacific Ocean, taken over the present states of Florida and California, and had driven the Mexicans out of the present states of Texas, Arizona and New Mexico. It had also absorbed Native American lands and acquired an overseas empire in the Pacific, becoming the dominant power in the Caribbean and Central America. By the end of the First World War in 1918, the United States had emerged as one of the great powers of the 20th century. Its population expanded from around 5.3 million in 1800 to 123 million in 1930. Arguably, the 20th century would be shaped more by the United States than by any other nation. This chapter traces the rise of the United States to 'Great Power' status.

Figure 3.1 The Oklahoma Land Rush, 1889 – part of the USA's westward expansion

Expansion in North America 1840s–90s

Westward expansion in America started almost as soon as the first settlers arrived from Europe, and it continued throughout the period prior to the recognition of American independence in 1783. Once independence was attained, expansion accelerated rapidly. In 1803, President Jefferson gained Louisiana (around 2,142,000 sq km/827,000 sq miles) by purchase (see page 8), doubling the size of the United States. Florida was taken from the Spanish in 1819. Settlers moved further and further west, towards and then across the Mississippi. Thousands moved into what is now the state of Texas, but was then a largely uninhabited part of Mexico. Mexico was weak and unstable, and these American settlers revolted against the Mexican government and set up the Republic of Texas as an independent state in 1836.

Figure 3.2 The expansion of the United States in the 18th and 19th centuries

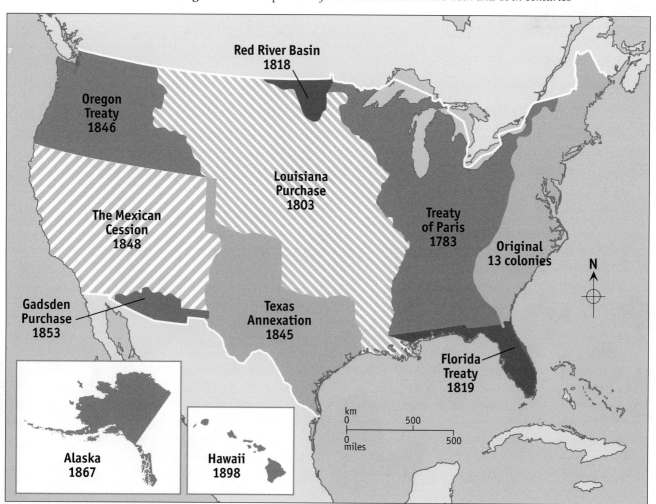

The concept of manifest destiny

'Manifest destiny' referred to the notion that the United States was destined to expand into, settle and rule over the whole North American continent.

> *This continent was intended by Providence as a vast theatre in which to work out the grand experiment of Republican Government under the auspices of the Anglo-Saxon race.*
>
> **Unknown congressman, speaking in 1845.**

> *There should be no interference by foreign powers aimed at limiting our greatness and checking the fulfilment of our manifest destiny to overspread the continent allotted to us by Providence for the free development of our yearly multiplying millions.*
>
> **John Louis O'Sullivan, *Democratic Review*, 1845.**

The term 'manifest destiny' was first used in this context in the 1840s, but the concept had been around for decades. The main ideas underpinning manifest destiny were as follows:

- US expansion to the Pacific was logical and inevitable.
- Aggressive US nationalism was desirable.
- The United States had the 'divine right' (a right given by God) to settle the whole North American continent, and to spread its Christian and republican values.
- Incorporation into the United States would bring liberty and freedom to other North American territories.
- If the USA did not acquire territories such as California, then some 'evil' colonial power might.

Some historians have argued that most of the points listed above can be seen as a justification for US aggression, imperialism and greed.

Areas of expansion

There were three main areas of US expansion in the period after 1840:

- to the South and Southwest, then part of Mexico
- to the West and to the Pacific, areas mostly belonging to Native Americans
- to the North and Northwest, where Native Americans, Russians and the British (in Canada) controlled the land.

US expansion into the Southwest, then part of the independent republic of Mexico, had long been envisaged. Texas was already separate from Mexico and looking to join the United States. There was a growing desire on the part of both the government in Washington, DC, as well as of thousands of potential American settlers, to move into the largely unpopulated Mexican areas of what are now the states of California, New Mexico, Arizona and Nevada.

The causes of the US–Mexican War

Several factors contributed to the outbreak of the US–Mexican War in 1846. These included:

- the earlier annexation of Texas
- Mexicans' fear that the United States wanted to take over the whole of the Southwest and destroy their republic
- the failure of US politicians to understand why the Mexicans did not like the idea of parting with 'spare' land that the USA could settle
- the US view of Mexicans as cruel and incompetent rulers, and the resulting claim that the territory would be much better run by the USA.

The main short-term cause for the US–Mexican War, however, was the election of President James Polk in 1844. A strong supporter of manifest destiny, Polk was determined to absorb Texas and California, and as much of the Southwest as he could, into the United States. Public opinion was overwhelmingly on his side. Seeing civil unrest in Mexico as an opportunity, Polk moved 4000 troops to the US–Mexican border. Some negotiations were attempted, but in truth there was little desire on either side to settle their differences.

The world has nothing to fear from military ambition in our government … our government cannot be otherwise than pacific. Foreign powers should therefore look on the annexation of Texas to the United States not as the conquest of a nation seeking to extend her dominions by arms and violence, but as the peaceful acquisition of a territory once her own … diminishing the chances of war and opening new and ever-increasing markets for their products.

President Polk's inaugural speech, 1845.

President Polk was spared the accusation of 'aggressor' when in early 1846 a Mexican army unit attacked US soldiers on what Americans viewed as 'their' side of the Rio Grande River. Eleven US soldiers were killed in the fighting. Polk and Congress took this as a declaration of war and ordered US generals to attack. President Polk wanted a short, contained war and a quick peace. He certainly did not want a long campaign that would be expensive in terms of lives and money. Generals Winfield Scott and Zachary Taylor initially had only modest success against Mexico, partly because the US army was not well supplied and equipped.

However, in 1847 a larger and much better-supplied army invaded deep into Mexico and took the capital Mexico City, bringing the war in Mexico to a close.

In addition, in 1846 **John Frémont** led a rebellion in California against the Mexicans and proclaimed an independent Republic of California. The US navy landed marines and claimed California for the United States, after a combined Native American/Mexican army was defeated at the Battle of the Plains of Mesa in 1847. With the loss of their capital as well as an enormous amount of territory, the Mexicans admitted defeat. The way was open for peace negotiations.

> ## Note:
> In 1848, gold was discovered in California, the most successful find in history to date. It played a key role in fuelling the economic and commercial expansion of the later 19th century, triggering a 'gold rush' as more than 80,000 prospectors (people searching for gold deposits) entered California in one year.

The Treaty of Guadelupe Hidalgo 1848

The Treaty of Guadelupe Hidalgo was the peace treaty that ended the US–Mexican War. The USA paid a price for its victory in the war: 1700 US soldiers had been killed, 11,000 had died of disease, and Congress had paid out over $100 million for the war effort. In addition, at least 50,000 Mexicans had been killed and the war resulted in a legacy of lasting bitterness in Mexico. However, there were also considerable benefits for the USA:

- Around 2.6 million sq km (1 million sq miles) of land was gained from Mexico, constituting the present states of California, New Mexico, Nevada and Arizona.
- In return for this huge area of land, Mexico received only $15 million 'conscience money'.
- The United States was now a major continental power.

Critics of the US–Mexican War felt it was simply the act of an aggressive bully attacking a poor and weak republic. The United States might have gained a continental empire, but its international reputation declined.

The gains of Guadelupe Hidalgo were 'rounded off' in 1853, when the USA purchased 75,000 sq km (29,000 sq miles) of land from Mexico for $10 million, in order to gain a suitable rail route to their new acquisitions in the Southwest. The Mexicans had little use for the land and a lot of use for the money, and were happy to agree to the purchase. This deal – known as the Gadsden Purchase after the US ambassador to Mexico at the time – was the last major acquisition, apart from Alaska in the North, for the continental United States. The age of expansion was over, and the age of development was about to begin.

Key figure

John Frémont (1813–90)

Frémont was a soldier and explorer, often known as the 'Great Pathfinder'. He was a key figure in the acquisition of California from Mexico. He became a 'goldrush' multi-millionaire and was one of the first senators from California. Hostile to slavery, he played an important part in the formation of the Republican Party.

Conflict against Native Americans

The history of the relationship between the European settlers in America and the Native American population was troubled and bloody. The English had used Native Americans as their allies against the United States in the War of 1812. The viciousness on both sides during the Creek Wars, which ended in 1814, also left a bitter tension between them. By the end of Andrew Jackson's presidency in 1837, most major Native American groups had been driven, by force or by bribes, across the Mississippi. These groups had been allocated around 800 million sq km (200 million acres) in compensation.

The usual European–American attitude towards the Native Americans was racist, regarding them as totally uncivilised. Factors such as the Homestead Act of 1862, which gave 65 hectares (160 acres) to any new 'white' settler, and the massive birth rate amongst settlers who moved west, put more pressure on what had been seen as Native American lands. This overpowering of the Native American population by the force of sheer numbers of whites has been called 'demographic imperialism'.

Native Americans tended to live in tiny social groups that migrated constantly and were largely dependent on the buffalo for their food. They were usually tolerant towards others, provided they were left alone. However, they naturally resented the seemingly endless westward expansion of millions of white settlers, soldiers, gold prospectors and railway and city builders. This mass migration by people with fundamentally different lifestyles, and largely insensitive attitudes towards the Native Americans, inevitably led to conflict.

A good example of this deteriorating relationship between Native Americans and white settlers occurred after 1851. The California Gold Rush led to thousands of settlers wanting to go west to search for gold. The USA signed a treaty with a large number of Native American tribes in 1851, in which the tribes agreed to allow wagon trains through their territory and permitted roads and forts to be built along the way. In return, the Native Americans received guarantees for the security of their territory and for payments in cash and commodities. This treaty was renewed in 1868. However, the US government did not keep its side of the bargain: US citizens settled on supposedly secured Native American land, and not all payments were made. Further discoveries of gold, the Homestead Act and the rapid development of railways west of the Mississippi meant that it was only a matter of time before this conflict became widespread, resulting in incidents such as the Sand Creek Massacre in 1864.

> **Note:**
> In the Sand Creek Massacre on 29 November 1864, a force of 700 soldiers from the Colorado Territory militia brutally killed between 70 and 163 Cheyenne and Arapaho Indians, mainly women and children.

This led to retaliation by the Native Americans, which inevitably led to further reprisals by the whites. With numbers, firepower and support from the government and army on their side, the whites were bound to win. Conflict spread across the plains west of the Mississippi. President Ulysses S. Grant strongly disliked Native Americans. Superficially, he tried a more tolerant approach, but in practice this involved further settlement by whites and more attempts to 'civilise' the Native Americans by converting them to Christianity and putting a stop to their traditional nomadic lifestyle. This only led to further conflict.

In 1876, the Great Sioux War broke out. Gold had been discovered in the Black Hills (now in South Dakota) and gold prospectors and settlers poured into Native American territory. Fighting started between the settlers and the Native Americans, with the US army initially trying to keep the settlers out. Ultimately, due to popular and political pressure by the white US majority, the decision was taken to remove the Native Americans from the Black Hills by force. After some setbacks, including the famous massacre of Colonel Custer and his troops at the Battle of the Little Bighorn in 1876, a large and well-equipped US army destroyed the Native Americans. There were sporadic incidents in the following years, which culminated in the appalling Massacre at Wounded Knee in 1890, when the army slaughtered more than 200 men, women and children of the Lakota tribe.

The same story continued across the United States in the period after the Civil War. During the war, regular soldiers were called up to fight. Dealing with the 'Indian problem' was often left to irregular, undisciplined local groups who detested the Native Americans and wanted to get rid of them. Brutality on one side was followed by further atrocity on the other. When gold was discovered in what is now Idaho and Oregon in the 1860s, prospectors once again flooded into Native American lands, followed by the inevitable settlers, and conflict resulted. The Snake Wars of 1864–68, in what are now the states of Oregon, Nevada and Idaho, and the Nez Perce War of 1877 followed.

In 1887, Congress passed the Dawes Act. This was designed to break up the Native American tribal system and assist the integration of Native Americans into 'normal' US society. Individual Native Americans were given land and the means to cultivate it, but often in places where the soil was totally unsuited for cultivation. Of the millions of acres that had been made available for Native American reservations before the Dawes Act, over two-thirds were taken away from them and given to 'white' settlement by the act.

Gradually, the Native Americans were worn down, killed or moved to new reservations. In 1900, by the end of what one writer called the 'Century of Dishonour' because of the white settlers' broken promises and treaties, as well as the killings, fewer than 350,000 Native Americans were left. This was almost half the population of 600,000 recorded in 1800. The contrast with the demographic explosion of white Americans is vast, and the ruthless treatment of Native Americans in the name of US expansion represents a shameful part of the USA's early history.

A study of the dates when new states were admitted to the Union is revealing. Between 1867 (with Nebraska) and 1890 (with Wyoming),

Note:
The Dawes Act authorised the US president to survey Native American tribal land and divide it into sections for individual Native Americans. Individual ownership of land was seen as an essential component of the Native Americans' assimilation into wider US society. There was also a provision in the act that any land 'left over' after the tribal land had been split up would be bought by the US government and made available for non-Native American settlers.

eight new states joined the Union. All were in the West, and all had been crucial areas for the Native Americans. They were now 'settled', and barbed wire and cultivated fields covered the land where the Native American tribes had formerly roamed.

The North and Northwest – Oregon and Alaska

Another of Polk's ambitions was to acquire the Pacific Northwest Coast, centring on the present state of Oregon. This was an area of around 1.3 million sq km (500,000 sq miles): a land of vast forests, good agricultural land and the superb port of Vancouver. The British, the Russians and the Spanish were all interested in the region. Apart from the Native Americans, the majority of the local population were of US origin.

49th parallel
A circle of latitude, like the 36° 30′ line (see page 22).

Ownership of this area was unclear, and the most likely cause of conflict lay with the British in Canada. Traditionally, the US–Canadian border lay along the **49th parallel**, but the Americans argued that the boundary should go much farther north. They argued that:

- they had settled in the region first
- they had explored it more thoroughly
- it was next to US territory and it made geographical sense for the USA to have it.

The British argued that:

- they had initially explored it
- their Hudson Bay Company had been trading there for years
- they needed the important Pacific port of Vancouver.

Note:
The numbers of people living in Oregon were tiny until 'Oregon fever' gripped the United States in 1841 and over 10,000 potential settlers headed west to settle this part of the 'promised land'.

Although some aggressive comments were made by both US presidential candidates, Polk and his challenger Henry Clay, in the 1844 campaign, the victor Polk was much more concerned with Mexico and the South. He did not want to fight a war on two fronts with his tiny army. The British, deeply involved in crises at home, were also in a conciliatory mood, and the Webster–Ashburton Treaty was signed between Britain and the USA on 9 August 1842. This continued the US border along the 49th parallel. The Oregon territory was added to the United States, giving the country an extensive Pacific coastline.

The purchase of Alaska 1867

The last North American acquisition was Alaska, then part of Russia. Russia found looking after Alaska a challenging administrative task. It was difficult to reach from Moscow and it had few settlers or resources, so it seemed to be sensible to sell the area when the USA made a cash offer. The Americans were keen to acquire Alaska for a variety of reasons:

- It would expand the Pacific coastline of the USA.
- There was good fishing there.
- It would spread US rule and keep the British out of the area.
- It made sense to stay on good terms with Russia.
- It would be a peaceful acquisition.

Congress was initially reluctant to acquire Alaska, but the secretary of state **William Seward** managed to push through the deal, paying the Russians $7.2 million for it. The acquisition of Alaska brought to an end the vast expansion of the United States in the 19th century.

The debate on US expansion

As always with such a major issue central to the development of the United States as a world power, there is a serious debate amongst historians as to exactly what the motives were for the USA's 19th-century expansion. Some of the arguments are that it was:

- largely accidental, it 'just happened'; there was no single overriding motive, just lots of separate incidents that took place at a very local level
- the result of simple demography; once the first settlers arrived, millions more immigrants followed and reproduced at a high rate, so westward expansion was inevitable until it hit the natural boundaries of the Pacific and the Rio Grande
- deliberate policy by citizens, states and the federal government
- entirely politically led; presidents like Jefferson and Jackson had started it, and presidents like Polk and Grant followed
- part of a special mission to bring the benefits of the American way and democracy and freedom
- ruthless and aggressive imperialism of the sort practised by the Spanish, French and British in North America in earlier centuries.

The present state of the debate is that most historians believe westward expansion was largely driven by politicians at state and national level, with great popular support, for political and commercial reasons.

Questions

1 Why did war break out between the USA and Mexico in 1846?

2 To what extent was the expansion of the United States within North America motivated purely by commercial factors?

Key figure

William Seward (1801–72)

William Seward was the US secretary of state from 1861 to 1869. Strongly anti-slavery, he was a US senator before the Civil War and a founder of the Republican Party. He was a committed supporter of Lincoln and Johnson during the Civil War and Reconstruction periods. A keen expansionist, he tried to obtain the Caribbean islands for the United States.

Central America and the Caribbean 1840–1930

In the period from 1840 to 1930, US policy towards islands in the Caribbean and the states of Central America changed considerably. Conscious of its strong status and protective of its interests, both strategic and commercial, the USA saw both regions as important to its security and prosperity. It carefully monitored developments in these countries, and was also prepared to use force to protect US interests.

Figure 3.3 US involvement in the Caribbean and Central America, from 1895 to the 1930s

Mexico
US troops and navy sent into Mexico in 1914 and 1916

Cuba
Spanish–American War, 1898
Platt Amendment, 1901
US forces in Cuba, 1906–09 and 1917–22

Haiti
US protectorate announced, 1915
US marines in Haiti, 1915–34

Puerto Rico
US acquisition from Spain, 1898
Organic Act of 1900
Puerto Ricans granted US citizenship in 1917

Dominican Republic
US marines sent into Dominican Republic, 1905
US protectorate, US marines stationed 1916–24

Nicaragua
US protectorate announced, 1912
US marines in Nicaragua until 1930s

Panama
Aid and support for Panamanian independence, 1902–03
Acquisition of land for Panama Canal, 1903; Panama becomes US protectorate
Panama Canal completed, 1914

US policy towards Cuba 1897–1940

Cuba provides an excellent example of US expansionism in the 19th century. It also demonstrates very well the USA's attitude to neighbouring countries that it felt were in its sphere of interest in the 20th century.

Cuba, with its position in the Caribbean and its proximity to the United States, became of increasing interest to Americans as the United States grew as a commercial and naval power. Cuba was the last Spanish colony in the region, and it was badly ruled. In 1868, the Cubans followed the example of many other Spanish colonies and revolted against their rulers, demanding independence.

With their own 'anti-colonial' background, as well as a lot of US capital investment in Cuba, people in the United States felt a certain amount of sympathy for the Cuban rebels. Roman Catholic Spain excluded Protestant missionaries from Cuba, and the Spanish were seen as brutal anti-democratic rulers. These factors caused widespread anger in the United States. In the 1890s, Cuba became an issue in US politics: in the 1896 election, 'Free Cuba' and support for Cuban independence were political party platforms.

Figure 3.4 Spanish government troops being ambushed by a rebel force, 1896

The newly elected US president, William McKinley, made a brief attempt to appease both US and Cuban opinion by trying to persuade the Spanish to reform their methods of government. However, events began to spiral out of control. A private letter from the Spanish minister in Washington, DC, was stolen and published. It accused President McKinley of being a 'weak bidder for the admiration of the crowd' in his Cuban policy. McKinley and the US public naturally found this highly insulting.

The situation reached crisis point when a US battleship, the *Maine*, was sent to Cuba to protect US citizens who had been caught up in the fighting there. The intention may have been to intimidate the Spanish as much as to protect Americans. However, the *Maine*, which was moored in a Cuban harbour, exploded and over 260 US sailors were killed. The press insisted that Spain was to blame for the deaths, and McKinley demanded 'forceful intervention' in retaliation. Congress voted in support of the extra money needed for the war, and passed a War Resolution. A naval blockade was established, and war with Spain followed.

Note:

The evidence now is that the *Maine* blew up not because of some deliberate act by the Spanish, but because a fire in a coal store next to the ship's ammunition store caused the ammunition to explode.

The debate on the reasons for the Spanish–American War

A variety of arguments have been put forward to explain why the United States went to war with Spain over Cuba. According to different sources, the war was:

- inspired by an aggressive and patriotic press campaign that inflamed public opinion
- intended to protect US business interests
- an unfortunate misunderstanding caused by the *Maine* incident
- inevitable, given the misrule of the Spanish and the geographical closeness of Cuba to the USA; the United States had to intervene to restore order
- the result of US fears of an independent Cuba that it could not control
- motivated by the USA's desire for more territory and business
- a 'Christian mission'
- a deliberate distraction for Americans to divert interest from their economic depression
- part of an American tendency to confuse selfish US interests with progress and the wellbeing of other peoples.

All of these factors probably played a part in bringing about the war. The strongly imperialistic attitude of McKinley and many influential Americans, coupled with popular support and the strategic importance of Cuba, were probably the most significant causes of the war.

The Spanish–American War

The war itself did not last long. It was largely fought at sea, as the USA had a large modern navy (which it was quite anxious to demonstrate) but only 30,000 soldiers. The US navy destroyed the Spanish navy at Manila Bay, in the Spanish colony of the Philippines, in 1898. A small number of US troops were landed at Santiago in Cuba. During the fighting, the future US president, Theodore Roosevelt, achieved considerable fame with his band of 'Rough Riders' in a charge up San Juan Hill in Cuba.

Note:
The 'Rough Riders' were a group of volunteer soldiers who joined up for the duration of the war in Cuba. The US army was very small and depended on such volunteers.

Figure 3.5 US troops charge San Juan Hill, 1 July 1898

There was a lot of hostility between the Cuban freedom fighters and the US troops. Cuban efforts were decisive in the victory over the Spanish. With their navy destroyed, and their army in Cuba defeated by the Cubans and Americans, the Spanish surrendered. Without the help of the Cubans, the USA might have had a great deal more difficulty in both landing in Cuba and defeating the Spanish. However, the USA ignored the Cubans' contribution and maintained that it was a purely American victory. They did not include or even seriously consider Cubans in the final peace settlement with Spain, and the treaty was signed in Paris.

In the 1898 Treaty of Paris, the USA gained Puerto Rico, Guam and the Philippines, and the Spanish were required to withdraw from Cuba. The US Senate only just passed the treaty, as some senators had real reservations about the United States becoming a colonial power. The Cubans naturally resented being treated as racial and military inferiors by the Americans, and the scene was set for a future of difficult relations between the two countries.

Cuba after the war

Once the Spanish had been defeated and had withdrawn from Cuba, a major debate started in the United States about what to do with Cuba. There were three possibilities. Cuba could:

- be given its independence and left alone
- become a colony
- come under some type of **protectorate** by the USA, in which it would be administered by its neighbour.

Prior to the war starting, in April 1898, Congress had passed the Teller Amendment as part of the decision to go to war with Spain. This stated that the USA should not annex Cuba, and that control of the island should be left to its own people.

Victory led to a change of opinion by the Americans, who felt that the Cubans were not yet ready to rule themselves. This belief was really a justification for their concern that US commercial interests might not be allowed to develop in Cuba if it was self-governed. As a result, in 1901 Congress passed the Platt Amendment, which was to govern US–Cuban relations until 1934.

Cuba became a republic in 1902, but a lot of control still lay with the United States. Cuba's final treaty with the USA was passed in 1903; quite a lot of pressure had to be put on the Cubans to make them give up a significant amount of the freedom for which they had fought. The presence of an American army in Cuba persuaded its people to agree to the treaty, which imposed a new political system on the country and made its economy heavily dependent on the United States. A far-reaching takeover of Cuban land by Americans followed, and American businesses began to move into Cuba on a large scale. The Cuban economy started to develop much along the lines the United States wished it to.

protectorate
A country under the protection of the United States, preventing other countries from taking it over, while at the same time giving the United States considerable control over the country itself.

Note:
The Platt Amendment gave the United States control of Cuban foreign, financial and commercial affairs. It limited Cuban sovereignty and gave the USA the right to intervene in Cuban affairs. It also gave the United States certain naval bases in Cuba.

The imposition of a political system that was alien to the Cuban people, restricting the right to vote to the rich, did not work at all well. Political instability simmered in the country right up to 1934, when the Platt Amendment expired and the Cubans gained greater autonomy. US forces returned to Cuba to keep order and protect US business interests on a fairly regular basis, in 1906–09 and 1917–22. After 1934, Fulgencio Batista, always willing to co-operate with the United States, controlled Cuba in a ruthless and undemocratic way until overthrown by the Communist leader Fidel Castro in 1958–59.

Cuba was a success story as far as the commercial and strategic interests of the United States were concerned, and US businesses flourished there. Whether the Cuban people saw the process as successful is arguable, although conditions may have initially been better than they were under the Spanish. American companies took over large amounts of Cuban land and they broke up the Cuban village system, which was based on communal ownership, in order to increase the production of sugar. This caused serious rural depopulation and many Cubans were reduced from the status of communal landowners to simple labourers. The education system was used to impose American culture on the Cubans.

Puerto Rico

The island of Puerto Rico, also a Spanish colony, had already been given a degree of independence by Spain before the war with the United States broke out in 1898. It was invaded in 1898 by American troops and after a little fighting the Spanish surrendered and withdrew. Under the Organic Act of 1900, Puerto Rico was to be administered by the United States. It developed more peacefully than Cuba, and was less important to the USA both strategically and economically. In 1917, it was given its own legislature for local matters and its citizens were granted US citizenship, although it did not become a US state.

> *The march of events rules and overrules human action. The Philippines, like Cuba and Puerto Rico, were entrusted to our hands by the war. It is not a trust we sought; it is a trust from which we will not flinch.*
>
> US president William McKinley, September 1898.

US policy in Central America and the Caribbean

The period after the USA's acquisition of Cuba and Puerto Rico showed a marked increase in US interest and direct involvement in the Caribbean and Central America. It is often known as the era of the Banana Wars and of **Dollar Diplomacy**.

Note:
In spite of unemployment in Cuba, several US companies imported cheaper and more compliant workers from Haiti and Jamaica, which further worsened relations between many Cubans and the United States.

Dollar Diplomacy
A term invented by President Taft to describe the US foreign policy of advancing American business interests, using military power if necessary.

Note:
Bananas were often a major crop of the Central American and Caribbean countries, such as Honduras, Nicaragua, Haiti and the Dominican Republic. All these countries became politically unstable at some point in this period, and the United States felt it necessary to intervene militarily in order to restore law and order. America intervened partly to ensure stability in the region, and partly to ensure good conditions for US business to flourish.

The US government was active in pushing the nation's business interests and investment, using force if necessary, to ensure its own strategic interests and to facilitate moneymaking by American businessmen. There was occasional embarrassment in the United States, with its libertarian, democratic, republican and anti-colonial traditions, at this involvement in what could be seen as aggressive and selfish imperialism similar to that practiced by European powers.

The United States and Mexico to 1920

The relationship between the United States and Mexico throughout the period after 1848 was always tense. Mexicans had inevitably bitter memories of the loss of so much of their territory. However, Mexico had limited economic potential and experienced constant political instability, and it was never in a position to be a threat to the United States. The USA disliked the fact that the Mexicans had chosen a 'monarch', the Emperor Maximilian, in the 1860s – partly because he came from Europe, and partly because of an ingrained ideological dislike of monarchical systems.

Mexican republicans captured and executed Emperor Maximilian in 1867, and this led to further political weakness in the country. However, by the late 1870s there was a degree of stability in Mexico, which encouraged some US investment and business expansion.

When Mexico descended into civil war after a liberal revolution in 1910, the United States became very concerned – particularly now that the Panama Canal was under construction (see page 82). President Woodrow Wilson, who used US forces in the region more extensively than any president before or since, sent troops and the navy into Mexico in both 1914 and 1916 to protect US interests and 'restore order'. He was anxious to ensure that there was no strategic threat to the United States from the south. The relationship remained tense until 1920, when a new administration in Washington, DC, and a greater level of competency in Mexican rule led to improved conditions.

Note:
One of the main reasons that the United States entered the war against Germany in 1917 was because of the Zimmerman telegram. This was a message from the German foreign minister to the German minister in Mexico, encouraging the Mexicans to invade the USA from the south (see page 88).

Panama and its canal

There had long been a desire in the United States to connect the Atlantic and the Pacific oceans. The journey round the tip of South America was long and often dangerous by sea. In the 1860s, US secretary of state William Seward, always a keen expansionist, had tried to start negotiations with Colombia (which then owned what is now Panama) for a canal, but the Senate stopped him.

There were three possible routes for a canal – through Mexico, Nicaragua or Panama. The best choice was Panama, but Colombia was not interested in the canal. So a French company, with considerable aid from the United States, stirred up a Panama independence movement around 1902. Panamanian independence followed in 1903, with rapid recognition by the United States, which naturally dissuaded any Colombian reaction. The US navy was very much in evidence off shore, to encourage the Panamanians and discourage the Colombians. The United States then permanently acquired a strip of Panamanian land – 16 km (10 miles) wide – through which the canal would be built, while at the same time making the new republic a protectorate.

corollary
A statement that follows on from another statement.

In 1904, President Roosevelt announced a **corollary** to the Monroe Doctrine of 1823. The Monroe Doctrine had intended to preserve the sovereignty of the independent states in the Americas, with a message for Europe to stay out of the region. Roosevelt now sanctioned US armed intervention when it was felt necessary to prevent financial and/or political collapse. Roosevelt's successors, from his departure in 1909 up to the late 1930s, would use this corollary to justify armed intervention in the region.

The Panama Canal was finished by 1914, built largely with American money and above all with US engineering skills and initiative. It played a major part in the development of the United States as a Pacific power.

Figure 3.6 The opening of the Panama Canal, 1914

Dominican Republic

The Dominican Republic proved to be another example of the United States actively using its 'police' power in the region. In 1905, Roosevelt sent the US marines to the Dominican Republic, allegedly to prevent European powers taking action to collect debts owed to them. However, protection of massive US investment was a more likely reason for American intervention.

With US warships off shore and marines ashore, the Dominican Republic became a US protectorate with Americans running the economy. The marines returned to 'police', or protect US interests, in 1916 and stayed there until 1924 when order was said to have been restored. By 1930, the Dominican Republic had come under the control of a US-marine-trained dictator, Rafael Trujillo, who ruled the country with great brutality for over 30 years. Trujillo allowed US business interests to dominate the economy of the Dominican Republic.

Nicaragua and Haiti

The US role in Nicaragua followed a similar process. Nicaragua's proximity to the possible Atlantic/Pacific canal site, as well as to the USA, in addition to the high level of US investment in the country, meant that the United States was bound to view Nicaragua through 'corollary to Monroe' eyes. Armed conflict with its neighbouring countries, such as Honduras and El Salvador, led Nicaragua and its president, Jose Zelaya, into serious debt.

> **Note:**
> In 1950, when the average annual income of an American was around $3000, the average income of a Haitian was $40. American 'protection' did not appear to bring many benefits to the protected.

With internal conflict and the inevitable threat to US business interests, a US protectorate was announced in 1912, and the US fleet and marines moved in. The USA managed Nicaragua's economy, and the marines stayed in the country until the 1930s. As with so many other countries in the Central American and Caribbean region, once an authoritarian, pro-American dictator was installed – in this case, the Somoza family – the marines withdrew and American business interests continued to dominate.

Haiti followed a comparable path: foreign debts, internal unrest and fear of intervention by others led to the arrival of the US marines in 1915, and they stayed until 1934. An estimated 10,000 Haitians were killed during the course of American occupation. A protectorate was initially proclaimed in Haiti and the USA controlled the economy while a series of brutal, pro-American dictators ran the country.

The economic depression after 1929, coupled with Roosevelt's **Good Neighbor policy**, brought to an end the age of intervention and the protectorates. The American policy from now on tended to be to prop up authoritarian dictators of varying brutality who supported US business and strategic interests.

Good Neighbor policy
Roosevelt promised to respect the rights of other nations in the Americas, and to place more focus on co-operation and trade and less on the use of military force.

US involvement in Central America and the Caribbean was driven by a mixture of commercial, business and strategic interests. Often the reasons given for the many interventions were altruistic in nature: to keep order; to bring stability, peace and democracy. However, the inhabitants of those recipient states seldom benefited, as real wages often fell and one harsh dictator succeeded another.

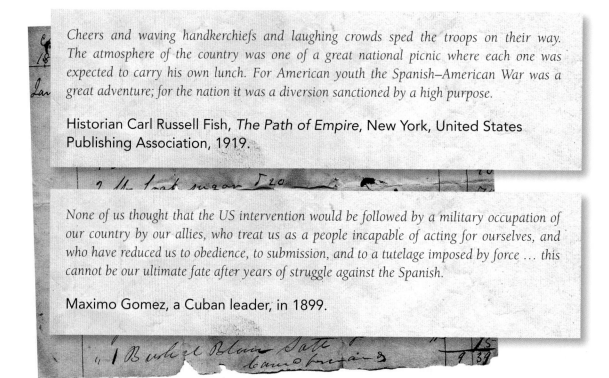

Cheers and waving handkerchiefs and laughing crowds sped the troops on their way. The atmosphere of the country was one of a great national picnic where each one was expected to carry his own lunch. For American youth the Spanish–American War was a great adventure; for the nation it was a diversion sanctioned by a high purpose.

Historian Carl Russell Fish, *The Path of Empire*, New York, United States Publishing Association, 1919.

None of us thought that the US intervention would be followed by a military occupation of our country by our allies, who treat us as a people incapable of acting for ourselves, and who have reduced us to obedience, to submission, and to a tutelage imposed by force ... this cannot be our ultimate fate after years of struggle against the Spanish.

Maximo Gomez, a Cuban leader, in 1899.

Questions

1 Why was the United States prepared to go to war with Spain over Cuba?

2 'While US policy in the Caribbean between 1890 and 1940 brought many advantages to the United States, it brought few to the Caribbean people themselves.' To what extent does your knowledge of US policy in the Caribbean support this view?

The USA's relationship with Europe 1840–1930

The relationship between the United States and the major European countries went through a variety of phases in the period 1840–1930. A large number of different factors influenced this relationship: traditional rivalries and alliances; the US Civil War; commercial developments in the United States; and its new position as a major player in world politics. The fact that the United States contained many ex-Europeans, with their own traditions and rivalries, also influenced policy. The large number of Irish people who settled in the United States, for example, often felt strong dislike for the British. Many Germans remained fiercely loyal to their former homeland. Not all immigrants were able to leave their own histories behind when they arrived at **Ellis Island**.

US relations with Britain and Germany until 1914

Of all the major European powers, Britain and Germany were the two that featured most prominently in the history of US foreign policy in the 19th and early 20th centuries.

Britain

Although the British started out as the hated colonial rulers of the USA, the two countries later enjoyed a mainly stable relationship. After the War of Independence in 1783 and again after the War of 1812, well-thought-out peace treaties removed most potential causes of friction. The British foreign secretary George Canning had strongly supported the Monroe Doctrine in the 1820s, and good sense on both sides prevented conflict over the border with Canada in the Oregon boundary issue (see page 74). Britain and the USA benefited enormously from trade with each other, with Britain buying vast amounts of the cotton and tobacco that the South produced, and selling enormous quantities of manufactured goods to the rapidly growing population of the United States.

The US Civil War could well have caused major problems for this relationship, bearing in mind that the Southern economy was so dependent on exporting cotton to Britain. The North blockaded the South and stopped most of its cotton exports to Britain. With its massive navy, Britain could easily have broken the blockade, which had led to mass unemployment in the Lancashire cotton industry. However, the British prime minister, Lord Palmerston, insisted that his country should remain neutral in the conflict.

Ellis Island
The island near New York where the vast majority of immigrants from Europe arrived and were processed.

In addition, Jefferson Davis was a poor diplomat who hated the English. He failed to capitalise on the support the South had in both British politics and the press. When the North had a grievance against the British because some assistance had been given to Southern blockade runners, the issue was intelligently dealt with by the British through **arbitration** and the payment of proper compensation to the United States. The relationship between the USA and Britain survived the American Civil War well.

arbitration
Using an independent referee to settle a dispute, and agreeing to abide by the judgement of that referee.

After the Civil War, there were no major issues between the USA and Britain. There were signs of a growing commercial rivalry in the 1890s, but there was also the feeling in both countries that a 'special relationship' was developing. They co-operated well over the Boxer Rebellion in China when their joint interests were threatened (see page 94).

Note:
The Boxer Rebellion was an anti-foreigner, anti-Christian-missionary peasant uprising in China in 1900, which had some official backing by the Chinese authorities. In one area of Beijing, the Boxers besieged many foreigners, who were rescued by troops from several countries, including the USA.

Germany

Germany only emerged as a unified country and major power in 1871, so no significant relationship existed with the United States until the later 19th century. Prussia, the state that had led the unification of Germany, had supported the North in the Civil War. By the 1880s, about 9% of the US population originated from what had become unified Germany, and many of these people still felt strong ties to the 'mother country'.

Note:
The United States intensely disliked the German colonisation of Samoa in the 1880s, which was felt to be very much in an American sphere of interest.

However, a stronger degree of rivalry than existed with the British began to emerge by the later 1870s. The aggressive nationalism of the Germans did not appeal to many in the United States. There was strong commercial and economic rivalry between the USA and Germany, particularly in the Far East and in Central and South America. One of the reasons that the United States was so keen to take over Guam and Hawaii in the Pacific was because it feared that the Germans might take the nations first. The relationship between the USA and Germany was becoming increasingly tense when the First World War broke out in Europe in 1914.

The growth of the US navy

Since the earliest days of the republic, the US navy had been a critical resource for the defence of American trade and commerce. A naval academy for training officers had been created at Annapolis in 1845, and the small US navy had played an important part in the US–Mexican War. During the Civil War, control of the seas was vital for the North.

However, the US navy, like the army, was cut right back in the 1870s. The public was tired of war and the strain it put on the country's resources; there were no real threats and no apparent need for a navy. A few small squadrons were kept in the Far East, the Mediterranean and the Caribbean to protect US commerce, but on the whole the ships were small and often old-fashioned. However, after 1890 several factors led to a rapid growth in the size and importance of the US navy:

- Three presidents in a row – Harrison, McKinley and Roosevelt – were all enthusiastic about naval expansion.
- European powers were starting out on a race to build more and better warships.
- The Japanese, with a growing navy, were seen as a threat.
- A book written by Captain A. T. Mahan, called *The Influence of Sea Power upon History*, argued that naval power was vital for a nation's greatness and prosperity, and this had enormous influence in the United States.
- The navy played a vital role in so many of the conflicts and acquisitions of the 'imperial' phase of US history after 1890, such as the acquisition of Cuba, that the American people could see that a navy was vital for US trade and prestige. Public opinion demanded a strong navy to protect US interests.

Naval expansion started under Theodore Roosevelt (a former minister for the US navy) and soon 16 new battleships were ready for action. Between 1907 and 1909, Roosevelt sent the ships on an international tour to make sure the world knew that the United States was now a major naval power.

The First World War

When war came to Europe in August 1914, the US president was the Democrat **Woodrow Wilson**. Able and knowledgeable, he was well aware that the USA was now a world power. Wilson was a highly principled man, deeply religious, and a believer in the importance of democracy and **self-determination**. He believed that the United States had a special role to play in world affairs. Outwardly he maintained that he disliked Dollar Diplomacy (see page 80) and imperialism, but his own track record in Central America and the Caribbean suggests otherwise.

However much he sympathised with the Allies (Britain, Russia and France) in the war, Wilson initially remained firmly neutral in policy. He had avoided any formal links with either of the two armed camps that had developed in Europe, and did all he could to mediate between the warring nations. When Britain blockaded Germany, it caused an immediate drop in the large trade between the USA and Germany, but the British took care to avoid upsetting the Americans. The USA benefited from the war, taking over both German and British markets in South America and making a great deal of money out of the war itself by setting up loans to countries involved in the conflict.

Key figure

Woodrow Wilson (1856–1924)

Wilson was a Democrat and a leader of the Progressive Movement. Before being elected US president in 1912, he served as president of Princeton University and governor of New Jersey. Wilson narrowly won a second term as US president in 1916. He introduced several major progressive reforms, as well as the famous Fourteen Points, during his time in office.

self-determination

The independence of the people of a given area, and their freedom to decide upon their own government.

Wilson maintained US neutrality in spite of the huge anti-German outcry in the USA caused by the deaths of 128 American citizens who were aboard the British liner *Lusitania* when it was sunk in the Atlantic, without warning, by a German submarine.

However, once Wilson was re-elected as president in 1916, the likelihood of war with Germany grew. The British blockade was severely damaging to Germany. Food and materials were in short supply. The Germans began to feel they were losing the war. In January 1917, Germany decided to begin a policy of unrestricted submarine warfare. The Germans would sink any ship from any country that they felt might be bringing supplies to its enemies. The German High Command felt that this would do immense harm to the British and French, who were so dependent on imports such as food and iron ore. This new German policy led to many US ships being sunk and many US citizens being killed. Popular opinion in the USA began to turn in favour of joining Britain and France in the war. Wilson broke off diplomatic relations with Germany, but he did not immediately go to war.

The real trigger for US entry into the First World War came early in 1917, when the British intercepted and then decoded a telegram from the German foreign secretary, Arthur Zimmerman, to the German ambassador in Mexico. This telegram ordered the ambassador to confer with the Mexicans about the possibility of Mexico invading the United States from the south if it entered the war on the side of Britain and France. The British – desperate for a new and powerful ally – made sure the Americans were aware of the content of the Zimmerman telegram. A furious Wilson did not find it hard to persuade Congress to declare war in April 1917. He had lost faith in the honesty and integrity of the Germans, and he wanted to 'make the world safe for democracy'.

The USA in the First World War

Once the decision was taken to enter the war, Wilson and the United States threw themselves into the conflict with enormous effort and commitment. The US navy played an important role in ensuring that the German submarines were finally defeated in the Atlantic, and that vital supplies for Britain and France, as well as US soldiers, could cross the ocean. Participation in the war had a major impact on the United States:

- More than 2 million American men crossed to France, and they played a key role in the fighting in 1918. By the end of the war, over 112,000 US soldiers had died.
- On the home front, Wilson organised a massive anti-German propaganda campaign.
- Huge sums of money were raised by taxation and borrowing to fund the war, and large loans were made to Britain and France.
- There was considerable federal government involvement in industry, to ensure that sufficient war materials were manufactured.

Like many of America's earlier wars, for the USA the First World War was short, successful and not fought on US soil, and it brought in a great deal of money and commerce. By 1918, the USA was the greatest financial power in the world, and had been able to take over a large number of former British and German markets. The war had proved to be very good for the American economy and American business.

President Wilson and the post-war peacemaking process

President Wilson was a central figure in the post-war peacemaking process in 1919. He faced enormous challenges as he hoped to end the tradition of the 'winner takes all' approach to peace treaties, believing that it simply led to greater resentment and conflict. When Germany had defeated France in 1871, it had imposed harsh terms on France. This meant that France was determined to seek revenge in 1918.

Wilson hoped to make the sort of peace that the USA had established with the British in 1783 – a peace designed to prevent further conflict and bitterness. To this end, he produced a remarkable plan, the famous Fourteen Points. Wilson hoped this would provide a basis for dealing with the enormous problems facing Europe, such as the collapse of the German, Russian and Austro-Hungarian empires, while at the same time trying to prevent future conflict.

The Fourteen Points

Over the course of 1918, Wilson took enormous care in preparing for the peace he knew would come. In January 1918, in a statement to the US Congress, he issued what became known as the Fourteen Points, his blueprint for a peace that might also prevent future wars. The most important of the Fourteen Points were:

- There should be open covenants (treaties/agreements), and no more secret treaties and alliances that might cause fear and suspicion between nations.
- There should be freedom of the seas, so nations could sail and trade freely.
- Armed forces should be reduced.
- Germany should leave France, and Alsace-Lorraine be returned to France.
- There should be agreement to 'reasonable' colonial claims by nations.
- The Germans should leave the Russians (now under communist control) to deal with their own future.
- Poland should be granted independence and access to the sea.
- Self-determination (the ability of a nation or people to decide its own future) should be a major principle in the settlement.
- There should be a general 'association' of all countries, guaranteeing the sovereignty and independence of member states; this was the League of Nations.

Note:
In the 1871 Treaty of Frankfurt, after France's defeat by Germany in the Franco–Prussian War, France lost its territories of Alsace and Lorraine and had to pay reparations (damages) to Germany.

There was no mention of any indemnities, reparations, loss of colonies by the losers, admission of war guilt or exclusion of any of the 'losers' from the peace settlement.

There were excellent ideas in the Fourteen Points, and in an ideal world they could have been adopted and been the basis of a Europe without future war. Wilson's allies had different views on the subject, however, and they had not been consulted about Wilson's plans. Some of their motivations were based on historical enmity and national advancement:

- Germany had imposed savage terms on the French in 1871, and on the Russians in 1918 at Brest-Litovsk, after defeating them in war. They felt it was now Germany's turn to be punished.
- With over 5.5 million casualties, and a huge part of northern France wrecked by the war, the French were not interested in showing Germany any leniency. They wanted to be sure that Germany would never again be strong enough to invade France.
- The British were hardly likely to be sympathetic to any attempt to reduce their naval dominance or colonial pre-eminence. Defending these things had been factors in their decision to go to war, and nearly 1 million British had died in the war.
- The Italians, who had also entered the war on the Allied side, had suffered badly in the fighting and were determined to revenge themselves on the Austrians.

The post-war peace talks were held in Paris, recently shelled by the Germans and, as one commentator put it, 'full of grieving widows and mothers'. Wilson's idealism stood little chance here.

The British and the French wanted to punish the Germans and, understandably, to secure their countries against future German aggression. In addition to these issues, Wilson lacked negotiating skills and his own advisors were divided. Colonel E. M. House was in favour of scrapping the Fourteen Points, while the secretary of state **Robert Lansing** argued strongly for letting Germany play a key role in the negotiating process rather than just presenting them with a **diktat**.

There were weaknesses in Wilson's draft for the Covenant of League of Nations. There was no system of arbitration built into his system; it was unclear whether it was a moral or a legal document. There was an inevitable conflict between the more detached idealist, Wilson, and the cynical and war-weary European leaders. Ultimately, now the war was over, Wilson had no means of putting pressure on the French and British to agree to his terms. The Treaty of Versailles went through with all its flaws. However, Wilson must be given real credit for what he did achieve, including:

- his constructive guiding principle that peace treaties should remove the causes of future wars
- his conception of the League of Nations

Key figure

Robert Lansing (1864–1928)

Robert Lansing was the US secretary of state from 1915 to 1920. Lansing was anti-German and supported the declaration of war against Germany. His relationship with Wilson broke down as he felt the Fourteen Points were too vague, and that Wilson should not personally go to Paris as a peacemaker. Although he supported the Treaty of Versailles and the League of Nations, he was sacked by Wilson in 1920.

diktat
A statute, penalty or settlement imposed in harsh terms upon a defeated party by the victor.

- his support for self-determination, which played a major part in resolving the situation in Eastern Europe and the Balkans
- his sound ideas on making Poland a viable independent state – for instance, giving it access to the sea.

Upon his return to the USA, Wilson had to persuade the Senate to ratify the Treaty of Versailles and the League of Nations. The midterm elections of 1918 had led to a swing to the Republicans, and the key figure in the Senate was the chairman of the Senate Foreign Relations Committee, Henry Cabot Lodge. He was the most influential figure on the committee, and the Senate as a whole tended to support the decisions of its committees. By and large, Lodge supported both the peace treaty and the League and just wanted some revisions – his 'Fourteen Reservations'. These were not profound changes; they were acceptable to Europe and they would have ensured passage through the Senate.

But Wilson would not compromise in any way. It had to be exactly the deal he had brokered in Paris. The result was that the Senate rejected the Treaty of Versailles and the League of Nations. Lodge was portrayed by Wilson as the real villain of this decision.

The debate on President Wilson and the First World War

Wilson was only partially successful in the post-war peacemaking process, as the memories of the war were too bitter for the other victors. Popular demands on elected leaders naturally favoured the idea of revenge, and the treaties that were finally signed played a part in causing the next war. The US Senate rejected the Treaty of Versailles, and refused to join the organisation that Wilson had intended to be the 'war preventer', the League of Nations.

In one sense Wilson could be seen as a failure, as he:

- failed to prevent war
- failed to keep the USA out of the war
- failed to attain the 'just and lasting peace' he had hoped for.

However, Wilson did:

- give sympathetic help to many nations wanting help to achieve self-determination
- stop the total break-up of Germany and Russia
- prevent too barbaric a peace settlement being imposed on Germany
- work very hard for peaceful settlement of disputes between nations
- provide a possible model and mechanism for the resolution of conflicts
- get the United States to play a major and often positive role in world affairs.

Note:
The Germans argued that they had only agreed to an armistice in November 1918 on the basis of Wilson's Fourteen Points. They had assumed they would only have to return Alsace-Lorraine and not suffer the admission of war guilt, the loss of colonies, the loss of land to Poland, the reparations and the exclusion from the peace negotiations and the League of Nations.

Note:
Wilson's claims of Lodge's villainy can be seen as unfair. Lodge did have some reservations about the Covenant of the League of Nations, as did many others. He also questioned the viability of the suggested peacekeeping methods. Later events were to prove him right.

US foreign policy 1920–1940

isolationism
A national policy of avoiding political or economic commitments to other countries.

It has been argued that once the First World War was over, the United States 'retreated' from the rest of the world and entered a period of **isolationism**. This did happen after 1933, but certainly was not the case during the presidencies of Harding, Coolidge and Hoover. There were three major events in the 1920s that showed the United States' willingness to involve itself in international affairs: the Dawes Plan of 1924, the Kellogg–Briand Pact of 1928 and the Young Plan of 1929.

The Dawes Plan constituted an effort by the USA, Britain, Italy, Belgium and France to aid the recovery of the German economy crippled by the effects of war and the reparations payments to the victorious Allied nations. The plan was led by, and named after, the American banker and politician Charles Dawes. The Dawes Plan was followed in 1929 by the Young Plan, which was again largely American-led. This plan reduced the reparations payments that Germany had to make, and attempted to find a long-term solution that would have a less damaging effect on the German economy. Both the Dawes Plan and the Young Plan helped Germany and were factors in the reduced tension in international affairs during this period.

The Kellogg–Briand Pact of 1928 was an international agreement not to use war to resolve disputes or conflicts between nations. It was named after its authors, the US secretary of state Frank B. Kellogg and the French foreign minister Aristide Briand. Many nations, including the USA and the major European powers, signed the pact. It was a fine ideal, but failed in practice. Many of the states that signed were at war by 1941.

US foreign policy changed fundamentally under Franklin D. Roosevelt. He was not involved at all with the World Economic Conference in 1933, and under him the USA avoided international commitments and pursued a policy of isolationism. The Neutrality Acts, passed by Congress in 1935, 1936 and 1937, forbade the USA from supporting any side in a foreign conflict. The USA remained detached from the Italian invasion of Abyssinia in 1935, and from the Spanish Civil War (1936–39). It was not until early 1941, when the United States became concerned that Britain would not be able to defeat Nazi Germany, that Roosevelt was prepared to support the Allied side in the Second World War. In December 1941, the Japanese attack on Pearl Harbor, followed by Germany's declaration of war on the United States, finally ended the USA's period of isolationism.

Questions

1 Why did the United States finally go to war in 1917?

2 'The great peacemaker'. To what extent does Woodrow Wilson deserve this title?

US relations with China, Japan, the Philippines and the Pacific Islands

In the 19th and early 20th centuries, the United States became interested in expanding its territory and influence in the Far East. The US treasury secretary said in 1848, after the USA's expansion to the Pacific Coast: 'Asia has suddenly become our neighbour with a placid intervening ocean inviting our steamships upon the track of commerce greater than all Europe combined.' The United States was anxious to develop the vast potential of the Chinese and Japanese markets. The British and the Dutch were already established in China and the East Indies by the 1840s, and making large profits. The Americans hoped to follow suit. By the early 20th century, the USA had acquired a large colony in the Philippines, strategic outposts in Hawaii and Midway Island (see page 97) and substantial commerce throughout the Far East.

The United States and China

The USA was well aware of the potential size of the Chinese market and the profits that could be made there. The British had forced open Chinese trade – at gunpoint – in the early 19th century (when the Chinese refused to trade, the British just bombarded their ports until they did). The Chinese were reluctant to permit foreigners to sell goods in their country, particularly as one of the main British products was opium (a highly addictive drug).

In 1844, under pressure from US merchants who were concerned that the British were going to dominate the Chinese market, the United States signed the Treaty of Wangxia with the Chinese government. This treaty allowed Americans to trade in China on the same terms as the British, known as the 'most favoured nation' policy. The treaty was supposed to be revised after 12 years, but China's intense dislike of foreigners meant that it continually avoided renewing the treaty. When the French and the British used force to persuade the Chinese to open their country fully to trade, the Americans did not join in, but were allowed to trade there under the terms of the Treaty of Tianjin in 1858.

This treaty opened all of China to US trade, allowed American Christian missionaries to come to China, and also allowed an American embassy in Peking (modern-day Beijing). China was now open for US business. The Treaty of Tianjin was renewed in the Burlingame Treaty of 1868, with the United States retaining its 'most favoured nation' status. This was what the Americans wanted, referring to it as an **Open Door policy**. Chinese immigration to the United States started, providing a large labour force for building the railways. Fears over a potential flood of immigrants, nicknamed the 'Yellow Peril' by the American press, led to restrictions in the Chinese Exclusion Act of 1882.

Open Door policy
A policy that gives multiple powers economic and trading access to a particular country, with an emphasis on free trade.

sphere of influence
An area where one country has dominant commercial, cultural, economic, political and/or military influence.

Unlike other countries, such as Britain, Russia, Germany and above all Japan, the USA never wanted to colonise or settle in China. Its main interest was in trade. After Japan's victory in the Sino–Japanese War of 1894–95, the USA did not join with Russia, France and Germany to stop Japan taking over large parts of China. Nor did the United States gain a 'sphere of influence' like Britain and Germany in the gradual break-up of China in the 1890s.

In 1900, an uprising known as the Boxer Rebellion, directed largely against foreigners, broke out in China. The USA sent a small number of troops to assist other countries in the rescue of the foreign embassies in Peking. Military intervention was considered necessary by the USA to ensure that commerce still flowed.

In 1911, the growing demand for radical change in China culminated in revolution. Foreign influences had disrupted the country's traditional ways, and economic change had led to demands for social and political change. The death of the 73-year-old empress, followed by the accession to the throne of a three-year-old emperor, sparked the revolution. Radical and reform-minded élites, often educated abroad and in Japan in particular, led to a radical, republican and comparatively peaceful revolt in 1911. The child emperor abdicated, and China became a republic on 1 January 1912.

Woodrow Wilson was anxious to prevent the exploitation of China: he broke up a US conglomerate that threatened the country's independence, did his best to stop Japanese aggression there in 1915, and made Japan return Shantung Province to China in the 1919 post-First World War peace settlements. The USA never made enormous profits from its trade with China, but still wished to preserve the territorial integrity of the country against its aggressive neighbours.

The United States and Japan

Japan, like China, became a target for US commerce in the early 19th century. However, it was even more determinedly isolationist. By the 1840s, American commercial interests started to put pressure on both Japan and the US government to open Japan to US trade. The Dutch had already gained access to the Japanese market and the Americans wanted a share. Another factor that encouraged the Americans to persist was that US whalers and those who traded with China wanted accessible ports for food and shelter en route to China.

The settlement of Oregon (see page 74) and the acquisition of California opened up the USA's Pacific Coast and led to a greater interest in the Far East. The first 'official' visit to Japan by a US warship, the USS *Preble*, was made in 1849. The ship was there to rescue US sailors who had been shipwrecked in Japan. The Japanese were reluctant to let the *Preble* into port, but after the threat of force it successfully retrieved the sailors.

The fact that the sailors had been harshly treated by the Japanese did nothing to assist early relations between the two countries.

This first contact was followed in a much more aggressive fashion by the visit of Commodore Perry in 1853 and in 1854, the purpose of which was to establish a trade treaty with Japan. As he arrived, Perry turned the ship's guns towards the town of Uraga and refused Japanese demands to leave. He demanded permission to deliver a letter from President Fillmore, which made it clear that the United States expected to be allowed similar, if not better, access to Japan than the Dutch. Tough terms were imposed on the Japanese, and the letter threatened large-scale violence from the USA in the event of any armed resistance from the country. It was not the best way to start a relationship.

Relations between Japan and the USA remained uneasy throughout the remainder of the 19th century and into the early 20th century. There was substantial Japanese immigration into both Hawaii and the United States, but legislation in 1900 stopped this movement. The openly racist nature of these laws upset the Japanese, as did the US annexation of the Philippines. The Americans felt threatened by the growth of a large Japanese navy and Japan's ambitions in China. The defeat of the Russians in the Russo–Japanese War – especially the destruction of a large Russian fleet at the Battle of Tsushima in 1905 – only heightened the USA's fear of a strong and powerful Japan.

President Theodore Roosevelt helped negotiate the end of the Russo–Japanese War in 1905. He was concerned about Japanese imperialism, but was keen to develop better relations. As a result, in 1908 the Root–Takahira Agreement was signed. The two countries agreed to respect each other's interests in China and to maintain the 'status quo' (or current situation) in the Pacific. The Open Door policy (see page 93) was confirmed for the USA. The United States agreed, without consulting the Koreans, to the Japanese 'right' to annex Korea. The relationship remained uneasy, however. Wilson did his best to stop continuing Japanese aggression against China in 1915, and in 1919 made Japan return Shantung Province to China. Increasingly, the USA saw itself as 'protector' of China against its aggressive neighbours.

[Japan] is a most formidable military power. Her people have peculiar fighting capacity. They are very proud, very warlike, very sensitive, and are influenced by two contradictory feelings; namely, a great self-confidence, both ferocious and conceited, due to their victory over the mighty empire of Russia; and a great touchiness because they would like to be considered as on a full equality with, as one of the brotherhood of, Occidental nations, and have been bitterly humiliated to find that even their allies, the English, and their friends, the Americans, won't admit them to association and citizenship.

Former US president Theodore Roosevelt on Japan, 1909.

The Washington Naval Conference

In 1922, as tensions in the Pacific continued after the First World War, the Washington Naval Conference aimed to settle two threats to global peace and stability: the international naval arms race and the unstable politics of the Asia Pacific region. Both of these issues were at least in part related to tensions between the USA and Japan. Nine countries attended the three-month conference: the USA, Britain, Japan, China, Portugal, France, Italy, Belgium and the Netherlands.

The USA, Japan, Britain, France and Italy signed a naval treaty, agreeing to limit their fleets of battleships and aircraft carriers, to destroy some of their existing ships and not to build any new warships for the next ten years. This was a significant measure of disarmament, intended to prevent the reoccurrence of the pre-war arms race that many thought had contributed to the outbreak of the First World War. In practice, however, the treaty would ensure Japan's naval dominance in the western Pacific region.

Two issues of power politics in the Asia Pacific region were addressed at the conference. The first was the competing ambitions of the USA and Japan: US politicians were alarmed by Japan's rapid rise as a regional power, while Japan had ambitions to expand its influence in the region even further. The USA, Britain, Japan and France agreed to consult with each other rather than act independently in any future crisis in the region. This treaty ended the 1902 Anglo–Japanese Alliance, which had provided British support for Japan in the event of conflict.

The other issue was China, not least because it was the focus of Japanese ambitions. All nine powers at the conference agreed to uphold the status quo in China, which included the Open Door policy advocated by the USA. At the same time, Japan's special interests in the Chinese province of Manchuria were recognised. All three of these treaties depended solely on the goodwill of the signatory states, but within ten years that goodwill had evaporated.

veto
A president is given the power to stop a congressional bill becoming law, and this known as applying a veto.

In 1930, President Hoover's refusal to **veto** the Smoot–Hawley Tariff (see page 141) hit Japan very hard, and was seen as an attack on the country. Then in 1931 the Japanese invaded Manchuria, left the League of Nations and began building up its army and navy prior to a series of attacks on British, French and Dutch colonies in 1941.

The US–Japanese relationship was always an uneasy one. Both were in a sense 'emerging' nations, anxious to establish their power and influence in the same region. Each saw the other as a threat – and with their very different cultures, values and traditions, conflict was likely.

US relations with Hawaii, the Philippines and the Pacific

The USA's acquisition of the Philippines in 1898, the growth of its trade in the Far East, and its internal expansion to the Pacific coast led the country to focus increasingly on the Pacific region in the late 19th century. One of the USA's major acquisitions was Hawaii. The British explorer Captain James Cook was the first European to land there, in the 18th century. American missionaries followed in the 19th century, as did US businessmen.

By the 1860s, such businessmen dominated the economy and the country had become an economic satellite of the United States. US citizens took over key roles in the islands, excluding anyone else from positions of importance. There were protests in 1889 by the indigenous people against this unofficial takeover by the USA. The islands were annexed in 1898; Hawaii became a US territory in 1900 and a state in 1959 – the 50th state of the USA. Economic takeover was followed by political takeover, as America argued that it knew what was best for the Hawaiians.

Another US acquisition in the Pacific included Midway Island in 1867. No one lived there but it had potential as a naval base, and the Americans wanted to lay claim to it before anyone else did. They acquired Samoa, Guam and Wake Island for similar reasons.

The United States and the Philippines

Events in the Philippines followed a similar course to those in Cuba (see pages 76–80). There was a revolt against Spanish colonial rule by the late 1890s, led by Emilio Aguinaldo. After the sinking of the USS *Maine* (see page 77), assistant secretary of the navy Theodore Roosevelt ordered the US Far Eastern Fleet to the Philippines. It destroyed the Spanish fleet in Manila in 1898, and US marines were landed to take over the islands.

Spain eventually withdrew from the Philippines. US military forces did not co-operate with the Filipinos and ensured that Aguinaldo played no part in the final victory over the Spanish and the peace settlement, which handed all the islands over to the United States. President McKinley ordered that the Philippines be transferred to US ownership. The USA did not think the Filipinos were capable of self-government, and viewed them in a similar way to the Native Americans.

> **Note:**
> The Philippines proved of limited commercial value to the USA in the long run. However, US possession of Philippines aroused hostility from Japan, which also had ambitions in the area. The Japanese were looking for raw materials, new markets and colonies, and they resented American presence in the region.

Figure 3.7 Injured Filipinos in a makeshift hospital during the American–Philippine War

benevolent assimilation
Describes the process of taking over a country in a way that brings some benefits for its inhabitants, thus reducing opposition to the occupation.

The United States' long-term policy towards the Philippines was one of **benevolent assimilation**: its stated plan was to bring the benefits of good and stable government. Aguinaldo and many Filipinos did not agree with this approach. Aguinaldo was proclaimed president of an independent republic, to the fury of the Americans. In 1899, war broke out between the United States and those it had come to 'free' from Spain. During the three-year conflict, both sides committed atrocities, but US tactics particularly affected Filipino civilians. The USA suffered 10,000 casualties, but there were more than 250,000 Filipino casualties.

President Wilson was a believer in self-determination and he disliked the aggressive imperialism that the US acquisition of the Philippines represented. Between 1913 and 1916, he did all he could to increase the participation of Filipinos in their own government. He pushed Congress for the Jones Act, which gave substantial autonomy to the Philippines. In 1934, Congress and President Franklin D. Roosevelt put through the Tydings–McDuffie Act, which promised full independence for the Philippines in 1946. In 1935, Manuel Quezon became the first president of the Commonwealth of the Philippines. Independence followed after the liberation of the Philippines from Japanese occupation in 1945.

The United States, like most of the major powers of the period, does not emerge with great credit from its 'imperial' phase. Indigenous populations were often badly treated and exploited. Simple greed was cloaked by claims of high ideals, and attempts to impose the values of one nation on another often proved both disruptive and dangerous.

Key issues

The key features of this chapter are:

- sustained westward expansion within the North American continent

- the treatment of native populations and other minorities encountered

- how business became the driving force behind much of the expansion

- the USA's willingness to use force to attain its objectives

- the USA's tendency to justify self-interest by claims that it was acting for the 'greater good'

- the emergence of the United States as a world power.

Revision questions

1 Why was the United States so keen to get involved with both China and Japan in the 19th century?

2 To what extent was US policy in the Pacific in the 19th century driven by commercial factors?

Further reading

Davies, E. J. *The United States in World History.* London, UK. Routledge. 2006.

Joy, M. S. *US Expansionism, 1783–1860: A Manifest Destiny?* (Seminar Studies in History). London, UK. Longman. 2003.

Link, A. S. *Woodrow Wilson: Revolution, War and Peace.* London, UK. John Wiley & Sons. 2013.

Pérez Jr, L. A. *The War of 1898: United States and Cuba in History and Historiography.* Chapel Hill, USA. The University of North Carolina Press. 1998.

Weeks, P. *Farewell My Nation: The American Indian in the United States in the Nineteenth Century.* London, UK. John Wiley & Sons. 2000.

Chapter 4

The Gilded Age
and the Progressive Era
1870s–1920s

Key questions

- Why were the 1870s and 1880s decades of rapid industrialisation?
- How great were the economic and social consequences of rapid industrialisation in the late 19th century?
- What were the aims of the Progressive Movement in the 1890s and 1900s?
- How successful was the Progressive Movement?

Content summary

- The causes of industrial growth in the 1870s and the stimulus of war.
- The population explosion after 1870.
- Land and transport.
- The role of the government.
- Innovators and big business.
- Agriculture in the United States.
- Economic growth and recession.
- The Progressive Era – immigration and urbanisation.
- The Progressives – their aims and methods.
- The impact of the Progressive Movement.
- The presidency of Theodore Roosevelt.
- The presidency of Woodrow Wilson.
- The constitutional and political changes of the Progressive Era.
- The end of the Progressive Era – the United States in the 1920s.

Timeline

Sep 1873	The Panic of 1873
Jul 1890	The Sherman Anti-Trust Act
May 1893	The Panic of 1893
Sep 1901	Theodore Roosevelt becomes US president
Jun 1906	Pure Food and Drug Act
Oct 1907	The Panic of 1907
Nov 1912	Election of Woodrow Wilson as US president
Feb 1913	16th Amendment to the US Constitution
Apr 1913	17th Amendment to the US Constitution
Dec 1913	Federal Reserve Act
Aug 1920	US women win the right to vote

Introduction

The period between 1870 and 1929 was a remarkable one for the United States. The country recovered rapidly from a devastating civil war, expanded and developed economically at a breathtaking pace. By the end of the 19th century, the USA had become the world's greatest economic power. Capitalism flourished to an extent previously unknown and some people made millions of dollars. The 'bad' side of capitalism, in the form of mass urbanisation, exploitation of labour and terrible housing, was revealed. Debates raged in the USA as to whether men and their businesses should be free from regulation by government, allowed to make millions of dollars at the expense of others. The Progressive Movement arose to challenge unregulated capitalism and to advocate key changes in both society and government.

Constitutionally and politically, 1870–1929 was also a period of evolution. The federal system created by the **Founding Fathers** in the 18th century had given power primarily to the individual states; the US president had only limited power over domestic and economic issues. Congress was expected to provide national leadership in such matters, but it proved to be an institution incapable of tackling major challenges and so the role of the president began to change. The United States struggled to adapt to the demands of a modern industrial economy, but two presidents, Theodore Roosevelt (1901–08) and Woodrow Wilson (1913–21), rose to the challenges of the time and provided remarkable leadership.

Founding Fathers
Members of the convention that created the US Constitution in 1787.

Figure 4.1 The symbol of American affluence – a gushing oil rig, in California in the 1920s

Industrial expansion in the 1870s and 1880s

There is no single reason why the United States underwent a remarkable economic transformation in the 1870s and 1880s. Many interrelated factors played a part, ranging from the availability of raw materials to the attitude of the government. There was no point in an entrepreneur building a factory if there was no transport system to service it, or labour and energy supply to keep it running. All the necessary factors for economic growth combined in the USA in the decades after the Civil War. This period is often known as the Gilded Age, because its relative prosperity functioned as a thin layer of gold masking serious social problems beneath the surface.

The impact of the Civil War

War, in spite of the death and destruction it brings, can often be a great stimulus to an economy. The US Civil War encouraged economic growth in a variety of ways:

- The North created a huge army. That army needed guns, ammunition, clothing and transport on a scale unknown before. The economy of the North had to adapt to this demand, and produce the huge amount of manufactured goods required. Economies of scale were discovered; mass production and distribution methods had to be developed.
- The government had to raise money to pay for the war, and this led to the development of a sophisticated capital-raising system centred on Wall Street in New York.
- During the war the government adopted a paper currency known as the United States Note or 'greenback'.
- The banking system had to evolve to cope with the increasing amount of money in circulation and the government's need to borrow money. This banking system was vital in ensuring that industrial expansion could be financed.
- Tariffs (taxes on imported goods from other countries) were raised – partly to gain income for the government, but also to protect American-produced goods, such as railway engines and wheat, from cheaper imports.

Note:
Tariffs were a great encouragement for American producers to invest in manufacturing in their own country, as they made overseas manufacturing costs more expensive.

Overall, the Civil War proved to be the start of a huge expansion of industry in the United States.

Population growth

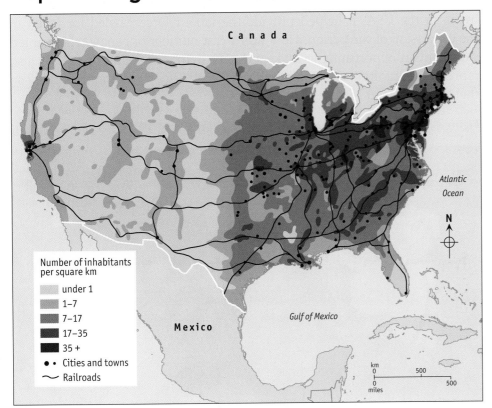

Figure 4.2 A map showing distribution of population and railways in the USA in 1900

Rapid economic expansion needs a labour force to make goods and consumers to buy them. In spite of nearly 500,000 dead in the Civil War, the population of the USA soared in the latter half of the 19th century. There was an ample supply of labour and consumers.

Year	Population
1860	31.5 million
1880	50 million
1900	76 million

Table 4.1 Population growth in the United States, 1860–1900

The reasons for this growth lay in the increase in incomes, which meant better food and housing, as well as advances in public health and medical knowledge that lowered death rates. There was also a high level of immigration to the USA.

Period	Total number of immigrants
1871–80	2.8 million
1881–90	5.2 million
1891–1900	3.6 million
1901–1910	8.8 million

Table 4.2 Immigration to the United States, 1871–1910

This was probably one of the greatest mass migrations in history, with people coming from Europe and Asia in search of a better standard of living in the USA. It helped provide the labour force needed for much of the expansion of the period. Here was a vast number of people who wanted work and an opportunity to make a decent living for themselves. They also represented additional consumers: they needed food, coal and clothes, so their demands fed growth.

Figure 4.3 A family of immigrants arrives in the United States, 1905

Availability of land

The 1870s and 1880s saw the massive expansion of the United States. New settlements required manufactured goods ranging from barbed wire to kettles, railway track to guns, and this created markets for US manufacturers. Some of the land settled was amongst the most fertile in the world, so there was plenty of food for all.

Much of the newly developed land was unsuitable for small-scale farming by families, but lent itself to larger-scale mass production of crops such as wheat, which enabled cities to be fed. This also led to the growth of a strong export market for food. Inevitably, this resulted in a demand for greater mechanisation in agriculture, which further fuelled demand for manufactured goods. An area much greater than the size of Western Europe was opened up in the USA for settlement in this period, so there was no problem in finding space for new cities, factories and farms.

Transport

Without the means to bring in the right raw materials and the coal needed to power the engines, and then distribute the finished goods, a manufacturer could do little. Initially, the United States had developed along the eastern coast and rivers such as the Mississippi. Most large cities were either on the coast or on navigable rivers. The railway changed all that. By 1900, every major city was a transport hub for its region, and states were linked by one of the most comprehensive railway networks in the world. Cattle could be transported from Texas to the Chicago meatpacking plants, and coal from the West Virginia coal fields to the factories of New England.

> **Note:**
> In 1860 there were 48,280 km (30,000 miles) of railway.
> By 1900, this had grown to 310,600 km (193,000 miles).

The railways employed nearly 1 million workers by 1900, and provided an example of how large organisations could function. They required a sophisticated capitalisation process, which further stimulated the money and capital markets. Above all, they stimulated demand. Railways that were 310,600 km (193,000 miles) long needed a lot of steel, and that steel needed a lot of coal to make it. Engines and rolling stock (railway vehicles) poured off the production lines, and fierce competition pushed prices down and led to a demand for technological improvement to improve quality. Railways enabled the American industrial revolution in the first place, and then facilitated its expansion. The rail centres required roads in order to distribute goods to outlying areas, and this again further stimulated growth.

Figure 4.4 Railway workers on a railway-building car, a so-called 'shoulder car', of the Boston and Maine Railroad Company, 1902

The role of the government

There was no tradition of state control or regulation of the economy in the United States. There was a tradition of freedom for the individual, and many came to the USA for just that freedom to make their living in any way they chose. Unlike in some European countries, the government in the USA was expected to play only one economic role, and that was to support business in all its forms. The Constitution gave the federal government virtually no role in managing the economy, and presidents and Congress had shown no great desire to intervene in economic matters, except in emergencies.

Sherman Anti-Trust Act
This statute, introduced by Congress in 1890, aimed to introduce more competition into the marketplace. It was not enforced properly by the federal government.

There were no laws restricting hours of labour. There were no taxes on profits. There were no rules about how business had to be conducted. State legislatures and judiciaries, in a position to bring in local rules and regulation, tended to be dominated by local business or agricultural interests. Business owners soon learned how to use money and pressure to ensure that what limited state control did occur did not harm their interests. The law provided no obstacles to entrepreneurship; the **Sherman Anti-Trust Act**, designed to exert a measure of state control over business, had no practical impact on matters.

Sec 1   Every contract, combination in the form of trust or otherwise, in restraint of trade or commerce among the several States, or with foreign nations, is hereby declared to be illegal …

Sec 2   Every person who shall monopolize, or attempt to monopolize, or combine or conspire with any other person or persons, to monopolize any part of the trade or commerce among the several States, or with foreign nations, shall be deemed guilty of a misdemeanor.

The Sherman Anti-Trust Act, 1890.

The USA also had no tradition of trade unions. What few unions there were tended to be divided between the aims of the skilled workers and the unskilled; those who were prepared to use peaceful methods to get better pay and conditions, and those who largely were not. When industrial disputes arose, often both state and federal authorities used troops to assist owners in defeating worker demands for improved pay and conditions. There was little to stop an employer managing his workforce in any way he wanted.

Social attitudes

Americans prided themselves on the absence of a class system, of living in a land where anyone had the chance to go from rags to riches. It was a very egalitarian society – as long as you were a white man. Respect and status came with wealth and achievement, and making money was seen as a highly respectable occupation. Business success led to social leadership. The 'celebrities' of the age were inventors and successful entrepreneurs.

Technological and business innovation

The 1870s and 1880s are full of examples of men who were prepared to experiment with, adapt to and develop new ideas, and who made vast sums of money. Two of the many examples are **Andrew Carnegie** in steel and **Thomas Edison** in electricity.

Andrew Carnegie and United States Steel

Until the 1860s, steel was costly to produce; the Bessemer process revolutionised its manufacture. Carnegie did not invent the process, but when he saw it in Britain he realised its enormous potential. Working with **Henry Frick** (see page 108), who controlled substantial amounts of the energy supply needed for Carnegie's steel mills, Carnegie built up a steel company that alone was producing more steel than the whole of Britain by 1900. His annual profit by 1900 was $42 million.

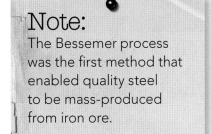

> **Note:**
> The Bessemer process was the first method that enabled quality steel to be mass-produced from iron ore.

Carnegie's companies not only developed the technology but also invested massively in new manufacturing plants and equipment. Carnegie controlled the whole process – from the raw materials needed, such as coal and ore, through the manufacturing process to distribution. He innovated, invested and kept prices as low as possible. In good times he banked profits to keep his plants operational in bad times. He ruthlessly opposed any attempts to form unions in his factories. When attempts were made by his men to organise for better pay and conditions, he brought in his own armed guards and used violence to stamp out the action. Several people were killed and wounded in this struggle.

Thomas Edison and electricity

Inventions are one thing, but the ability to spot the commercial potential of an invention is another. It was Michael Faraday in Britain who made the key scientific discoveries about electricity, but it was Thomas Edison in the USA who made electricity 'commercial'. There are three main reasons why Edison is such a good example of the entrepreneurship of the age:

- He was responsible for a large number of actual inventions, such as the electric light bulb.
- He had the skill to industrialise those inventions, make them commercially viable, and produce and sell them on a large scale.
- He developed the first great industrial research laboratory, with chemists, engineers and mechanics, to work on more similar inventions.

Edison was helped considerably by the Patent Acts passed by Congress in the late 18th century and early 19th century, which stopped other manufacturers from copying his ideas.

Key figure

Henry Frick (1849–1919)

Frick was a highly successful but ruthless businessman. He founded his own company, which manufactured a fuel called coke, and he later became chairman of the Carnegie Steel Company. Frick was sometimes known as the 'most hated man in America' for his brutal treatment of trade unions and colleagues for whom he had no further use. During one strike, nine locked-out workers were attacked and killed by the security forces that he had hired.

Figure 4.5 Thomas Edison listening to the first phonogram sent to New York from England

Availability of capital

Entrepreneurs need capital, especially if they are, for example, trying to build generators that can provide electricity for a whole city and lay the hundreds of kilometres of cable needed as well. By 1870, largely due to the stimulus provided by the Civil War – when the government needed money to pay for the war, and the arms manufacturers needed capital to build their factories – a highly developed stock market, where the necessary capital could be raised, had developed in New York.

The huge profits generated by the war were invested in this stock market, and the capital needed to build a railway across the continent or steel mills in Pittsburgh could be raised. By 1865, the annual turnover of the New York Stock Exchange was over $6 billion, and by 1880 it had become the second largest money market in the world. The finance for the industrial revolution could be raised here, and fortunes could be made by those who speculated in stocks and shares.

The rise of the corporation and the trust

The complete absence of any rules or regulations meant that businessmen were free to create organisations that could cope with massive nationwide expansion. The 'corporation' emerged.

A corporation could own, for example, a large number of railways. It could hire the management it wanted to run it, it could sue and be sued, and it could buy, sell and own property. It could merge with other railways or take over companies that made railway engines. It could attract investors and speculators, and its managers could own shares in the company and run it for their own benefit. There were no rules about keeping accounts or reporting to anyone. It proved to be the perfect vehicle for the growth of giant industries.

The other vehicle for massive expansion was the trust. Some states had old laws that forbade a company set up in that state from owning property in other states or owning shares in other companies. A man named Henry Flagler found a way around this by creating a 'trust'. The secretary of Standard Oil, Flagler appointed himself as a 'trustee' for stocks and property that the company was not allowed to own. In the end, three employees of Standard Oil at its headquarters in Cleveland, Ohio were the 'trustees' of all the properties and assets outside the state, and did just as they were told to do by their boss, **John D. Rockefeller**. It was a simple, but perfectly legal, device to get around one of the very few barriers in the way of an organisation that could end up controlling the entire US oil industry.

Protective tariffs

As Congress was largely dominated by business interests, and presidents and their Cabinets were highly responsive to the needs of US industry and overseas trade, the commercial policy of the government also helped expansion. Congress was happy to impose protective tariffs to ensure that foreign-manufactured goods were more expensive than home-produced ones. Duties could be as high as 50% of the cost of the imported goods.

However, tariffs were controversial – especially in the 1880s and 1890s. Although manufacturers liked them because they reduced competition from abroad, the farmers of the South and the West opposed them because they increased their operating costs. The Republican Party supported tariffs, while the Democrats did not, and tariffs were an important issue in the 1888 presidential election campaign. Republican dominance in the late 19th century meant that high tariffs remained in use.

With a rapidly expanding population, and protective tariffs ensuring that US-manufactured goods were cheaper than those from abroad, demand soared. Energy supply was sufficient: in 1870, 40 million tonnes of coal was extracted in the USA; by 1900, 270 million tonnes were dug out. The unions were weak. Conditions in the United States after the Civil War were perfect in every way for an industrial revolution.

Key figure

John D. Rockefeller (1839–1937)

Rockefeller created the Standard Oil Company through very aggressive business methods, and dominated the oil industry in the United States. He was the first American billionaire. When he retired, he devoted his life to charitable works.

Questions

1. What role did the federal government in the USA play in the decades of industrial expansion?

2. How far were the railways responsible for US industrial expansion between 1870 and 1900?

The economic and social consequences of rapid industrialisation in the late 19th century

Agriculture

Agriculture did not enjoy the same success as manufacturing in the USA during the late 19th century. While some made millions on the stock market or in manufacturing, few made much more than a reasonable living out of farming. Many were reduced to subsistence farming and a life of debt. There was growth, but not profitability.

Between 1890 and 1900, a million new farms were established. The earlier Homestead Act of 1862 (see page 72) had opened huge areas of the West to settlement and farming. However, many farmers found that owning their own land did not lead to the success they had envisaged. There were a variety of reasons for the problems that faced farmers and the agricultural industry:

- borrowing for purchase and mechanisation, which led to debt
- bad weather conditions and poor use of land
- overdependence on unreliable overseas markets and high costs of transportation
  - deflation that caused debt to rise and made credit more costly
  - too many small farmers trying to compete with big 'agribusinesses' in a tough world market
  - the fact that much of the new land was marginal and 'ecologically fragile'
  - lots of tenancy farming, where there was little incentive for the farmers to improve the quality of land because they did not own it
  - overdependence on a single cash crop, such as cotton.

While there was never the squalor and destitution that was present in the inner cities, there was also never the huge wealth and ostentation that could be seen in the suburbs of the new cities. Many felt that the opportunity promised by the American dream of 'owning your own place' simply had not come true. Prices kept on dropping, and so did returns. It is hardly surprising that so many of the populist and protest movements, such as the Grangers, the Greenbackers and the Populists, had their roots in rural areas. It was not until another war brought increased demand for foodstuffs that farming underwent a brief revival.

Note:

Established in 1867, the Grangers was an alliance of US farmers committed to fighting monopolies over grain transport and storage. The Greenbackers were an anti-monopolist and anti-deflation group active between 1874 and 1889. The Populists were a more radical and democratic group, in favour of a wide range of social reforms.

Growth and recession

Even a brief look at the statistics that illustrate US economic growth in the late 19th century will give a clear picture of the remarkable development. The average annual output per iron and steel plant increased by a factor of 25 between 1860 and 1900. The annual turnover of the average meatpacking plant (once the American invention of the tin can had been adopted) went from $110,000 to $1.4 million in the same period. Output of everything soared and new mass production, distribution and management techniques were adopted. Two examples – cigarettes and oil – give some idea of the economic development in this period.

Cigarettes

In 1870, there was no cigarette industry as such. Those who wanted to smoke a cigarette bought the tobacco in bulk and rolled it by hand. In 1884, James Duke, who had little experience in the tobacco industry, spotted a new machine invented by a Virginia teenager called James Bonsack, which could produce 120,000 neatly rolled cigarettes a day. Duke bought out Bonsack, and started production. He pushed the price of cigarettes down, improved their quality and managed to reduce the tax on tobacco. With brilliant sales and marketing techniques, distribution deals with the railways and direct links to tobacco growers, Duke won control of the supply chain. Within a decade he was selling 834 million cigarettes a year. By 1900, simply by buying out weaker rivals, his American Tobacco Company had a monopoly of cigarette production in the United States, and Duke was a multi-millionaire.

Oil

In 1860, about 2000 barrels of oil a day were produced and refined in the United States. By 1900, it was 60 million. The bulk of the oil came from lots of small wells in Pennsylvania. Two smart young businessmen, John Rockefeller and Henry Flagler, realised that enormous profits could be made out of oil. They recognised that they could not control the output, which was in the hands of the owners of many different local wells, but that they could dominate the entire industry if they could control the refining process and then the distribution of the oil.

By 1880, Rockefeller and Flagler controlled over 80% of the oil-refining industry and its distribution. Their methods were ruthless. They bought out rivals with cash or stock, and if they would not sell then they would undercut their prices until they were bankrupt. Rockefeller used his rail monopoly to prevent his rivals distributing oil. However, the two men brought stability to the market and the price of oil dropped throughout the period.

Note:
The downside of monopolies was that a monopolist tended not to take risks and was not usually inclined to innovate. He also did not have to pay much attention to the consumer, who had no alternative but to buy from him.

Economic disasters

It was not always continuous growth and economic stability in the United States in the late 19th and early 20th centuries. As mentioned above, agriculture was never a great success story, especially in the South. There were also three occasions when real disaster struck the growing American economy.

The Panic of 1873

Like many of the 'panics', or economic crises, this had its roots in the poor state of the American banking system. There was no overall regulation and control of banks. Anyone could set up a bank and operate it independently – and many did. Local banks depended on the larger (also privately owned and unregulated) New York banks for cash supply, and also kept their deposits there. The New York banks would use those deposits for investment purposes. They could invest unwisely, as when many were involved in lending $100 million to Jay Cooke, a railway speculator. In 1873, Cooke's company went bankrupt and dragged down with it hundreds of other companies and banks. The New York Stock Exchange had to close, and unemployment temporarily soared.

The Panic of 1893

In 1893, the instability of the American financial system struck again. Unexpected bankruptcies in industries, ranging from banks to railways, sparked a crisis. There was an acute shortage of cash, and prices and output both dropped. Industry laid off thousands of workers, and unemployment went from 3.7 million in 1892 to 12.3 million in 1894. With no welfare state, millions of people suffered severe hardship. The rich lost savings and investments, but the unemployed faced destitution. The widespread poverty created by this economic crisis was a great spur to Progressive thinking.

The Panic of 1907

This economic crisis was caused by the failure of a large trust that led to the collapse of banks. In this case, action by President Roosevelt and the great financier J. P. Morgan prevented the crisis from spreading, but once again it highlighted the flaws in and fragility of the financial system.

Immigration and its impact

Between 1860 and 1900 at least 14 million immigrants arrived in the USA. The majority, particularly those from eastern and southern parts of Europe, headed for the cities and provided the cheap labour force that the industrial revolution demanded. They were crammed into the cities and often had to put up with appalling housing and living conditions. Those from north-western Europe tended to head west and farm the new territories: because many of the original American settlers came from Northern Europe, these newcomers often found it easier to assimilate, as there were fewer cultural and religious differences. Another cause of immigration was the flight of Jews escaping the violent **anti-Semitic pogroms** in some parts of Europe. Many Jews went to New York to work in the clothing industry.

By and large, the immigrants assimilated well into US society. They formed the unskilled workforce in the rapidly growing industries, and because of the great demand for labour they were not usually regarded as a threat by American workers. Business liked immigration. It kept wages down and provided an endless supply of cheap labour that was not unionised and did not, initially, make demands about reasonable working hours and conditions. The migrant was grateful for a job, an opportunity and a roof over his head. It was estimated that by 1900 over two-thirds of those who had arrived in the United States in the previous 20 years existed below the subsistence level. It was this 'submerged' two-thirds that many Progressives aimed to assist.

While employers seeking cheap labour may have liked mass immigration, others did not. Some Americans who were liberal in other areas saw immigrants as an obstacle to reform, as they were prepared to put up with appalling conditions. The 'older' immigrant could often be hostile as the many new immigrants kept wages down and were often used by business as strike breakers.

In 1887, the American Protective Association was formed to try to put pressure on the government to reduce immigration. The concerns this group put forward were that the Anglo-Saxon, Protestant 'traditions' that dominated American culture would be undermined, and also that the current racial stock would be 'diluted'. Such concerns were more racist than economic, and the group was not usually vocal when the economy was strong. Although no major brake was put on immigration before the First World War, the 'racist' elements of anti-immigration forces attained their objective in the Chinese Exclusion Act of 1882, which stopped immigration from China. In 1908, immigration from Japan also ceased.

The immigration into the United States in the decades between 1870 and 1910 was one of the greatest mass migrations in modern history. The fact that so many were absorbed so peacefully must be seen as a tribute to the American system. America provided these immigrants with a sense of opportunity that their native countries did not. In return, the immigrants provided the labour force for the USA's mass industrialisation in the 19th century.

anti-Semitic pogroms Starting in Russia, and spreading to parts of Eastern Europe by the late 19th century, these pogroms were violent, state-condoned mob attacks on Jews and their properties.

The realities of urbanisation

Before 1860, there were 16 cities in the United States with a population of 50,000 or more; by 1900, there were 109. The growth in the number and size of cities was perhaps one of the most visible features of the industrial revolution in the second part of the 19th century. Chicago, for example, went from 30,000 inhabitants in 1850 to over a million by 1890, and became the fifth largest city in the world. It was a remarkable period of urban growth.

Note:
Within the towns and cities, diseases such as tuberculosis and cholera – caused by poor housing, malnutrition and bad sanitation – spread easily and caused thousands of deaths.

Two major problems arose out of this rapid and enormous increase. The first was the spread of slums, and the second was the establishment of corrupt and inefficient systems for managing these new cities.

A city needs a transport network, clean water, sanitation, policing, schools, utilities, housing and streets. It needs good government to provide them. Often the first thing to be built in a US city was a factory; this was followed by some basic housing, often of poor quality. Then came the rapid influx of labour, and these people's priorities were work and some shelter. The other necessities seldom followed. Those with wealth migrated to the suburbs, benefiting from rail networks to commute into the centre. The rest were crowded into insanitary slums that sprung up with no regulation or utilities. The slum, with its dreadful overcrowding and pollution, became the dominant feature of the majority of American cities.

The rapid growth of the 'new' cities was a major problem. They often developed very quickly from small towns that needed little government to places where people congregated from all parts of the world, with no experience of democracy and no involvement in government at any level. Without an established government or a tradition of central authority, the way was wide open for the unscrupulous and the corrupt to take advantage. This became known as the 'Boss' system. The 'Boss', usually the mayor, controlled the city. In all urban areas, there was a huge demand for transport, housing and utilities, and many businesses wanted to provide these things. The Boss simply sold the rights to many of the utilities to the highest bidder. Corruption became endemic. All city employees, from street cleaner to police chief, owed their job to the Boss. The Boss was elected and re-elected as he provided immigrants with all social services, ranging from employment to housing, and in return the Boss's employees ensured that immigrants, or African-Americans from the South, repaid the favour with their votes.

The slum and the Boss were two of the features that disfigured the Gilded Age, and they would become two of the main targets of the Progressive Movement.

Figure 4.6 Tenements in New York's crowded immigrant neighbourhood on the Lower East Side, 1912

Questions

1. What was the impact of mass immigration on US society between 1875 and 1900?

2. Evaluate the impact of rapid industrialisation on American society in the period 1875–1900.

The aims of the Progressive Movement 1890s–1910s

What became known as the Progressive Movement sprang up in the United States in the 1890s. It was a loose grouping of many individuals and organisations, with no easily identifiable leaders and no clear set of aims. It arose for several reasons, protesting against appalling working and living conditions, corruption in government and widespread unemployment. Over time, the movement developed different, and at times conflicting, aims – from political reform and regulation of working hours through to votes for women and major constitutional changes. It employed a variety of methods to achieve its aims, ranging from pressure politics to journalism. The movement's members, known as the Progressives, were responsible for some significant achievements: they caused the Constitution to be amended, radical reform to take place in many cities and states, and the role of the federal government to change in a way that would have a great influence on much of the 20th century.

What led to the rise of the Progressive Movement in the 1890s?

No single factor led to a growing desire by many to change the way in which people lived and were governed in the USA. The heavily indebted sharecropper (see page 62) in the South had different grievances from the unemployed steelworker in Pittsburgh, who received no welfare benefits and lived in poor housing. The college-educated middle-class woman who wanted the vote, and to end the sale and consumption of alcohol in the United States, had different aims from other groups, who sought bank regulation, for example. Amongst the principal reasons for the movement were:

- **Recession and unemployment:** in 1893, recession struck in the United States. Unemployment was severe, especially in the industrial cities of the North, and it remained at around 12% for much of the rest of the 1890s. Businesses cut wages to sustain profits, so the living standards of many in work dropped as well. Many banks collapsed during the recession, particularly small local ones that held many people's savings.
- **No welfare system in the United States:** there was no unemployment pay, no sick pay and no compensation for industrial accidents. Being out of a job meant destitution and eviction. There was no safety net at all for a working man and his family.

- **Bad living and working conditions:** living conditions were terrible in many cities. Overcrowding was severe and vital utilities such as clean water and sewage disposal could be totally absent. Streets were dangerously filthy and whole families had to live in single rooms. Working conditions could also be poor: serious injury was a statistical inevitability in both Carnegie's steel mills and in the mines that produced the coal he needed. There was no restriction on anyone's working hours. As a result, the six-day, 72-hour week was common.

- **Serious decline of agriculture in some areas:** the rapid expansion in the 1880s into the virgin farmlands of the North and West had had a real impact on farming elsewhere. The small farmers of the Northeast could not compete with the large-scale farming in the West. The price of wheat dropped from $1.19 per **bushel** in 1881 to 28 cents in 1890. Drought in 1890 worsened the situation for farmers. The Southern sharecroppers fell deeper into debt.

- **Failings of the political parties:** while the Republicans dominated politics in the period after the Civil War, and virtually through to 1912, neither party seemed to be interested in the poor. The Democrats, strong in the South, were deeply conservative and were primarily concerned with repressing African-Americans and preventing further Northern domination of the South. They appeared to have little interest in the grievances of the two most disadvantaged groups in the region – the sharecroppers and the African-Americans. The Republicans, who dominated Congress and most cities and states, seemed to have become the party of big business and the banks.

- **People's hostility to business, trusts and monopolies:** the growing power of Wall Street and a few individuals, such as Rockefeller, Morgan and Carnegie, was widely disliked. Many people felt that the interests of the masses were being subordinated to the vast profits of a few. There was a growing demand for government regulation of business, to control its size and reduce its dominance. There was also a fear that the Sherman Anti-Trust Act (see page 106) was being ignored. Trade unions were weak and often divided. Attempts to improve matters were broken up – using force – by owners and the government. A famous example of this ruthless treatment of workers is the Pullman Strike of 1894, one of the first almost-national rail strikes involving the Pullman Company and the newly formed American Railway Union. Over 250,000 workers were involved, and 30 people were killed in the violence.

- **Fear of revolution:** some Americans were concerned about the growth of socialism and radicalism, and felt that unless concessions were made to the working class there might be revolution. This was a factor amongst middle-class reformers who, while disliking the new 'aristocracy' of the super-rich, were also worried about threats from the poor.

---

bushel
A unit for measuring crops; for wheat, a bushel was about 27 kg (60 lb).

Note:
In the 1890s, 4200 companies merged into 257 corporations, and 200 individuals owned 40% of the nation's wealth.

laissez-faire policy
This is a policy of non-intervention by government. It means a government does not try to manage the economy, leaving it to market forces, and does not regulate employers or require health and safety legislation.

- **Desire for women's rights:** some women wanted the vote and were involved in the Progressive Movement in order to get it. A number of women wanted the vote in order to bring change to the society in which they lived.
- **Demands for change from economists and social scientists:** economists were challenging the whole idea of *laissez-faire* policy (see page 116) in the USA. They pointed out how governments could successfully intervene to regulate and provide welfare benefits, as in Germany.
- **Criticism from brilliant journalists and writers:** people such as **Ida Tarbell**, Lincoln Steffens, Jacob Riis and Upton Sinclair highlighted in their writing what they saw as the evils present in the United States. With a cheap press to publicise their ideas and a high literacy rate amongst Americans, they had a major impact. They became known as the 'Muckrakers'.
- **Rise in immigration:** increased immigration in the period led to a desire for a restriction of immigrants. This became one part of the movement that was not seen by all as 'progressive'. There were also strong conservative tendencies within the Progressive Movement, such as the desire by some for segregation in the South.
- **The positive example of individual politicians:** the work done by **Robert La Follette** in Wisconsin and Tom Johnson in Cleveland to 'clear up' their respective state and city showed what could be done to improve the quality of life for citizens.

What were the aims of the Progressive Movement?

One of the problems in assessing the success of the Progressive Movement is that it had such a wide range of aims. Some members wanted very specific changes, such as making employers pay compensation to workers injured at work, while others had much broader objectives, such as 'regulating big business' or creating a form of welfare state. Some were radical, others much more conservative. The white middle-class educated élite, who dominated the movement, had their own priorities, and often had little sympathy with unions or small farmers. Broadly speaking there were three categories of aims represented by the Progressive Movement: the political, economic and social.

The political and constitutional aims of the Progressives

- **Changing the Constitution:** some argued that the Constitution needed changing to make it more suited to the 19th century. Women should be able to vote; senators should be directly elected to make them accountable to the people, rather than being appointed by state legislatures often dominated by political party and business interests; a federal income tax should replace tariffs as the main source of income for the government.

- **Reform of the federal government:** there were two broad ideas suggested for reform. The first was for the federal government to adopt a more regulatory and interventionist role in the economy and society. The second was for the federal government to utilise the powers that it had more efficiently, such as enforcing the Sherman Anti-Trust Act (see page 106) more aggressively and intervening on the side of the workers rather than employers in strikes.

- **Radical reform of the management of cities and states:** many cities were run by corrupt officials. Often mayors and the police, judiciary, local officials and providers of water and transport lacked any sense of public duty. There was no accountability. Many citizens experienced increasing taxes despite a deterioration in the quality of local services. There were many examples, such as Boss Tweed and Boss Platt in New York, where private gain was the main feature of local leaders' administrations. The Progressives argued for a much more open and democratic system for electing mayors and other public officials.

- **Reform of political parties:** US political parties were often in the hands of tiny minorities or wide open to business influence. The way in which Rockefeller's Standard Oil Company dominated the politics of states such as Ohio is a good example. Candidate nomination, whether for local mayor or for president of the United States, often lay in the hands of a small group of businessmen who mixed business and politics to their own advantage. There was a real desire to open up the whole political process to a wider electorate, and one of their demands was for the open **primary election**. This is one of the success stories of the Progressive Movement, as the primary election is still the main method of choosing candidates for the presidency and Congress.

primary election
An early stage of voting in which the whole electorate can choose a political party's candidates for election, rather than having the candidates chosen for them by the parties.

The main economic aims of the Progressives

Broadly, the Progressives wanted greater regulation of business by federal or state government. They thought the government needed to play a different role in the economy – being not just the encourager, but also the regulator. They wanted government to be a force for protecting citizens against business excess and exploitation, ensuring that business was run in the interests of the whole community and not just in the interests of the super-rich. They wanted a new relationship between capital and labour.

The specific aims of the Progressive Movement were:

- tougher enforcement of existing legislation, such as the Sherman Anti-Trust Act and the Interstate Commerce Act
- new legislation such as:
  - recognition of trade unions by employers
  - regulation of hours at work, and of female and child labour
  - compensation for injury at work
  - insurance schemes for unemployment, sickness and old age
  - regulation of banks, insurance companies, the stock market and business
  - consumer protection against adulterated food, rigged prices, monopolies and dirty water
  - conservation legislation to protect the environment
- altering the basis of the currency, which was traditionally based on gold. Many, especially the Democrats led by **William Jennings Bryan**, wanted to introduce a silver coinage that they felt would raise prices for farmers and reduce the power of the trusts and big business. There was little economic sense in this objective, but it was immensely popular.

Key figure

William Jennings Bryan (1860–1925)

The democratic candidate for president in 1896 and 1900, Bryan was a well-known orator and was in favour of many of the radical reform ideas of the Progressives. He later became secretary of state for Woodrow Wilson.

Figure 4.7 The 1912 National Progressive Convention in Chicago

Social aims

The social aims of the Progressives were varied and could be conflicting, but they shared a common desire for a better quality of life for people. Some of these aims were:

- **Emancipation for women:** in 1890, two major women's groups formed the National American Woman Suffrage Association to campaign for women to have the right to vote. Many of the supporters of female suffrage were also strong supporters of other Progressive policies.

Figure 4.8 Five American campaigners for women's suffrage – including President Roosevelt's niece, Maud Roosevelt (centre) – pose with US flags

- **Welfare reforms:** there was never the demand in the United States for the degree of state-funded welfare benefits, such as pensions and health care, that countries like Germany and France were adopting. However, there was growing pressure to provide at least a safety net for people facing times of acute distress, such as occurred in some cities after the recession of 1893. Many Progressives were shocked by the poverty and squalid living conditions the journalists and writers known as the Muckrakers (see page 117) revealed, and felt that action should be taken to prevent the worst failings of capitalism. The social work of **Jane Addams** was an example of the type of programme that many Progressives wanted to see all over the USA.

(see page 117)

Key figure

Jane Addams (1860–1935)

Addams was a pioneering social worker in Chicago who founded an organisation for women and children to combat poverty. This organisation was called Hull House, and it proved to be an excellent example of welfare work in the USA that was followed in many cities.

There is a pronounced increase in child labour … in the cotton industries of the South … in the textile mills of the Northern states … this piteous army now numbers 2 million. The children are hurried from the cradle into the factories, with no childhood, no sweet memories of childhood or of home, nothing for them but work from morning till night and only 15 minutes to eat a cold lunch … these little white slaves of the 20th century are mostly American children. In this free land they are toiling under the glorious flag of liberty to satisfy the greed of commercialism.

Women's clubs attack child labour in a petition to the US Senate from 1906.

- **The abolition of the manufacture and sale of alcohol:** in 1893 the Anti-Saloon League was founded by Howard Hyde Russell. A pressure group focusing on a single issue, its aim was to close places where drink was sold and eliminate the damage that alcohol did to society as a whole.
- **African-American rights:** in some parts of the North, where many African-Americans had moved to escape the poverty of the South, black and white Progressives both aimed to improve African-Americans' situation.

The Populist Party

In the 1890s a new political party, the Populists, developed in the southern and western parts of the USA. This was very much a 'people's party' that appealed to many small farmers suffering from the agricultural depression and low farm prices. They shared many of the views of the city-based Progressives and added to the pressure on the government to act. Small farmers were often seriously in debt and wanted prices to rise so they could pay off their debts. The main programme of the Populist Party in the presidential election of 1892 (where it earned 1 million votes) was based on:

- regulation of railways, particularly the freight prices that many felt were artificially high
- regulation of monopolies
- far more government regulation at both state and national level in areas such as farm prices
- postal savings banks that would be secure and safe places for savings, and would not close as a result of speculation
- graduated income tax that would take away dependence on tariffs as the main source of government income, and place the financial burden much more on the rich; tariffs were felt, with some justification, to hit farm prices hard
- direct election of senators, which would ensure that all citizens would be able to choose the two senators from each state who went to Congress in Washington, DC, to represent the interests of that state.

Ultimately, most of the Populists' policies were put into practice. Although the Populists never got into power, their pressure combined with many of the other Progressive groups to persuade the government to start to regulate the economy.

The Progressive Movement – success or failure?

In many ways, the Progressive Movement could be seen as a success story. Largely as a result of the Progressives' campaigning:

- the Constitution was amended in several ways
- federal and state governments took on new powers of regulation
- laws were passed to deal with issues such as working hours
- the first moves towards a social security system took place
- women won the vote
- the sale of alcohol was banned.

However, events in the late 1920s proved that not all 'progress' lasted. Banks collapsed, destitution spread, farming proved a disaster area again and black lynchings continued. It was not until the 1960s that major changes were made to the welfare system and the rights of African-Americans.

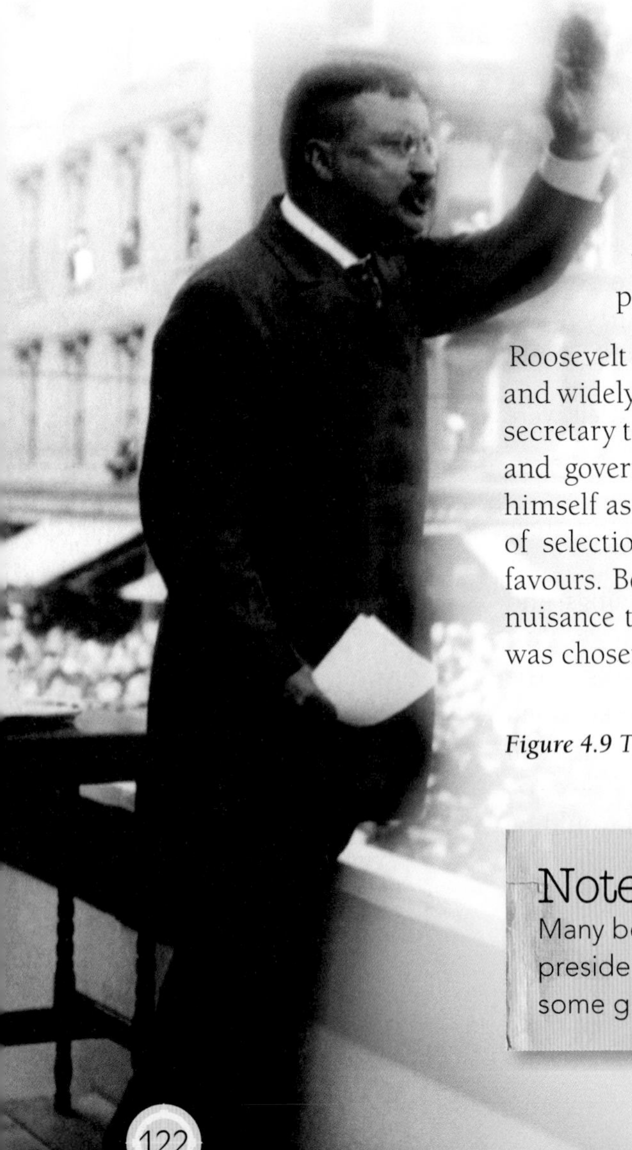

The presidency of Theodore Roosevelt

The Progressive Movement got its greatest supporter by accident. In 1901, the conservative Republican president William McKinley was assassinated. Under the terms of the Constitution, the vice president takes over office for the rest of the four-year term, which meant that Theodore Roosevelt became president of the USA.

Roosevelt was born in 1856 into a wealthy family; he was highly educated and widely travelled. He had experience in national government as assistant secretary to the navy in 1898, and later in New York as police commissioner and governor of the state. In the latter two roles, Roosevelt established himself as a reformer, trying to end corruption and to introduce methods of selection for key posts by merit and not by party bosses returning favours. Becoming a national hero in the Spanish–American War – and a nuisance to the Republican Party because of his reform ideas – Roosevelt was chosen as the vice presidential candidate in 1900.

Figure 4.9 Theodore Roosevelt delivering a speech in 1902

Note:
Many believe that Roosevelt was chosen as vice president partly to keep him quiet and partly to add some glamour to the dull McKinley's campaign.

Roosevelt was a remarkable man: an author, traveller, conservationist and soldier. He also aroused a huge amount of controversy. He felt that the federal government had a role in the economy, and he maintained that it should intervene in the relationship between capital, labour and agriculture. Roosevelt had advanced ideas on society and the economy, and he was flexible and had a great sense of responsibility. Criticised for being too cautious by liberals, he was seen as a dangerous radical by many in his own party.

Roosevelt's record as a Progressive needs to be judged by what developed during his presidency between 1901 and 1908. He displayed inevitable caution until 1904 because he had to seek re-election for a second term. Nevertheless, he was able to help push through some significant achievements. Roosevelt brought the presidential office of the United States firmly into the arena of social and economic reform. Although never a radical, and always democratic, Roosevelt did feel strongly that a US president should use his obvious influence, authority and publicity to highlight important issues such as tariff reform. He placed on the nation's agenda many of the issues that were of greatest concern to the Progressives, and he kept them there, using his status to assist in their development. Roosevelt's first **State of the Union Address** to Congress after taking office, while appearing a little bland and conservative, actually indicated that he was thinking seriously about trusts, rail regulation, tariff reform and conservation issues. This delighted the Progressives.

In 1902, Roosevelt instructed his attorney general Philander C. Knox to start proceedings under the Sherman Anti-Trust Act against the **Northern Securities Company**. Men like Rockefeller and J. P. Morgan were involved, and there was concern that the company was using its monopoly to create excess profits. The courts declared the company illegal and ordered its dissolution. The government had struck the first blow against the great trusts. In the remaining years of Roosevelt's presidency a further 44 corporations were prosecuted, including the Standard Oil Company.

Roosevelt was unusual in that he believed that unions had a right to exist. In 1902, 50,000 coal miners went on strike for higher pay, union recognition and better working conditions. The mine-owners refused to compromise, and a serious coal shortage threatened. Although ultimately Roosevelt's threat to send in troops to run the mines forced a compromise and ended the strike, he was also the first president to take a neutral stance in such a dispute and to call the unions and owners to the White House for arbitration. His predecessors had always been on the side of the employers.

As his presidency continued, legislation encouraged by Roosevelt started to be pushed through Congress:

- The Expedition Act of 1903 employed more lawyers to work for the government so that more actions under the Sherman Anti-Trust Act could be undertaken.

State of the Union Address
The US president's message to the country at the start of a new session of Congress.

Northern Securities Company
This was a vast holding company that controlled several railways in the north-east of the USA.

- The Elkins Act of 1903 started the process of regulating railways.
- The Pure Food and Drug Act of 1906 (inspired by Upton Sinclair's *The Jungle*, a novel about the American meatpacking industry) started the process of ending food adulteration.
- The Department of Commerce and Labor Act of 1903 created a new Department of Commerce with a Cabinet secretary.

The Department of Commerce had the power to collect data from any business that dealt in interstate commerce. That data could be vital in identifying the need to regulate business if it showed monopoly or price fixing. Roosevelt played a key role in getting this legislation passed by Congress, particularly by persuading the public to put pressure on their senators and congressmen to pass the bill. Similar pressure was used by Roosevelt to pass the Newlands Reclamation Act to help construct dams and, above all, start plans for conservation. Major measures were put through to establish national parks and preserve American forests.

Once safely re-elected in 1904, Roosevelt's State of the Union Address contained many Progressive elements, including:

- employer liability proposals, meaning that employers had to compensate for employees' injuries sustained at work
- limitation of working hours
- safety measures for the railways
- more regulatory powers for the government
- regulation for the insurance industry
- child labour restrictions
- factory inspections
- slum clearance measures.

The final two years of Roosevelt's administration, 1906–08, showed a marked shift to the left. The progressive reform movement was pressuring from below in states such as Wisconsin. Roosevelt was leading the assault on plutocracy (government by the rich) from the top. He would continue the pressure to reform until the very end of his period of office. In his final State of the Union message in 1908, he laid down an agenda that his Democratic successors would put into practice. He attacked the ownership and influence of excessive wealth and he made several recommendations, including:

- inheritance and income taxes
- further regulation of all interstate business
- further regulation of railways
- postal savings banks
- a more effective system of dealing with labour disputes
- an eight-hour working day
- compensation for injuries at work
- regulation of stock market speculation.

The notable thing about his two presidential terms is the multitude of things he has said and done from the initiative of his own brain … he dared tackle the combinations of wealth and compelled them to cease their unfair competition … he has demanded a square deal, and we have loved him for the enemies he has made. It would have been vastly easier to keep quiet … but he wanted the just thing done … he has purified the civil service as well as business methods, protected our forests, ended conflict with miners and investigated agricultural conditions.

Extract from an article entitled 'An Assessment of Theodore Roosevelt's Presidency', *Independent Magazine*, 1909.

The Progressive Movement under President Taft 1908–12

Although Roosevelt had a legal right to stand again as the Republican candidate in 1908, he chose not to. His successor was the lawyer **William Howard Taft**, who was an able administrator but was also lazy and conservative, and known for his hostility to trade unions. Much of Taft's administration was spent dealing with tariff reform, which actually had limited effect on the economy and split his own party. He earned the dislike of many Progressives by sacking Gifford Pinchot, the great conservationist whom Roosevelt had appointed. However, Taft did initiate a federal corporation tax and federal income tax, both of which later had huge significance in covering increased government spending. He also initiated many more prosecutions under the Sherman Anti-Trust Act, so his presidency was not a complete failure from the point of view of the Progressives.

Questions

1 What were the principal aims of the Progressives?

2 How far can Theodore Roosevelt be seen as 'the greatest Progressive of them all'?

The presidency of Woodrow Wilson 1913–21

The high point of the Progressive era came with the election of Woodrow Wilson. For the first time in decades, a Democrat took up residence in the White House. Wilson had successfully managed to bring together the very different elements that made up the Democratic Party: the deeply conservative and openly racist South, the liberal élite and the industrial working class from the Northern cities.

William Bryan (see page 119) also aided Wilson's election by appealing to former Populists, helping to prevent the Democrats from being just a conservative group of Southerners obsessed with race. Wilson's victory was also helped by the Republicans splitting badly between Taft and Roosevelt, who stood as a third-party candidate. Wilson had gained a reputation as a reformer in his position as governor of New Jersey, where he had copied many of the ideas of La Follette of Wisconsin (see page 117). He dominated government, but took great care not to offend Congress and tried hard to win its co-operation. Although distracted later by foreign policy and war, he helped pass a remarkable list of acts of Congress, as well as major Constitutional Amendments.

These are some of the major changes put through during Wilson's presidency:

- **The Federal Reserve Act of 1913:** this was an act typical of Woodrow Wilson, as it maintained a balance between the interests of big business and the needs of the wider community. It set up a Federal Reserve Board to oversee the banking system, and aimed to ensure that money was available where and when needed. Many see this as one of Wilson's most important campaigns, as it was hoped it would put a stop to 'Panics' like that of 1907 and bring stability to the banking system.
- **The Underwood Tariff Act of 1913:** tariffs had been a major political issue for decades. Wilson and the Democrats, who had a majority in Congress, reduced tariffs in this act. Many people regarded this as an attack on big business, which favoured high tariffs, and an aid to smaller businessmen and farmers.
- **The introduction of income tax:** income tax was intended to replace the government income lost when tariffs were reduced or abolished. Initially, income tax only had to be paid by those with an income of over $4000, which at the time was over four times a good industrial wage. The income tax gave the federal government a major source of income.
- **The Clayton Act of 1914:** this gave more powers to those enforcing the Sherman Anti-Trust Act in order to break up monopolies and trusts.

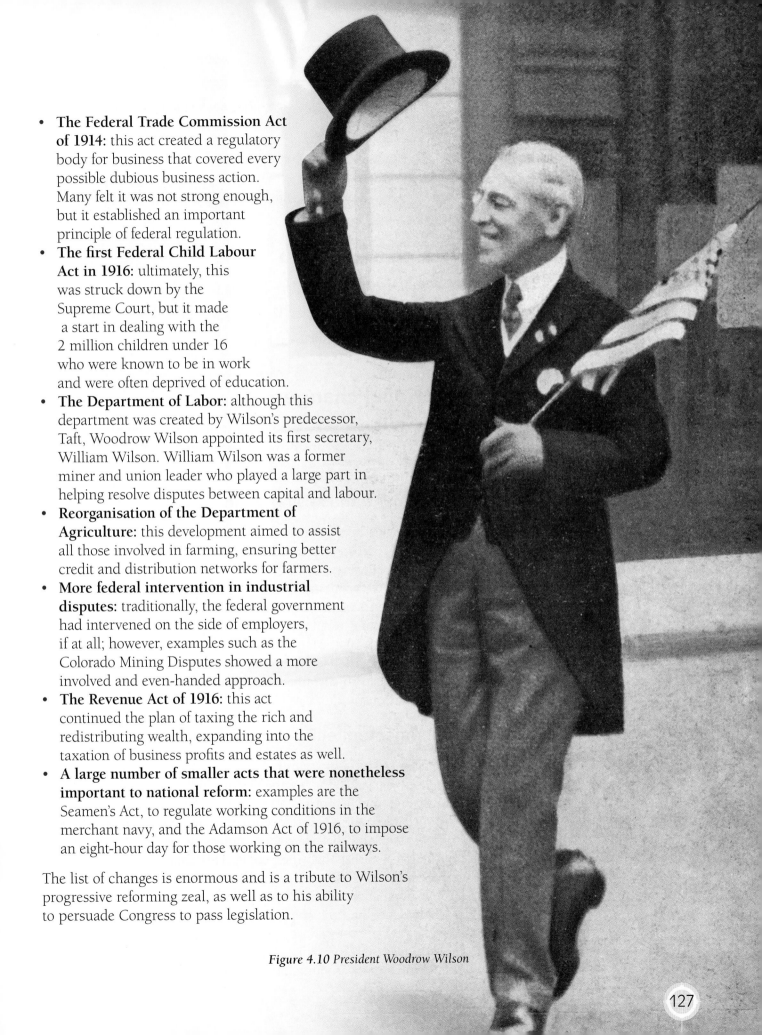

- **The Federal Trade Commission Act of 1914:** this act created a regulatory body for business that covered every possible dubious business action. Many felt it was not strong enough, but it established an important principle of federal regulation.
- **The first Federal Child Labour Act in 1916:** ultimately, this was struck down by the Supreme Court, but it made a start in dealing with the 2 million children under 16 who were known to be in work and were often deprived of education.
- **The Department of Labor:** although this department was created by Wilson's predecessor, Taft, Woodrow Wilson appointed its first secretary, William Wilson. William Wilson was a former miner and union leader who played a large part in helping resolve disputes between capital and labour.
- **Reorganisation of the Department of Agriculture:** this development aimed to assist all those involved in farming, ensuring better credit and distribution networks for farmers.
- **More federal intervention in industrial disputes:** traditionally, the federal government had intervened on the side of employers, if at all; however, examples such as the Colorado Mining Disputes showed a more involved and even-handed approach.
- **The Revenue Act of 1916:** this act continued the plan of taxing the rich and redistributing wealth, expanding into the taxation of business profits and estates as well.
- **A large number of smaller acts that were nonetheless important to national reform:** examples are the Seamen's Act, to regulate working conditions in the merchant navy, and the Adamson Act of 1916, to impose an eight-hour day for those working on the railways.

The list of changes is enormous and is a tribute to Wilson's progressive reforming zeal, as well as to his ability to persuade Congress to pass legislation.

Figure 4.10 President Woodrow Wilson

Business is in a situation in America which it was never in before; it is in a situation to which we have not adjusted our laws. Our laws are still meant for business done by individuals; they have not been satisfactorily adjusted to business done by great combinations, and we have got to adjust them. I do not say we may or may not; I say we must; there is no choice. If your laws do not fit your facts, the facts are not injured, the law is damaged; because the law, unless I have studied it amiss, is the expression of the facts in legal relationships. Laws have never altered the facts; laws have always necessarily expressed the facts; adjusted interests as they have arisen and have changed toward one another.

Politics in America is in a case which sadly requires attention. The system set up by our law and our usage doesn't work,—or at least it can't be depended on; it is made to work only by a most unreasonable expenditure of labor and pains. The government, which was designed for the people, has got into the hands of bosses and their employers, the special interests. An invisible empire has been set up above the forms of democracy.

An extract from a campaign speech given by Woodrow Wilson in 1912.

Constitutional changes

Pressure from the Progressives led not only to a large number of laws that resulted in greater government regulation, but also in changes to the US Constitution itself.

16th Amendment: the raising of an income tax 1913

The USA's Founding Fathers (see page 101) had not envisaged that the federal government would need a substantial income; they had felt that tariffs would be sufficient. However, by 1900 many were arguing that tariffs were harmful to trade and the economy. It was also felt that the federal government was now expected to involve itself in areas other than defence and foreign policy, such as economic regulation and welfare, and it needed a source of income to deal with that. Many Progressives advocated income tax, as it could be structured to fall most heavily on those best equipped to pay. The Supreme Court had ruled earlier that income tax was unconstitutional, so a change in the Constitution was required.

17th Amendment: direct election of senators 1913

The original US Constitution required that the two senators from each state were chosen by the state's own legislature. Often a single party (and sometimes just one 'boss') controlled the state legislature. There were also states where the railway or oil trusts were very powerful, and they ensured that the senators sent by that state to Congress worked primarily in the interests of the trusts rather than the people. This change to direct election of senators meant that these politicians, like congressmen, were directly chosen by the population of their state. Many states introduced primary elections, where voters had the chance to elect the party candidates before the main election, where they chose between the different party candidates. This system survives to the present day, and has played an important part in making the Senate a more accountable and democratic body.

18th Amendment: prohibition of alcoholic beverages 1919

Elements of the Progressive Movement had always been strong opponents of the 'saloon' culture in many states; these Progressives linked alcohol consumption to many social problems. By 1914, several states had gone 'dry' (had banned the consumption of alcohol) and Congress had attempted legislation that banned the transport of alcohol from 'wet' states into 'dry' states. The pressure continued throughout Wilson's presidency, and finally, in 1919, the Constitution was amended to ban altogether the sale and transport of alcohol in the United States. Arguably, this proved to be one of the less successful of the Progressive measures, particularly in the light of later events in the 1920s, when a large illegal industry grew up to provide for Americans who still wanted a drink.

Note:
It should be noted that not all Progressives supported Prohibition. Many felt that it was too great an intrusion into people's private lives.

Figure 4.11 Workers demonstrating against prohibition in the streets of New York

19th Amendment: votes for women 1920

A serious campaign for female suffrage had begun before 1900, and by 1920 several states had already granted women the right to vote. The pressure for female suffrage was strengthened in this period by the growth in education for women and the increased number of women working outside the home – rising to 25% of women by 1914. Over 1.5 million women worked in war industries during the First World War, and by the end of the conflict the pressure for the vote was unstoppable. Wilson, sympathetic rather than enthusiastic, helped to get the Amendment through Congress.

Note:
A greater proportion of women in the USA went to college than anywhere else in the world in the last quarter in the 19th century.

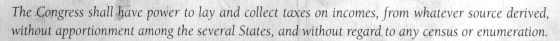

The Congress shall have power to lay and collect taxes on incomes, from whatever source derived, without apportionment among the several States, and without regard to any census or enumeration.

United States Congress, 16th Amendment to the US Constitution, 1913.

The Senate of the United States shall be composed of two Senators from each State, elected by the people thereof, for six years; and each Senator shall have one vote. The electors in each State shall have the qualifications requisite for electors of the most numerous branch of the State legislatures.

United States Congress, 17th Amendment to the US Constitution, 1913.

After one year from the ratification of this article the manufacture, sale, or transportation of intoxicating liquors within, the importation thereof into, or the exportation thereof from the United States and all territory subject to the jurisdiction thereof for beverage purposes is hereby prohibited.

United States Congress, 18th Amendment to the US Constitution, 1919.

The right of citizens of the United States to vote shall not be denied or abridged by the United States or by any State on account of sex.

United States Congress, 19th Amendment to the US Constitution, 1919.

Given the tremendous effort that had to be put into amending the Constitution, the Progressives could look back on their work with great satisfaction. All these constitutional changes would have a profound impact on American politics and society, although not always in the way that was anticipated. The vote for women did not lead to speedy progress towards equality, and Prohibition led to the rise of organised crime. The Senate still largely remained a 'rich man's club', and wartime emergency needs showed that income tax could hit the lower-paid as well as the rich.

The Progressives' impact on the states

Every state in the USA has its own governor and legislature, and is entitled under the Constitution to administer itself and pass its own laws in areas allowed under the Constitution. As early as 1900, many Progressive states were passing laws in areas such as consumer protection and the restriction of working hours, which were later followed by Congress and applied to the whole United States. Some also passed new laws in an effort to break the powers of the party 'bosses' and to give their state a much more democratic system of government. Amongst the many changes that Progressives brought in to states were:

- **Direct election and the direct primary:** where officials in a state had been appointed by the state legislature, they now had to be directly elected by the people, and they had to go through the primary process (see page 118).

- **The referendum:** all the voters in a state were asked to decide on an issue by voting, such as whether the state should go 'dry' (ban alcoholic drinks) or not.
- **The initiative:** once sufficient numbers requested it, citizens could actually put a new law through, or have one abolished, by holding a direct vote.
- **The recall:** citizens in a city or a state could demand the 'recall' or retirement from office of any elected official, such as the governor of the state.
- **The commissioner system in cities:** a city manager was appointed with specific powers, worked with the police, fire and education chiefs, and was accountable to an elected body. This was designed to remove party politics from essential local services, and break the boss system in many cities.
- **Votes for women:** many states allowed women the vote long before they got the vote in national elections.

Although it was often individual states that pioneered many of the great changes brought in by the Progressives, it should be remembered that some states, particularly those in the South, used their powers to exclude African-Americans from the vote and to deprive them of many of the rights and liberties normally seen as part of a democracy.

The USA in the 1920s: still part of the Progressive Era?

With the defeat of the Democrats in the presidential and congressional elections of 1920, and the return of the Republicans to power in the White House until 1933, this period is not always seen as part of the Progressive Era. The economy boomed for many (but not for all), employment remained high and consumer goods and cars poured out of the factories, so there was little demand for change and less desire on the part of Republican presidents to reform.

President Harding (in office 1921–23) and President Coolidge (in office 1923–29) were not active types like Wilson and Roosevelt. Their administrations were reluctant to disturb business, and felt that self-regulation for corporations made sense. The believed the government's role in the economy should be to encourage and not to direct. However, these presidents did little to change what the Progressives had already achieved.

Both presidents appointed some very able members to the Cabinet, such as Andrew Mellon and Herbert Hoover, who made use of the regulatory powers that had been given to the federal government. The enormous accumulations of wealth by a few might continue, but the 'monopoly' did not return. The dreadful exploitation of labour diminished, and shorter working hours and weeks become more common. The public showed little appetite for any more radical action. There were three particular areas of Progressive interest where there was actually a backslide during the 1920s:

- **Prohibition:** with the Constitution amended to ban alcoholic drinks, and federal and state governments empowered to stamp out the distribution and sale of alcohol, the dream of many (but by no means all) Progressives had come to the USA. However, with President Harding leading the way, mass evasion of the law commenced. Saloons closed their doors and reopened as illegal 'speakeasies', paying corrupt police to ignore them. Criminals rapidly realised the huge profits that could be made, and criminal empires developed that have lasted to this day. The Constitution was amended once more in 1933, ending Prohibition with hardly any resistance.

Figure 4.12 People in a bar raise their glasses after the repeal of Prohibition

> **Note:**
> From 1917 onwards, a fear that revolution might spread from communist Russia heightened a growing suspicion of foreigners in the USA. This resulted in a nationwide panic, known as the Red Scare, in 1919–20.

- **Immigration:** large numbers of immigrants had arrived from Europe before the First World War, alongside increasing numbers from China, Japan and the US colony of the Philippines. War had slowed the rush, but just after the war over 800,000 immigrants arrived, many from the devastated south and south-east of Europe, raising fears of the USA being 'swamped' by undesirable aliens. The Emergency Quota Act of 1921 restricted immigration numbers for the first time, but it also tried to ensure that the majority of those that came were from northern and western Europe, where it was felt that the 'culture' was most in sympathy with that of the United States. This was followed by the Immigration Act of 1924, which put tighter controls on immigrant numbers and excluded people from specific Asian countries. These racist acts both demonstrated a preference for white 'Nordic' peoples.

- **Race relations:** the First World War, with its demand for labour in both the North and the South, had often helped the economic conditions of African-Americans. However, there had been no progress towards eliminating segregation and racial discrimination. In fact, conditions worsened as the Ku Klux Klan rose again in many Southern states during the 1920s. Lynchings (see page 39) continued, with two a week on average during the Progressive Era.

Figure 4.13 A 1922 protest against lynching; more than 3000 African-Americans took part in this parade through Washington, DC, to call the government to action

The profoundly racist and conservative Ku Klux Klan used terror and violence to ensure that African-Americans were too frightened to vote. Through its powerful senators and congressmen, it also managed to prevent legislation such as anti-lynching laws from being passed. Discredited by financial scandals and violence, the Klan died out as a major force by the late 1920s. However, it was not until well after the Second World War that attitudes about race began to change in the USA, and even then it took enormous pressure from the president to ensure any progress.

The debate on the Progressive Era

The debate on how much the Progressives actually achieved continues, as does the debate about the role the federal government should play in economic matters. If the Progressives had been more united and clearer in their objectives, much more might have been achieved. Some argue that the movement did little more than highlight issues such as exploitation, corruption and monopoly, and relied on tough-minded politicians like Roosevelt and Wilson to actually change things. However, most of the broad objectives of the Progressives were achieved, and soon another Roosevelt would take their ideas much further.

Note:

The aim of the Ku Klux Klan was to ensure white Protestant supremacy. It was not only anti-black, but also anti-Semitic, anti-Catholic and anti-foreigner. It always argued in favour of the rights of individual states to impose such views against what members saw as an over-powerful central government.

Key issues

The key features of this chapter are:

- the causes of rapid industrial growth after the Civil War

- the impact of economic growth on US society

- the role the government could and should play in the management of the economy

- the extent to which the government should regulate capitalism

- the nature and extent of reforms after 1900.

Revision questions

1 Why was Woodrow Wilson able to instigate so many reforms during his presidency?

2 How successful was the Progressive Movement by 1920?

Further reading

Clements, K. *The Presidency of Woodrow Wilson*. Lawrence, USA. Kansas University Press. 1992.

Gould, L. *America in the Progressive Era*. London, UK. Pearson. 2001.

Hofstadter, R. *The Age of Reform*. New York, USA. Alfred A. Knopf. 1956.

Palmer, N. *The Twenties in America: Politics and History*. Edinburgh, UK. Edinburgh University Press. 2006.

Chapter 5

The Great Crash, the Great Depression and the New Deal 1929–41

Key questions

- What were the causes of the Great Crash and the Great Depression, and how great was their impact?
- How effective were the strategies used by presidents Hoover and Roosevelt to deal with the enormous domestic problems facing the United States between 1929 and 1939?
- What forms did opposition to the New Deal take, and how effective was it?
- How far does Franklin D. Roosevelt deserve his reputation as one of the greatest US presidents?

Content summary

- The Great Crash and the Great Depression, their causes and events.
- The economic, social and political impact of the Great Crash and the Great Depression.
- The policies of Herbert Hoover.
- The politics of Franklin D. Roosevelt, the First 100 Days and the First New Deal.
- The Second New Deal.
- The strategies and tactics of Roosevelt.
- Opposition to the New Deal.
- The debate on Roosevelt and the New Deal.

Timeline

Nov 1928	Election of President Hoover
Oct 1929	Beginning of the Great Crash
Jun 1930	Smoot–Hawley Tariff Act
Jan 1932	Creation of the Reconstruction Finance Corporation
Jul 1932	Emergency Relief and Construction Act
Nov 1932	Election of Franklin D. Roosevelt
Mar–Jun 1933	The First 100 Days
May 1933	The Agricultural Adjustment Act
May 1935	Schechter Case
Aug 1935	The Social Security Act
1935–36	The Second New Deal
1936	The Supreme Court Packing Plan; re-election of Roosevelt
1937	Recession returns to the United States

Key figure

Herbert Hoover (1874–1964)

Hoover was elected president in November 1928 and took office in March 1929. He was a Republican, and the party thought he was an excellent candidate. Hoover came from a modest background, trained as an engineer and made a fortune in the mining industry. As an administrator appointed by Woodrow Wilson, he had played a great part in bringing relief to war-torn Europe in 1918–19. He had been made secretary of commerce in Coolidge's Cabinet in 1921 and had retained the post for the next eight years. He was seen as partly responsible for the 'boom' years, which helped his victory in 1928.

Introduction

The period between 1929 and 1941 was traumatic for the USA and its people. The 1920s were a period of remarkable economic growth and social change, but this prosperity came to an end in 1929 and the United States entered an era of economic depression and unemployment that lasted until war came in 1941. Two presidents, **Herbert Hoover** (in office 1929–33) and **Franklin D. Roosevelt** (in office 1933–45) tried to solve the great economic and social problems, with varying degrees of success. In the process, the USA underwent enormous changes that last to this day. Perhaps the most important of these changes was in the responsibilities of the federal government, which went from playing a minor role in the economy to being a major force. It now regulated business, directed farming, regulated banks and created a welfare state.

This transformation was not always smooth, and mistakes were made in what became a process of experimentation by Roosevelt and his government to help the unemployed, the destitute farmers and the bankrupt banks. Opposition to Roosevelt's policies was often prolonged and bitter. However, the president provided a democratic solution to a dreadful crisis, steering a path between extreme capitalism on one side and the sort of solutions provided by the socialist or fascist states on the other.

Figure 5.1 Homeless jobseekers, victims of the Great Depression, travel on a freight train through the United States

The causes and impact of the Great Crash and the Great Depression

A traditional view is that the Great Crash occurred when the United States stock market, based in New York's Wall Street, collapsed in the autumn of 1929 in what was called 'an orgy of speculation'. This dragged down the rest of the economy, leading to mass unemployment, bank failures and a collapse in investment. However, this is now seen as an incorrect interpretation of events. The contemporary view is that the Great Crash was caused by the economic depression that had already set in.

Many reasons have been suggested as to why, between 1929 and 1941, the United States entered the longest economic depression in its history. The principal reasons are:

- the impact of the First World War
- the policies adopted by US governments in the 1920s
- weaknesses in US banks
- agricultural decline
- the policies of President Hoover between 1929 and 1933
- overproduction of commodities and manufactured goods
- rash speculation and lack of investment
- declining export markets and tariff wars
- external factors, such as the collapse of European economies in 1931.

The Great Crash

After a brief recession in the early 1920s, caused by adjusting from a wartime to a peacetime economy, the United States had entered a period of growth, especially in manufacturing. The stock market boomed, with shares in major companies continuously rising. The **Dow Jones Index** went up by 400% between 1921 and 1929, and by 1928 many shares were being bought and sold for a great deal more than they were actually worth. Companies and individuals bought the shares in the expectation that they would rise in value and could then be sold at a profit. This practice was called speculation. Of course, if the share price went down then they would make a loss, but the upward trend across the last decade gave people confidence. In 1928–29, several factors occurred to bring about the eventual stock market crash:

- In 1928, the **Federal Reserve Bank** (see page 138) increased interest rates on borrowed money and cut the money supply to the country as a whole.
- The head of the Federal Reserve Bank was dying, and there was no leadership from the Bank.
- There was a growing awareness that depression was setting into the United States, and this led to a loss of confidence in the markets.

Dow Jones Index
Created in 1896, this records prices and stock market activity on the New York stock exchange.

Federal Reserve Bank
Created in 1913, this bank had a limited regulatory role over other banks and also influenced interest rates and money supply.

- Large numbers of banks, insurance companies and businesses became heavily involved in speculating on the stock market rather than investing wisely.
- Much of the speculation was financed by borrowing. A bank, for example, could buy a share for 10% of its value. The seller of the share would 'lend' the remaining 90%, using the share itself as security for the loan. The share then would rise in value (hopefully), and by the time the 90% outstanding had to be paid off, the share had risen so much in value that this loan could be paid.

In October 1929, for the reasons outlined above, confidence collapsed on Wall Street and shares dropped in value by as much as 40% in a single day. Thousands of individuals were ruined, and many small banks and insurance companies went bankrupt.

The stock market recovered slowly in the course of the next two years. Some argued that what happened was necessary, and that it ended unwise speculation by banks and businesses. However, it was a severe blow to confidence and did little to encourage new investment. Less than 3% of US citizens had stocks and shares, but many lost their life savings in the collapse of banks and insurance companies that had been speculating with clients' money.

Figure 5.2 'Black Thursday' in the USA (24 October 1929): stockbrokers and stockholders gather near Wall Street in New York to try and withdraw their money

The causes of the Great Depression

There is inevitably a great debate over the principal causes of the Great Depression, and whether these causes originated in the USA or abroad. The role of the government is much debated, with questions about whether it did too little or took the wrong actions.

Some historians and economists argue that the Great Depression should be blamed on long-term, deep-rooted factors over which there was no immediate control, such as the switch to new high-tech consumer-oriented industries that had different investment and labour needs from the USA's traditional areas of production. However, several factors undeniably played a part in triggering the Great Depression:

- **The decline in agriculture:** a combination of factors meant that agriculture, which then still involved a substantial section of the population in the South and West of the USA, was struggling throughout the 1920s and not sharing in the 'boom' years. Serious drought devastated many areas, and overproduction led to up to a 60% drop in prices for farm produce. Attempts to help farmers were vetoed by President Coolidge.
- **Overproduction in industry:** by 1929, for example, 4.5 million cars a year were being produced in the United States. When demand dropped, as it did by 1929, this affected not only the motor industry but also the linked industries such as steel and coal.
- **The US banking industry:** the central bank, the Federal Reserve Bank, had limited regulatory powers. Most US banks were small and served only their local communities. They had few reserves and many were deeply involved in the speculation that led to the Great Crash, when they collapsed.
- **Growing tariff wars:** tariffs were designed to 'protect' US industries from foreign competition, but inevitably other countries would respond by 'protecting' their industries. High foreign tariffs on exported goods were very damaging to the USA, which in 1929 produced 42% of the world's manufactured goods and was the world's largest exporter.
- **Lack of investment:** too much money had gone into speculation and not enough into the new plants, equipment, research and training that was necessary for industrial and business development.
- **Deflation:** prices dropped, in manufacturing as well as agriculture, which discouraged investment and led to further contraction in the economy. It was this, combined with the huge drop in spending by the American people, that was really damaging the US economy by 1930.

The impact of the Great Depression

The Great Depression devastated huge areas of the United States. By 1933, 25% of men were out of work. Purchasing power was radically reduced, so demand for the products made by those in work was further reduced. Hundreds of thousands of families were unable to pay their mortgages, so were made homeless or were forced to leave their farms.

The majority of small banks closed, taking the life savings of their investors with them. Thousands of men roamed the country looking for work. There was no welfare state to provide a safety net. There was no unemployment pay. What little assistance there was, provided by individual states or by charities, was unable to cope with mass unemployment. State income dropped and states were unable to pay teachers and the police. The economic system of the United States had ground to a halt.

Men, young and old, have taken to the road. Homes in which life savings were invested have been lost and never recovered. There is no security, no foothold, and no future to sustain them. Savings are gone and debts are mounting with no prospect of repayment. Women and child labour further undermine the stability of the home. Food rations are pared down, rents go unpaid and families are evicted. Idleness destroys not only purchasing; power, lowers the standards of living but destroys efficiency and finally breaks the spirits.

An extract from 'Report and Recommendations of the California State Unemployment Commission', Sacramento, 1932.

Figure 5.3 Impoverished citizens of New York are given food parcels, 1929

What surprised many observers was how peacefully the vast majority of Americans reacted to the crisis. In countries such as Germany, citizens looked to radical solutions such as those provided by Hitler. In the United States there was little serious unrest, and a general willingness to remain within the democratic process to find a solution.

Questions

1. What role did the banking system play in causing the Great Depression?

2. To what extent was the Great Crash the cause of the Great Depression?

Strategies for domestic problems by Hoover and Roosevelt in the 1930s

The presidency of Herbert Hoover 1929–33

The traditional view of Herbert Hoover and his policies towards dealing with the Great Depression were that he did too little to help and in some cases actually made the situation worse. To be fair to Hoover, there were real limits to what a president could do under the Constitution at the time. Hoover felt that it was not the job of the president to intervene extensively in the economy, as this might cause more harm than good. He also felt that much of the blame for the US crisis lay with other countries, over which he had no control. It is also worth noting that the worst of the crisis did not come until 1932 and early 1933, and before this time Congress and the public were more conservative about intervention in the economy.

The policies of Herbert Hoover

Hoover felt strongly that the president should have a limited role in economic matters. The Founding Fathers had not anticipated the way in which the US economy would develop, and so economic matters had traditionally been firmly in the hands of either Congress or the individual states. It was widely believed that the president should focus primarily on defence and foreign policy. However, the Great Depression presented a new challenge: neither Congress nor the states had the ability to respond to a national crisis of this size, so in the 1930s all looked to the president for action and solutions. Hoover did not feel that it was his role to actively manage the economy, nor did he feel that it might help to intervene, but he was determined to do what he could.

However, several historians argue that some of the actions Hoover took actually made the situation worse rather than better:

- He did not persuade the Federal Reserve Bank to increase the supply of money in the economy. This might have reversed **deflation** and increased demand.
- He did not use his veto to stop the Smoot–Hawley Tariff Act in 1930. He had promised a tariff on agricultural imports in 1928 to help farmers, but as the bill went through Congress, many manufactured goods were added to the list of protected goods. This led to retaliation by other countries and played a key part in the collapse of world trade, which was catastrophic for the United States and its manufacturers and producers.

deflation
This describes a general drop in the prices of goods and services.

Note:
US exports were worth $5.2 billion in 1929 and had dropped to $1.1 billion by 1932.

Note:

The Gold Standard was an international monetary system in which the standard economic unit was based on the fixed weight of gold. It placed a value on a currency and was also used to compare one currency with another for exchange rates.

- In 1931, when many European banks started to collapse and Britain came off the Gold Standard, Hoover and his treasury secretary insisted on 'defending' the dollar and staying on the Gold Standard. This was another massive error that limited investment and borrowing. It also cut the supply of money in the USA, and led to further deflation.
- In 1931, concerned about the Federal Budget being unbalanced, with more money going out than was coming in as taxes, he decided to recommend an increase in taxes to balance the budget. Congress agreed, and of course this cut money supply even further.
- In 1930, Hoover opposed an attempt by the Senate to bring in unemployment insurance, fearing the creation of a welfare-dependent class.

Two schools of thought quickly developed in our administration discussions after 1929. First was the 'leave it alone liquidationists' headed by Secretary of the Treasury Mellon who felt that government must keep its hands off and left the slump liquidate itself … it will purge the rottenness out of the system. People will work harder and live a more moral life … But other members of the administration believed with me that we should use the powers of the government to cushion the situation. To our minds the prime needs were to prevent bank panics. To mitigate the privation amongst the unemployed and the farmers …

Herbert Hoover, *The Memoirs of Herbert Hoover*, 1953.

Figure 5.4
Herbert Hoover

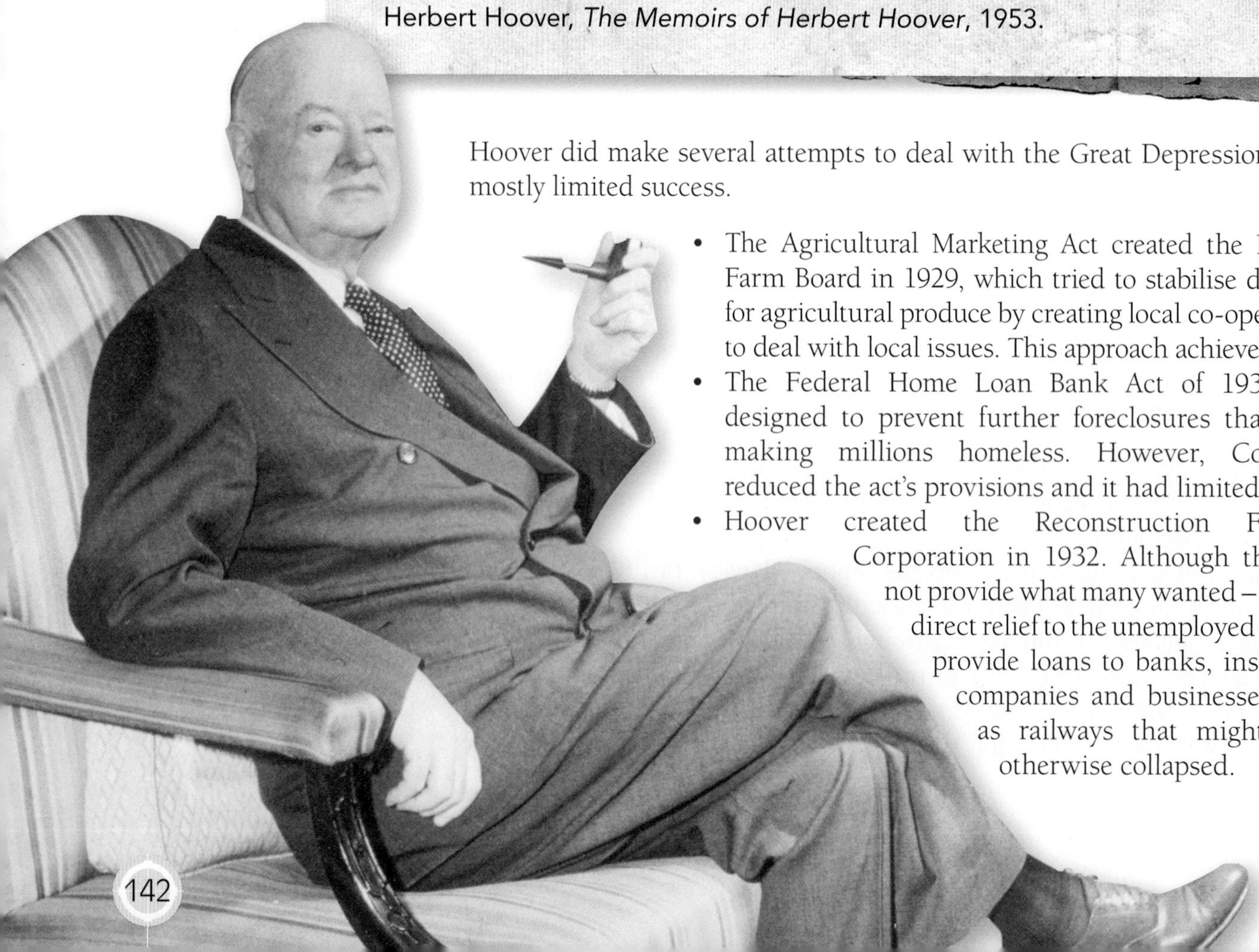

Hoover did make several attempts to deal with the Great Depression, with mostly limited success.

- The Agricultural Marketing Act created the Federal Farm Board in 1929, which tried to stabilise demand for agricultural produce by creating local co-operatives to deal with local issues. This approach achieved little.
- The Federal Home Loan Bank Act of 1932 was designed to prevent further foreclosures that were making millions homeless. However, Congress reduced the act's provisions and it had limited effect.
- Hoover created the Reconstruction Finance Corporation in 1932. Although this did not provide what many wanted – that is, direct relief to the unemployed – it did provide loans to banks, insurance companies and businesses such as railways that might have otherwise collapsed.

- He persuaded Congress to pass the Relief and Reconstruction Act in 1932, which allowed for $1.5 billion of federal spending on public works, such as roads, to create jobs. It also allocated $300 million to the states to help with welfare – basically feeding the hungry. It was simply too little to have much effect on mass unemployment.

Hoover faced re-election in 1932, and it was bitterly remembered that in 1930 he had cheerfully announced 'The depression is over'. With unemployment at 25% of adult males, hunger and destitution spreading across the USA, wages falling and the majority of US banks suffering a total collapse, Hoover stood no chance of winning.

In addition to this, although Hoover was able and intelligent, he lacked charisma, and he often came across as uncaring and cold. This was highlighted in 1932, in the middle of the campaign, when army veterans from the First World War marched to Washington, DC, to claim payment of their 'war bonuses'. The veterans were driven off and treated very harshly by the US army. For many, this confirmed their impression of Hoover's lack of compassion. The Democratic candidate, Franklin D. Roosevelt, won easily in the 1932 election.

Franklin D. Roosevelt and the New Deals

Roosevelt came from a wealthy family and was educated at Harvard University. He was the vice presidential candidate for the Democratic Party in 1920 and then governor of New York State from 1929–32. He had been crippled by polio in the early 1920s and was unable to walk unaided for the rest of his life.

> **Note:**
> Those who had served in the US army in the First World War had been promised a sum of money as a reward, to be paid in 1944. They wanted it sooner, and staged a march in an attempt to achieve this.

Roosevelt offered few policies to ease the crisis in the course of the election campaign of 1932. In some cases, such as stressing the need for a balanced budget, his policies were similar to those of Herbert Hoover. However, while Hoover placed much of the blame for the economic crisis on the First World War and the situation in Europe, Roosevelt implied that it was more to do with structural and institutional failings within the United States. His main slogan was to promise a 'New Deal' for the American people. He won the election by a massive majority. Some of the principal reasons for this great victory were as follows:

- Many Americans blamed Hoover and the Republican Party for the economic crisis, and wanted somebody different in power.
- Roosevelt managed to generate optimism and hope, and convinced people that he had solutions to the crisis.
- Roosevelt had far more charisma than Hoover, and his excellent use of the new medium of radio carried his message to a wide spectrum of the public; he also had substantial support in the press.

- Roosevelt was an outstanding politician, able to get the very different elements that made up the Democratic Party to work together and appear united.
- Roosevelt's record as governor of New York showed he cared about the plight of the unemployed and was prepared to take action to help.

Some signs of Roosevelt's principles had emerged by 1932, which also helped his election and indicated the sort of policies he might implement as president. He felt that the federal government had a larger role to play, and should do more to control the economy in order to ensure that the interests of the United States as a whole were not subordinated to the interests of the rich.

Roosevelt believed in trying to replace selfish individualism with voluntary co-operation. He had a real sympathy for the poor, and he felt that there was a need to provide greater welfare and social security. Roosevelt was aware that complete economic individualism, with no regulation at all, did not sit comfortably with democracy. He had also indicated by his attitude towards the supply of key utilities, such as water, gas and electricity, that the private sector was not always the best way of providing these services to the public. In addition, Roosevelt was an enthusiastic environmental conservationist.

I want to speak not of politics but of government. I want to speak not of parties, but of universal principles … The issue of government has always been whether individual men and women will have to serve some system of government or economics, or whether a system of government and economics exists to serve individual men and women … the task of government in relation to business is to assist the development of an economic declaration of rights, an economic constitutional order.

Franklin D. Roosevelt, in a campaign speech delivered in San Francisco, 1932.

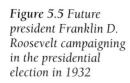

Figure 5.5 Future president Franklin D. Roosevelt campaigning in the presidential election in 1932

In the months between Roosevelt being elected (November 1932) and actually taking office as president (March 1933), the economic crisis within the United States dramatically worsened. Hoover wanted Roosevelt's co-operation in dealing with the crisis in the way Hoover saw fit. Roosevelt declined. As a result, by the time Roosevelt was inaugurated:

- there was a major banking crisis, and all the banks in 32 states had closed
- there had been a huge withdrawal of cash from banks
- a Senate committee had revealed corruption and incompetence on Wall Street, and the New York Stock Exchange had closed
- there was a massive flight of capital and gold from the USA
- national unemployment was at over 13 million and rising, and welfare assistance had run out.

Roosevelt was not idle in the months between election and taking office. He built up a team of advisors, many of them young academics, known as the 'Brains Trust'. Their analysis of the origins of the crisis was that internal factors were the main cause and that the focus of the remedy should be on and within the United States. They felt that the federal government ought to play a much larger role in the regulation of the economic life of the country. The Brains Trust advisors were democratic and pro-capitalist, but also very progressive, adaptable and above all pragmatic. How right they were in their analysis of the causes and in their suggested solutions is subject to immense debate.

> **Note:**
> The role of the Brains Trust was to debate, analyse and argue in order to come up with ideas that provided solutions to the crisis and which fitted in with Roosevelt's broad principles.

> *The New Deal was an incident in American history which arose out of the great depression ... most of its characteristics, however, developed from traditional progressivism and most of its devices were accepted items in the general armoury of government ... it would be almost true to say that the New Deal of the thirties constituted of postponed items from Wilson's programme which had been abandoned in favour of preparation for war in 1916.*
>
> **Rex Tugwell, 'The Experimental Roosevelt',** *Political Quarterly,* **1950.**

Under the US Constitution, the president does not have many powers when it comes to domestic policy:

- All Cabinet members have to be approved by the Senate.
- All new laws have to pass through Congress, and both the House of Representatives and the Senate can reject a bill.
- If the president vetoes a bill, Congress can overturn his veto by a two-thirds majority.

Note:

The nine judges of the Supreme Court have tremendous 'blocking' power. They can decide that an action by the president himself, or by any member of his/her government, is unconstitutional and put a stop to it.

Key figure

Frances Perkins (1880–1965)

Perkins was the first woman in the US Cabinet. A committed radical and humanitarian, she was a great advocate for the Civilian Conservation Corps (see page 147) and issues such as minimum wages, restriction of child labour and maximum hours of work.

- The president's budget has to be passed by Congress.
- If the president does get a law through Congress, the independent Supreme Court could declare that law unconstitutional and ban its implementation.

Roosevelt had to work within these limitations. Initially, he had a fairly easy task. The newly elected Congress had a large Democratic majority, many from Northern cities where the Depression was most severe, and it wanted action. There was a huge public demand for change and solutions to deal with the crisis. Roosevelt appointed some moderate Republicans to his Cabinet, including Harold Ickes as secretary of the interior and Henry Wallace as secretary for agriculture (both key appointments on the domestic front) to show a united approach to solving the serious problems facing the United States. He also appointed the first woman Cabinet member, **Frances Perkins**, a former social worker with an extensive knowledge of poverty in cities, as secretary of labor.

Figure 5.6 Franklin D. Roosevelt giving an interview in Albany, New York State, in 1932

The First 100 Days and the First New Deal

Roosevelt was incredibly active in the first 100 days of his presidency. In fact, no other US president had ever passed more legislation through Congress in such a short amount of time. There were at least fifteen major pieces of legislation put through in Roosevelt's legendary First 100 Days. In addition, Roosevelt regularly gave radio broadcasts, known as his 'Fireside Chats', to help restore public confidence in the US system and explain what he was doing and why.

The series of acts of Congress that he initiated in the spring and summer of 1933, together with some other government actions, are collectively known as the 'First New Deal'. They include:

- summoning an emergency meeting of all bankers, closing all banks for four days to try and curtail the panic, and stopping all transactions in gold
- summoning a special session of Congress to deal with the crisis and to put through the laws he wanted
- getting Congress to pass the Emergency Banking Act, which gave the federal government greater control of the banks, interest rates and money supply
- persuading Congress to repeal Prohibition, the ban on making and selling alcohol, which started to bring in revenue as alcohol was taxed
- cutting government spending on some salaries and pensions (the Economy Act)
- coming off the Gold Standard, which meant the dollar dropped in value compared with other countries, helping get international trade and US exports moving again
- creating the Civilian Conservation Corps (CCC), which initially employed 250,000 young men on public works that had a focus on conservation, reforestation, flood control and the national parks; ultimately, over 3 million men were employed on this programme – it helped reduce the number of unemployed and also injected money into the economy
- establishing the Agricultural Adjustment Administration (AAA) and the Farm Credit Administration, which gave the head of the AAA and the secretary of agriculture (Henry Wallace) considerable powers to deal with agricultural problems
- setting up the Federal Emergency Relief Administration, which was designed to deal with relief to the unemployed; it represented the first time that the federal government had ever intervened in this area of the economy
- creating the Public Works Administration, which would spend $3.3 billion on public works to provide employment
- putting through the National Industrial Recovery Act, which many saw as the most remarkable innovation as it gave the federal government power to regulate not only things like maximum hours of work, but also minimum wages, guaranteed union rights and prices and production
- establishing the Tennessee Valley Authority (TVA), a publicly owned corporation that built dams for flood control; this generated electricity and played a key role in transforming a severely depressed part of the South
- getting Congress to pass The Glass–Steagall Banking Act, which prevented banks from speculating with their customers' money and reduced the risk of bank collapse
- ensuring the federal insurance of bank deposits, which further improved confidence in the banking system.

Note:
When faced with serious opposition from Congress, one of Roosevelt's techniques was to use his 'Fireside Chats' on a Sunday evening to appeal to the American people and suggest they put pressure on their senators and congressmen to support the measures he was advocating.

Note:
The Emergency Banking Act encouraged people to put their savings back into banks and helped restore confidence in US banks. Credit and money started to flow again.

A national emergency productive of widespread unemployment and disorganisation of industry is hereby declared to exist. It is hereby declared to be the policy of Congress to remove obstructions to the free flow of commerce and to provide for the general welfare by promoting the organisation of industry for the purpose of cooperative action … to increase consumption by increasing purchasing power, to reduce and relieve unemployment …

United States Congress, Section 1 of the National Industrial Recovery Act, 16 June 1933.

It was a remarkable achievement in a short space of time. The bank panic ended and banks reopened. The principle of federal regulation in a variety of areas, such as banks, industry and farming, was established. The federal government made a start on providing jobs and welfare, and some optimism and confidence was injected into American society. Money started to move again and the stock market was on the up by the autumn of 1933. It has been argued that this First New Deal was not a particularly coherent plan, just a series of experimental and innovative measures to deal with a crisis of a type previously unknown in US history. Its critics stressed the lack of coherence and its comparatively limited impact in terms of jobs, production and investment. However, by the end of 1933 the situation had certainly not got any worse and there were genuine signs of improvement. Arguably, the American system, both economic and political, had been saved.

> **Note:**
> To this day, the Securities and Exchange Commission (SEC) regulates the US stock market and tries to prevent the sort of crisis on Wall Street that occurred in 1929.

The Second New Deal

By the end of 1933, a degree of confidence had been restored. Unemployment had begun to drop and the economy had started to move again. Some further reforms continued into 1934, such as the creation of the Securities and Exchange Commission (SEC).

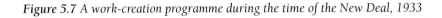

Figure 5.7 A work-creation programme during the time of the New Deal, 1933

By January 1934, the Civil Works Administration had 4.2 million men at work (building roads and so on), being paid a minimum wage, which was putting money into the economy and increasing purchasing power. However, there were still major problems:

- Unemployment remained high – it was still 20% in 1935.
- Agriculture had shown limited improvement: there was still serious drought in some areas, farmers were being evicted for debt in other areas, and there was still overproduction of some crops. Some felt that the AAA (see page 147) was more helpful to big commercial interests than to small farmers.
- Millions were still living in poverty.
- There was a genuine fear of radical action being taken in agricultural areas and possibly in the cities.
- Some aspects of the New Deal were clearly not working: the Public Works Administration and the National Industry Recovery Act were having limited effect; they had created lots of jobs for bureaucrats, but had done little else.
- Opposition was growing to the New Deal from the right wing.
- The Supreme Court was challenging the constitutionality of some of the New Deal.

Despite the continuation of the Depression and a growing hostility to the New Deal, the Democrats did well in the midterm Senate elections in November 1934. In January 1935, Roosevelt set out on his 'Second New Deal'.

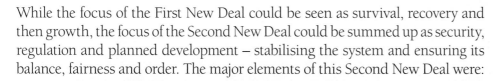

I knew Roosevelt long enough and under enough circumstances to be quite sure that he was no political or economic radical. I take it that the essences of economic radicalism are to believe that the best system is the one in which private ownership of the means of production is abolished in favour of public ownership. But Roosevelt took the status quo (the existing capitalist system) as much for granted as his family … He felt the system ought to be human, fair and honest and those adjustments ought to be made so that people would not suffer from poverty and neglect and so that all would share.

Frances Perkins, *The Roosevelt I Knew*, 1947.

While the focus of the First New Deal could be seen as survival, recovery and then growth, the focus of the Second New Deal could be summed up as security, regulation and planned development – stabilising the system and ensuring its balance, fairness and order. The major elements of this Second New Deal were:

- **The Emergency Relief Appropriation Act:** this was often known as the 'Big Bill'. It was designed to inject over $4 billion into the economy (the greatest peacetime allocation of money by Congress to the federal government in US history to date) to spend on creating employment. It gave work to 3.5 million jobless people, who would be employed on labour-intensive projects such as building roads, schools, hospitals, airports, electrification projects and aircraft carriers. Ultimately, 8.5 million people gained work through this project.

- **The Social Security Act:** this was put forward by Frances Perkins, the secretary for labor. It brought in a system of unemployment insurance that would ensure some income when a worker was laid off. The employee and the employer contributed to the scheme. The same system was applied to old-age pensions.
- **The 1935 Banking Act:** this gave the Federal Reserve Bank, the nearest the USA has to a central controlling bank, a much greater role in regulating the money supply and the money markets.
- **Wealth tax:** this was designed to tax the highest earners. It did not actually bring in much income to the government, but it did appeal to Roosevelt's more left-wing critics.

Note:

Part of the initial plan for the Social Security Act had been to include health care, but Congress felt this was too radical and so it was dropped.

Overall, the acts – particularly the Social Security Act – were not as radical as first hoped. Health care was excluded from the Social Security Act, and over 9 million citizens (many of them African-Americans) were not covered. However, 26 million people were covered for the first time, and because of the principle established about the role of the federal government in social security, the Social Security Act is considered the most important piece of social security legislation in the country's history. It brought a degree of security into the lives of millions and relieved two of the greatest fears of many workers: how to deal with unemployment and with old age.

Figure 5.8 A map showing areas of economic decline and the distribution of economic relief, 1933–39

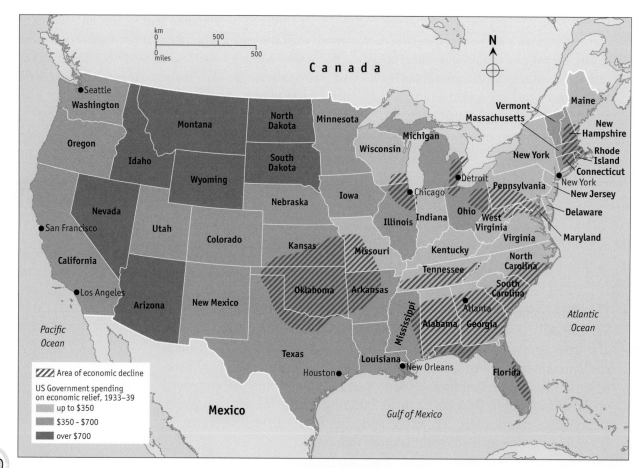

The political strategies of Franklin D. Roosevelt

It was not just popular demand that enabled Roosevelt to bring about both New Deals; he also had great ability as a politician. As well as considerable charm and charisma, and ability as a public speaker, he had a great sense of what was possible in the highly complex structure of US politics. He had experience at both national and local level, which was an enormous asset. He was also a skilled radio broadcaster and he was the first major politician to use this medium effectively. Roosevelt's ability to manage the press was impressive, too. He made himself available to journalists, both individually and in larger press conferences, to answer questions and to put forward arguments in favour of his policies. He was an excellent communicator who made good use of the mass media available at the time.

Roosevelt always faced problems with his own political party, the Democrats. His Democratic predecessor, Woodrow Wilson, had done an impressive job in bringing together the very different, and often conflicting, elements that made up the Democratic Party. Roosevelt continued the process, as the Democratic Party was still made up of very different elements.

- **The South:** Democrats in states such as Mississippi were deeply conservative and very hostile to anything that might challenge white supremacy. Their senators and members of the House of Representatives often sat in Congress for decades, which made them a very powerful force and enabled them to block a president's legislation. Roosevelt had to be careful not to antagonise such men. Most African-Americans in the South were excluded from voting in the Southern states, so the fact that he stood to lose white votes but not gain any votes from African-Americans may have been a consideration for Roosevelt. One of the reasons why Roosevelt was so keen on the Tennessee Valley Authority (see page 147) was because it would bring aid in a variety of forms to the South, which would help the poor without offending Southern Democrats.
- **The Northern industrial cities:** the immigrant and working-class vote tended to support the Democrats in the big industrial cities like Chicago. However, the management of these cities was often in the hands of 'bosses' who could be both very powerful and extremely corrupt. Their 'machines' provided housing and jobs for workers, but the workers were expected to repay these favours with their votes. Often these bosses could play a major role in national politics, and Roosevelt knew he had to manage them carefully. Often, the interest of a Northern industrial worker and his boss conflicted with the interests of a deeply conservative cotton farmer from the South, so Roosevelt had to use great skill to keep both elements of his party happy.
- **The educated and liberal élite from the Northeast:** most of Roosevelt's 'Brains Trust' and some of his other key advisors fell into this category. Many of the ideas behind the New Deal came from such people. They tended to be much more tolerant on issues such as race.

- **The trade unions:** the trade unions did not constitute a united movement, and contained many different forces. Some union leaders were deeply conservative, particularly those who led the unions for skilled men. Those leading the unskilled were more radical – some were even socialist. Union leaders disagreed on whether the unions or the government should provide benefits such as pensions.

Note:
The trade unions were major cash contributors to the Democratic Party.

- **An enormous range of other people with a wide variety of interests:** in order to ensure re-election, Roosevelt had to also bear in mind those who could be persuaded to vote Democrat. A potential voter might be a migrant farm worker in California, a teacher from Oregon or a small farmer in Kansas.

The success of the Democratic Party in the midterm elections of 1934 was largely due to the New Deal, which demonstrated positive action to address the problems of recession. The electorate was prepared to give the Democrats and their president more time to solve the problems facing the USA.

As always, Roosevelt went on the 'stump' – travelling around the country by railway, giving speeches – to drum up support, and his Fireside Chats, by then a popular institution, were extremely helpful in keeping confidence in the Democratic Party growing. Many of the Democrat congressmen and governors who were elected or re-elected in 1934 clearly owed their positions to Roosevelt and the New Deal, and this helped to gain support from the states as well as easing the passage of legislation through Congress.

The re-election of 1936

Note:
US political parties hold a convention in the summer of a presidential election year to choose a candidate for the presidency.

In the 1932 election, Roosevelt had been cautious about committing himself to specific policies. At the Democratic Convention in 1936, he was much more specific and arguably made a significant move to the left in terms of policy. With the two New Deals on his record, a recent tax on undistributed corporate profits and payment of the War Bonus to veterans, he argued that he had already done much to help ease the Great Depression.

At the Democratic Convention, Roosevelt launched an attack on 'the economic tyranny of the few' and 'organised money', and almost went out of his way to attack big business and Wall Street. Some felt that he was making unnecessary enemies, but Roosevelt thought that, with growing radicalism in the USA, he might lose working-class votes to more extreme candidates unless he made it clear which side he was on. There was still serious unemployment in the cities, and drought was affecting the farm states in the Midwest.

Roosevelt's Republican opponent, Alf Landon, offered little that was different in terms of domestic policy. The New Deal was clearly very popular and showed signs of working. Landon differed from Roosevelt on foreign policy, but what was happening outside the USA was of little interest to the vast majority of American people.

Not only was Roosevelt comfortably re-elected for his second term, but the Democrats were successful in elections for the Senate and the House of Representatives. The Democrats also fared well in elections for many state assemblies and governorships. This massive endorsement from the American people proved useful for Roosevelt when facing up to his many critics and opponents.

There were several key reasons why Roosevelt won the election:

- The New Deal was immensely popular and a clear majority of Americans supported it.
- Always the able politician, Roosevelt was extremely clever in his use of patronage – not only in major government appointments such as the Cabinet, but also in the way the New Deal ensured that Democratic bosses in cities and states were able to use the new jobs to support their own position and reward supporters.
- His criticism of the Supreme Court and its role in blocking New Deal actions was popular.
- He had tremendous support from the labour movement and from African-Americans who had the vote, particularly those who had moved to the North and found it easier to register as voters.
- Those employed by the Public Works Administration were naturally enthusiastic supporters of a man whose opponent might well end the scheme.
- The 4 million homeowners whose homes were saved from foreclosure were obvious supporters.
- The millions of people whose bank deposits and life savings had been saved in the dark days of 1933 were grateful to him; gratitude is not always a strong factor in voting behaviour, but in this case it was.

Questions

1. What measures did Herbert Hoover take to deal with the Great Depression?

2. Discuss the view that Roosevelt's First New Deal actually had little impact.

Opposition to the New Deal

The New Deal was not universally supported, and there was opposition to it from a variety of sources. Some came from political quarters; Republicans could be expected to oppose as a matter of course. One major adversary was ex-president Hoover, who was bitter about losing in 1932. There was opposition from the states, the Supreme Court and Congress, based on the powers given to them under the Constitution. The US Constitution is very clear on what the federal government can and cannot do.

- The individual states were expected to play the major governing role in the lives of US citizens. Issues such as education, welfare and any form of regulation in economic life were expected to be the responsibility of a state. State assemblies and their governors tended not to like taking orders from Washington, DC, which could be well over 1600 km (1000 miles) away and unaware of local feelings and issues.
- Congress, consisting of the Senate and the House of Representatives, can impose legislation on an unwilling president, block any legislation he might want by a simple majority in either House, block or amend his budget and reject any of his appointments to the Cabinet. However, for much of the New Deal period Congress was not a huge barrier to Roosevelt's wishes, as the president's polices proved to be enormously popular.
- The federal judiciary, with the Supreme Court at its head, deals with all matters linked to the federal government and Congress. The Supreme Court can examine an act of Congress and decide whether that act is constitutional. If the court decides that the act is not in accordance with the principles of the Constitution, the act can be struck down. The Supreme Court also has the power of **judicial review**. However, the Supreme Court cannot itself initiate the process of declaring an act or action invalid: it is purely an appeal court, so it has to wait until somebody appeals a case to it, which can take time. This is why it was not until 1935 that the Supreme Court proved to be a major obstacle to the New Deal.

Some opposition came from the left, which argued that Roosevelt was not nearly radical enough in terms of his legislation and spending. Some wanted much greater investment in welfare; others were keener on creating equality. Some argued for greater power for unions (which were often bitterly divided amongst themselves about what their objectives should be). Some opponents, such as Huey Long, were **demagogues** out for power and influence for themselves; others were utopians hoping to create a better world. One advantage that Roosevelt had was that there was little or no unity or common aim from his opponents on the left, and a 'divide and rule' policy could work. However, the left influenced Roosevelt's thinking and played a part in the welfare focus of the Second New Deal and in his campaign for re-election in 1936.

Note:
Roosevelt had to be cautious about offending the major figures in Congress, as Congress had the ability to do serious harm to his programme.

judicial review
The power of a court to review the legality of actions by a legislature or government body.

demagogues
Leader who have mass appeal and often try to stir up the public to win votes.

Other opponents came from the right of the political spectrum. Some were hostile to what they perceived as an unjust attack on their wealth. Others felt that Roosevelt was aiming at a type of dictatorship, and he was undermining the Constitution of the United States. There were strong conservative forces that did not like the idea of the government getting involved in areas such as business. Businessmen did not like their profits being taxed or being ordered to pay their workers a minimum wage. The impact of the opposition from the right is more difficult to measure, but it would certainly play a role in ensuring that little of a radical nature occurred after Roosevelt's second term of office.

Opposition from the Supreme Court

The Supreme Court has the ability to declare any act of Congress unconstitutional and stop it operating. The court is made up of nine judges that are appointed for life, and it is virtually impossible to remove them. When there is a vacancy because a justice (judge) has either died or retired, the president can nominate a successor but the Senate has to approve the appointment. All the nine judges in 1933 had been appointed by Roosevelt's predecessors, and he had no means of influencing them in any way. It is not unusual for the Supreme Court to take decisions that have enormous impact on the United States. For example, in the 1857 *Dred Scott* v *Sandford* case (see page 26) the Supreme Court upheld the rights of slave owners over their slaves, and this played a part in the causes of the US Civil War.

There is a tradition of litigation in the United States: if someone does not like a decision, then they can take the issue to court to challenge it. If they do not like the decision they get there, they can appeal against it to the very highest court. This is precisely what happened to aspects of the New Deal. The Schechter Case illustrates this well.

In the 1935 *Schechter Poultry Corp* v *United States* case, often known as the 'Sick Chicken Case', the owners of a chicken company that slaughtered and processed chickens were fined and imprisoned for not following the regulations laid down by the National Industrial Recovery Act. They appealed, and the Supreme Court ruled that the federal government did not have the power under the Constitution to make such regulations. Effectively, the Supreme Court struck down the National Industrial Recovery Act and its administration. It was a major blow to the whole New Deal. Further Supreme Court decisions struck down the AAA and 11 other New Deal acts. However, the opposition from the Supreme Court did not last long. In February 1936, it decided that the TVA and the National Labor Relations Act were constitutional.

Roosevelt made a mistake in his initial reaction to the Supreme Court's decisions to strike down some of the New Deal. He criticised the 'nine old men' who he thought wanted to take the USA back to the 'horse and buggy era' and who failed to support his attempts to bring relief to the unemployed and hungry. He tried to increase the number of judges so he could appoint

Note:
In the 1937 *Parrish* case, the Supreme Court upheld the ability of the government to regulate business, and the Supreme Court stopped being a major barrier to the New Deal.

those who might not vote to strike down the New Deal legislation. However, this angered both public opinion and Congress, which opposed any major change to a revered institution. Roosevelt had to back down. The tide turned in his favour by 1937 with justices retiring or changing their minds, so there was no further opposition from the Supreme Court.

Opposition from the left

There was a broad range of opponents to the New Deal and Roosevelt. They often had very different views from each other, so stood little chance of working together or actually attaining power in any way. However, in a variety of ways they still had an influence on the president and the New Deal. The main groups of the left were:

- **Liberal Republicans:** the two main parties in the United States, the Republicans and the Democrats, both represented a wide range of views on issues. Some Republicans were much less conservative than others, and the liberal Republicans did not like Roosevelt's very cautious monetary policy. They felt that he was putting too little money into the economy, and wanted the government to spend much more money to stimulate the economy. It was helpful to Roosevelt to have his main opposition party divided over this issue, as many other Republicans wanted the government to spend a lot less money and balance the budget.
- **Intellectuals and academics:** many intellectuals from the universities wanted Roosevelt to expand the role of the government. They thought the government should regulate economic life to a far greater extent, including areas such as utilities and banking.
- **The Communist Party:** although other countries that suffered mass unemployment in the Great Depression were drawn to communism, in the USA the Communist Party remained small and isolated. Communism was regarded by the vast majority of Americans as dangerous and 'un-American'. Communist ideas did not sit well with the American tradition of 'rugged individualism' and free enterprise.

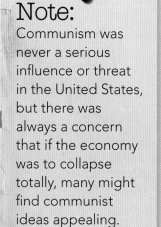

Note:
Communism was never a serious influence or threat in the United States, but there was always a concern that if the economy was to collapse totally, many might find communist ideas appealing.

Figure 5.9 Women demonstrate in Boston for the American Communist Party and better working hours

- **The Old Age Pension movement:** this movement was led by **Dr Francis Townsend**, and proposed giving all those over 60 a pension of $150 a month (later $200). The pension would be paid for by the federal government imposing a tax on the sale of all goods. This would stop those over 60 having to work, freeing up jobs for the young, and would also pump a great deal more money into the economy. The organisation he set up to promote this quickly rose to 5 million members. There was also a 20-million strong petition by the movement's supporters to Roosevelt during the course of the Second New Deal, which played a part in influencing Congress to pass the Social Security Act.

- **Father Coughlin:** Charles Coughlin was a Roman Catholic priest who had initially been a supporter of the New Deal. By 1934, however, he felt that Roosevelt was not being nearly radical enough and he became a strong critic. He founded the National Union for Social Justice in 1934, which allegedly had over 8 million members. The government could not ignore Coughlin as he had a huge following in the Northern industrial cities and the Midwest, areas vital for Roosevelt's re-election. Coughlin was a brilliant organiser, journalist and speaker on the radio. By 1936 his radio programme had an estimated weekly audience of over 30 million, and he was getting up to 80,000 letters of support every week. There was little religious content in his broadcasts, which mainly advocated a huge programme of nationalisation of major industries, wider state control of economic life and many more rights to workers. He became a bitter critic of Roosevelt, saying he should follow a programme similar to that adopted by Mussolini in Italy and Hitler in Germany. Coughlin also became very anti-Semitic. In the end, Roosevelt was able to stop Coughlin broadcasting.

- **Huey Long:** like Coughlin, Long was an early supporter of the New Deal but soon turned against Roosevelt and the New Deal for not being radical enough. He founded his 'Share our Wealth' Society in 1934, which proposed heavy taxation of the rich, old age pensions and a grant of $500 for each family, in addition to huge public works to create employment and much greater spending on education and welfare. An outstanding speaker who became a senator in 1932 and enjoyed widespread public support, Long was seen by Roosevelt as a real challenge.

The death of Huey Long removed the most serious threat to Roosevelt and the New Deal from the left. These forces were certainly an influence in keeping Roosevelt's focus on the welfare aspect of the New Deal. Perhaps more importantly, they persuaded Congress to pass the legislation and may have influenced the opinions of the Supreme Court justices.

Key figures

Dr Francis Townsend (1867–1960)

A retired doctor, Townsend was appalled by the way in which poverty affected the elderly. His attempt to get involved in politics in 1936 failed totally, but it did show the power of public opinion.

Huey Long (1893–1935)

Governor and then senator for Louisiana, Long was a powerful speaker feared for his forceful, populist tendencies. He could have been a serious threat to Roosevelt's re-selection but he was assassinated by a man named Dr. Carl Weiss in 1935.

Opposition from the right

Unlike opposition from the left, there were no clearly identifiable figures who 'led' from the right. Opponents from the right included:

- **Republicans:** as mentioned earlier, the Republican Party was not always totally hostile to the New Deal. Its more liberal elements were in favour of developments such as the TVA and wanted the government to spend more money. However, a substantial group of Republicans, led particularly by former president Hoover, were fundamentally opposed to the New Deal. Hoover argued strongly that Roosevelt was taking on 'dictatorial' powers and involving the government far too much in the management of the economy. Fortunately for Roosevelt, this group was not initially strong in Congress.
- **Democrats:** members of the Democratic Party came to Washington, DC, from all over the United States, and represented very different interests and ideas. While some came from heavily industrialised states such as Michigan, or from urban, liberal, often immigrant-dominated states such as Massachusetts, others came from deeply conservative, largely rural and often quite racist states such as Mississippi. The senators and representatives from many of the Southern states tended to be frequently re-elected, and consequently wielded great power in Congress. They were therefore in a position to either ignore Roosevelt's ideas or to join up with the more conservative Republicans and prevent much in the way of innovation after 1936 in terms of New Deal legislation.

Overall, the opposition from the right, like the opposition from the left, was often divided and encompassed very different aims and objectives. However, after 1936 this opposition became increasingly effective in stopping Roosevelt from doing what he wanted to do and not giving him the authority to carry out his wishes effectively. An unofficial 'conservative coalition' would form a serious obstacle to any further radical changes, as this group had powerful components:

- Southern Democrats in Congress
- Republicans in Congress and state governors and legislatures
- a middle class largely unaffected by the Great Depression, who were frightened of trade union power, wage rises for their employees, reduced profits, regulation, higher taxes and lower dividends, and what they saw as too much support for African-American people.

Opposition from institutions

The New Deal constituted a significant change to the role of the government, introducing regulation of, and intervention in, aspects of society that had largely been left to run according to free market and individualist principles. Institutions such as business, the press and the trade unions offered varying degrees of opposition to Roosevelt's plan:

- **Business, stockbrokers and the big banks:** inevitably, big business and the banks and those involved in the stock markets in the United States resisted and then opposed many aspects of the New Deal. They did not like the way in which Roosevelt and the many New Dealers blamed them for causing the crisis. They felt that the New Deal violated their freedoms and prevented them from making profits; in their opinion, it was anti-capitalist, hindered business and probably did a lot more harm than good. They blamed the rise in unemployment in 1937, when the economy declined, on the New Deal and they argued that it was causing a lack of business confidence and was directly responsible for stopping investment. Any organisation or person that might oppose Roosevelt – such as Alf Landon and some key senators and governors – received a great deal of financial support from this group.

The New Deal is nothing more or less than an effort sponsored by inexperienced sentimentalists and demagogues to take away from the thrifty what the thrifty and their ancestors have saved and give it to others who have not earned it … And thus indirectly destroy the incentive for all future accumulation. Such a purpose is in defiance of all the tenets (basis) on which our civiliation has been founded.

Pamphlet from the American Liberty League (founded by businessmen opposed to the New Deal), 1935.

- **Trade unions:** some trade unions were great supporters of Roosevelt and the New Deal. Others were not supportive and resented the government intervening in issues such as hours and wages, which they felt was their role. Naturally, this group did not get on well with business, so there was quite a degree of division within the opposition from institutions.
- **Press:** much of the press, both local and national, was highly supportive of Roosevelt in 1932. However, by 1935 a significant proportion of the newspapers, which were very influential in the USA at the time, began to oppose the New Deal. They accused Roosevelt and the government of taking on unprecedented powers and making decisions that were not in the best interests of the United States and its economic recovery.

Questions

1 Why was the Supreme Court able to stop New Deal measures?

2 To what extent was Congress the main obstacle to both the First and Second New Deals?

Roosevelt – a great American president?

Although praised by many for his work on the New Deal (as well as for many other aspects of his work as president, such as his leadership of the United States in its victory in the Second World War), Roosevelt also attracted criticism for his work between 1933 and 1941. Some see him as the man who saved American democracy and its people by steering the USA on a moderate path between the two extremes of unregulated capitalism on one side and fascism or communism on the other. Others argue that his work had limited economic impact, that he did more harm than good to the economy, and that getting more power for the federal government to regulate the economy and the workplace was destructive to the 'American' values of individualism, self-sufficiency and free enterprise.

The case for Roosevelt:

- He wished to bring stability and security to the American people.
- He held firm principles, but was prepared to experiment, adapt and innovate to stop the spread of the Depression and to alleviate poverty and unemployment.
- Unemployment did drop substantially, the banking system stabilised and the stock market recovered and rose steadily from 1933 onwards. The capitalist, the consumer, the worker, the employer, the pensioner, the banker and the investor all benefited from his work. Only agricultural subsidies and pensions would have long-term cost implications.
- He did not involve the government in the economy unless he had to. The SEC, for example, brought in openness, sensible reforms and cost-free regulation that would benefit all. His other regulatory reforms, such as those for civil aviation, rail transport and communication, have lasted successfully.
- He played a major part in getting trade unions accepted and supported, and did an enormous amount to ensure greater security in the workplace.
- He brought sense and more stability into the housing and mortgage market.
- He made a start in tackling the terrible problems facing US agriculture – overproduction, excessive competition and tenant farming.
- He started regulation of vital utilities such as electricity and gas supplies.
- He modernised the American system of government, providing real leadership in an era of crisis. This enabled the United States to face the serious challenges of the Second World War.

Figure 5.10 Civilian Conservation Corps workers reforesting waste land

The case against Roosevelt:

- He could be inconsistent. At times he was drawn towards those who advocated huge spending by the federal government to encourage the economy; at other times, he wanted to cut spending. Sometimes he tried to co-operate with business, at other times he attacked business leaders for their selfishness. At times he favoured planning by the state, sometimes he favoured *laissez-faire* policy and market forces.
- He failed to resolve the Great Depression. Unemployment remained high until 1941 and ultimately it was the Second World War that ended the Depression. His inconsistent policies may have done more harm than good. Many of the programmes seemed impressive at a national level, but actually had little impact at local level.
- By bringing the federal government into so many different aspects of American economic life he over-regulated and micro-managed, and actually harmed the economy, which would have naturally recovered. Government spending caused inflation, union demands bankrupted cities and companies, and above all the entrepreneurial spirit that had made America great was destroyed.
- His actions on the New Deal prevented the investment that would have really been the key factor in helping end the Great Depression. His policies of taxation and regulation distorted the market.
- He behaved unconstitutionally by acquiring more and more power for the president and by getting the federal government to take on responsibility for areas that the Founding Fathers intended states or individuals to deal with.

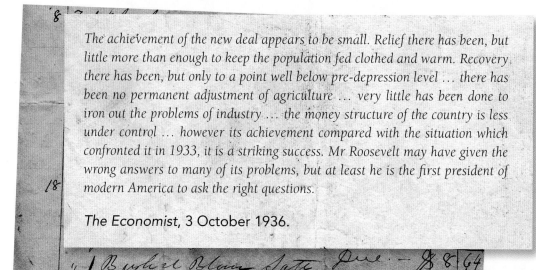

The achievement of the new deal appears to be small. Relief there has been, but little more than enough to keep the population fed clothed and warm. Recovery there has been, but only to a point well below pre-depression level … there has been no permanent adjustment of agriculture … very little has been done to iron out the problems of industry … the money structure of the country is less under control … however its achievement compared with the situation which confronted it in 1933, it is a striking success. Mr Roosevelt may have given the wrong answers to many of its problems, but at least he is the first president of modern America to ask the right questions.

The Economist, 3 October 1936.

The debate on the New Deal

There was a huge debate at the time on the merits and demerits of the New Deal. The view from Wall Street was very different from that of a dispossessed and hungry farmer and his family. In the years that followed the New Deal, conservatives attacked Roosevelt for introducing 'socialism', while liberals praised him for getting the federal government to solve the problems that Congress or the states could not. Some argue that all real economic gains made since 1945 have been the work of the government; others argue that all the crises faced since 1945 have been caused by the government.

Some later historians have said that the New Deal saved capitalism and enabled it to carry on exploiting workers and racial minorities. Others have argued that the New Deal was not a popular reform movement with great mass support, but rather a movement by the rich to save themselves and their corporations – merely a movement to buy off radicals. It is also felt by some that the Great Depression was an opportunity for radical social and economic change and that Roosevelt should be criticised for doing far too little. The debate will continue on this remarkable period in American history.

Key issues

The key features of this chapter are:

- the causes of the Great Crash and the Great Depression

- the link between the Great Crash and the Great Depression

- Herbert Hoover and the role of the US government

- the aims, objectives and impact of the First New Deal

- the aims, objectives and impact of the Second New Deal

- the nature and extent of opposition to the New Deal

- an assessment of the presidencies and legacies of Hoover and Roosevelt.

Revision questions

1 What were Roosevelt's aims for the Second New Deal?

2 'A very skilful politician, but no economist.' Discuss this view of Roosevelt in the period 1933–39.

3 Why did Roosevelt come into conflict with the Supreme Court?

4 What best explains the opposition to the New Deal?

Further reading

Adams, D. *Franklin Roosevelt and the New Deal*. London, UK. Historical Association pamphlet. 1979.

Kennedy, D. *Freedom from Fear: The American People in Depression and War 1929–45*. Oxford, UK. Oxford University Press. 2001.

Major, J. *The New Deal*. London, UK. Longman. 1968.

Sobell, R. *Herbert Hoover and the Onset of the Great Depression*. New York, USA. Lippincott. 1975.

Venn, F. *The New Deal*. Keele, UK. Keele University Press. 1998.

Chapter

6 Examination skills

Key questions

- What skills will be tested in examination, and how?
- What types of question will you meet?
- How should these questions be addressed?
- How should you prepare for examination?

Content summary

- Assessment Objectives – the skills being tested in an exam.
- The different types of question you will face.
- General tips for preparing examination answers.
- Knowledge and understanding questions and how to address them.
- Analysis and evaluation questions and how to address them.
- Primary and secondary sources.
- Different types of historical source and how to use them effectively.
- Source-based questions and how to address them.
- Revision and preparing for examination.
- General tips about examination techniques.

Introduction

In order to achieve success at AS Level History, you will need to develop skills that were, perhaps, less important in earlier examinations you may have taken. Generally, pre-AS Level examinations require you to demonstrate your knowledge and understanding of certain historical events. Now you will be required to *analyse* and *interpret* your knowledge in much greater depth.

This has implications for the way in which you study the subject. Your teacher will be able to help you by providing background knowledge, developing your historical skills and providing resources for you to work with. However, your teacher cannot tell you what to think or what opinions to have. At AS Level, you will have far more responsibility for developing your own ideas, views and judgements. To do this effectively, you need to acquire independent learning skills. In particular, this means reading as widely as possible around a topic, so that you gain access to different interpretations of the same issues and events. This will also give you an insight into the methods historians use to put across their ideas; you will be able to adapt these methods for your own use when answering examination questions.

History is not a series of universally accepted facts, which, once learned, will provide you with a detailed and accurate understanding of the past. Just as historical events were perceived in many different (and often contradictory) ways by the people who experienced them at the time, so they have been interpreted in many different (and often contradictory) ways by people who have studied them subsequently. The historical debates discussed at the end of each chapter in this book have shown that historians are not all in agreement about the reasons for, or the significance of, certain key events.

Although history deals with facts, it is equally about opinions, perceptions, judgements, interpretations and prejudices. Many of the questions you will face in examination do not have *right* answers; they are asking for your *opinion/judgement* about a certain issue. Provided you can justify it – support it by the appropriate and accurate use of evidence – your opinion is just as valid as any other. Sometimes, your friends and colleagues might disagree with your opinion and be able to provide convincing evidence to demonstrate why. Sometimes, they might convince you to change or refine your opinion. Sometimes, you will be able to convince them to change or refine theirs. Sometimes, you might just agree to differ. It is this ability to see things in different ways and to have the confidence to use your knowledge and understanding to make judgements, form opinions and develop arguments, that makes history so interesting, challenging and exciting.

What skills will be tested in examination, and how?

During a lecture delivered in the late 1960s, the historian A. J. P. Taylor said: 'History is not about answering questions; it is about knowing what questions to ask.' This may seem like a rather strange statement – not least because your own success in your history examinations will depend on your ability to answer questions effectively. However, as you will discover in this chapter, there is much truth in what Taylor said. The most impressive answers to exam questions come from students who have done more than simply acquire knowledge – they have developed the skills required to analyse information, interrogate evidence and form their own reasoned opinions. In short, they know what questions to ask.

Examination questions are not designed to 'trick' you or catch you out. On the contrary, questions are carefully designed to give you the opportunity to demonstrate how well you have mastered the required historical skills – as outlined in the Assessment Objectives.

You will be confronted with three main types of question, which are outlined below.

> ## Note:
> Assessment Objectives are lists of the historical skills on which you will be tested in examination. They can be found in an examination board's documentation for the particular course/syllabus you are following (available on the board's website).

Knowledge and understanding questions

Knowledge and understanding questions are testing your ability to:

- understand the question and its requirements
- recall and select relevant and appropriate material
- communicate your knowledge and understanding in a clear and effective manner.

> ## Key point
>
> These questions are testing *understanding* as well as *knowledge*. Remembering a relevant point is one thing; showing that you understand its significance is more important.

Analysis and evaluation questions

Analysis and evaluation questions are testing your ability to:

- understand the question and its requirements
- recall and select relevant and appropriate material
- analyse and evaluate this material in order to reach a focused, balanced and substantiated judgement
- communicate your argument in a clear and effective manner.

Key point

Your answer should contain a clear judgement/argument that is:

- focused – addresses the actual question set
- balanced – shows understanding of alternative viewpoints
- substantiated – supported by evidence.

Source-based questions

Source-based questions are testing your ability to:

- understand the question and its requirements
- comprehend source content in its historical setting
- analyse and evaluate source content
- reach a focused, balanced and substantiated judgement
- communicate your argument in a clear and effective manner.

Key point

Your answer should contain a clear judgement/argument that is:

- focused – addresses the actual question set
- balanced – shows understanding of alternative viewpoints
- substantiated – supported by evidence
- analytical – not dependent on a basic comprehension of source contents, but on a detailed evaluation of their reliability, etc.

In this chapter, we will look at some examples of each type of question, analysing the skills you will need to apply in order to answer them effectively.

Knowledge and understanding questions

These questions usually require you to explain why a particular event took place or why a particular course of action was taken. For example, you might be asked the question:

Why was the USA able to expand westwards to the Pacific Ocean in the mid 19th century?

Here are two typical responses to this question.

Response 1

Information on the USA's expansion can be found on pages 67–75.

> *There are many reasons why the USA was able to expand westwards in the middle of the 19th century. There was a rapid increase in the amount of exploration, aided by technological advancements. Unconquered lands west of the Mississippi provided the opportunity for Americans to expand and gain access to riches such as diamonds and gold. The West, as it became known, was strategically important, and improvements in the types of weapons available to Americans made it easy for them to take over western lands. Americans also needed land in the West because of their need for independence. Some Americans believed that they had a duty to bring civilisation and religion to the Native Americans of the West.*

Response 2

> *One major reason for America's ability to expand into the lands to the west of the Mississippi was the lack of serious opposition. When it became independent of Britain in 1873, the USA felt insecure. It covered only a small part of the North American continent. European colonial powers such as France and Spain to the west, as well as Britain to the north, threatened American security. All had their own interests in North America. All regarded the upstart American state with some suspicion. In addition, Native Americans, known then as Indians, were a potential threat to new American settlements.*

By the mid 19th century, the threats from the European powers had receded. There was no European state able to stop the westward expansion of the USA. France had withdrawn as early as 1803, when Napoleon sold a huge slice of North America to the USA. The British stayed in North America but from 1846 they remained north of the 49th parallel, giving the USA the freedom to expand westwards to the Pacific in Oregon. Spain had retreated in the face of opposition in Mexico. This made a newly independent Mexico a more immediate threat. The USA forced a war in 1846. Within two years it defeated Mexico. It helped itself to huge amounts of land in the south and west, including California on the coast.

The example of the US–Mexican war is significant. It shows the USA in a new, more offensive mood, aiming to assert its dominance over most of North America. A journalist of the time, John O'Sullivan, coined a phrase to justify this expansionist mood. In 1845, he wrote of America having a 'manifest destiny to overspread the continent', in order to justify the USA's right to expand westwards. And just as Mexico was handing over California to the USA in 1848, gold was discovered there. News of this discovery slowly spread. People rushed to California from the east over land and from the west by sea. This is another reason why the USA was able to expand to the Pacific: many people were keen to move westwards. 'Go West, young man' became much quoted advice from the 1860s. America had people arriving in the east from Europe in large numbers, as from Ireland following its famine in the 1840s. The relatively empty spaces in the West attracted them. Some thought of making their fortune. Others, such as the Mormons, wanted to escape persecution further east. The West became the land of opportunity. Without this steady stream of people moving in their tens and hundreds of thousands, the USA would have found it much harder to expand westwards.

New technologies also helped the USA to reach and settle in the West. Railways were of great importance. While coast-to-coast links were not completed until 1869, the expansion of the railway before then made going west easier and more rapid than it had been by stagecoach. The US economy was able to fund this all-important infrastructure.

Thus we can see that the USA was able to expand to the west coast because it had the superior resources – men, money and machines – that ensured its victory over obstacles to its expansion. Whether those obstacles were natural – the mountains and the climate, or human – resistance from others with claims to the region, the USA triumphed. Americans believed that it was right because it was the manifest destiny of the USA to do so.

Both responses contain much the same basic information. Both are based on the recall and selection of accurate, appropriate and relevant factual material (*knowledge*). However, Response 2 demonstrates a greater *understanding* of why these factors led to the westward expansion of the USA. The points it makes are fully explained and supported by evidence. It shows how various factors link together – for example, the fact that **gold was discovered** in California meant that many American people were **keen to move westwards**, and this movement was made easier by **the expansion of the railway**. On the other hand, Response 1 makes a number of rather vague and unexplained statements, which suggests that the writer does not fully understand the significance of the points made. For example:

> **Note:**
> An explicit connection is one that is fully and clearly expressed. The opposite of explicit is implicit – when a point is implied rather than fully and clearly expressed. An explicit point is easier to reward than an implicit one in an examination. Always make arguments as explicit as possible.

- 'Americans needed land in the west because of their need for independence': there is no explanation of why Americans needed independence.
- There is no explanation of how and why 'improvements in the types of weapons available to Americans made it easy for them to take over western lands'.
- No explicit connection is made between 'Some Americans believed that they had a duty to bring civilisation and religion to the Native Americans of the West' and the ability of the USA to expand westwards.

So, the key points to remember when addressing this type of question are:

- You need to read the question carefully in order to ensure that you fully understand what it requires. [*Skill: comprehension*]
- You need to be able to recall and select appropriate factual material. [*Skills: knowledge and effective revision*]
- You need to show the relevance of this factual material to the question, something that Response 1 does not always achieve (for example, by not explaining *how* technological advancements helped to cause the westward expansion of the USA. [*Skill: understanding*]
- You need to argue a case, demonstrating analysis and judgement rather than just listing reasons. Prioritise the reasons, arguing which was/were the most important and why.
- You should always prepare a brief plan before starting to write. A quick and easy way of doing this is to draw a table with two columns. Record the key points in the left column. In the right column show how each key point helps to address the question. This serves three purposes:

1 It ensures that you don't miss anything out, which is easy to do under examination pressure.
2 It ensures that you keep fully focused on the requirements of the question.
3 It ensures that you demonstrate the relevance of each point – you provide evidence for how the point helps to answer the question.

Take the question:

Why did it take the North four years to win the Civil War against the South?

A plan might look something like this:

Information on the US Civil War can be found on pages 38–53.

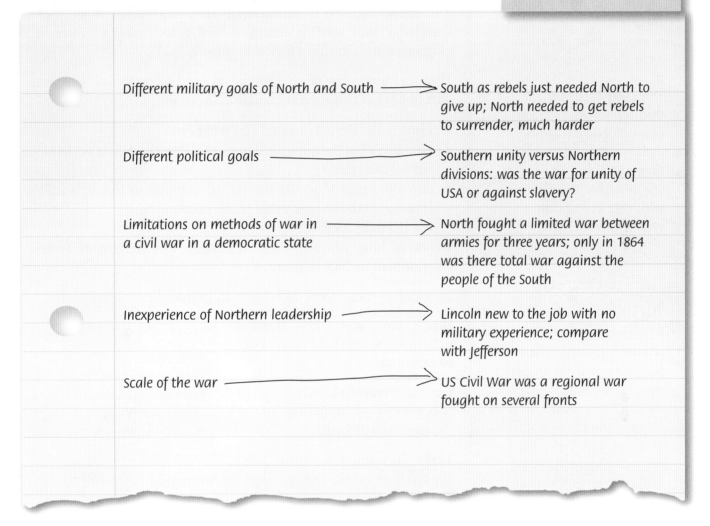

Different military goals of North and South ⟶ South as rebels just needed North to give up; North needed to get rebels to surrender, much harder

Different political goals ⟶ Southern unity versus Northern divisions: was the war for unity of USA or against slavery?

Limitations on methods of war in a civil war in a democratic state ⟶ North fought a limited war between armies for three years; only in 1864 was there total war against the people of the South

Inexperience of Northern leadership ⟶ Lincoln new to the job with no military experience; compare with Jefferson

Scale of the war ⟶ US Civil War was a regional war fought on several fronts

Your plan may not need to contain quite so much detail and can, of course, make use of abbreviations. It is entirely for your benefit – although it will be looked at, it will not be marked. One final point – do remember to *use* the plan when writing your response.

Analysis and evaluation questions

Note:

In examination, you may have at best a few minutes to carry out these tasks. You can practise them throughout your course of study, before writing initially untimed and then timed answers. The more you practise, the better your chances of doing well in examination.

Note:

Remember that the question is asking you to make a *judgement*. Many students provide evidence that could be used to support both sides of the argument. This confirms that they have a balanced understanding of the issue, but, in itself, does not answer the question. You must make sure that you do *reach a judgement* – show which side of the argument you find most convincing and why. The only exception to this rule is if you can make a valid (and substantiated) case to show why it is impossible or not advisable to make a judgement.

These questions require you to do rather more than just show your knowledge and understanding. They require you to *use* your knowledge and understanding in order to make a reasoned judgement and develop a logical argument.

There are a number of vital tasks you need to perform *before* you start to answer this type of question. These are:

- identify the factual material you will need
- establish what the question is actually asking you to do with that factual material
- develop a plan that lists the factual material so that it is fully focused on the requirements of the question
- reach a judgement
- decide how you are going to explain this judgement as an argument in your answer.

Let's look at these specifically, relating to the following question:

How far was US foreign policy between 1919 and 1939 isolationist?

Factual material: US foreign policy 1919–39; understanding of the term 'isolationist'.

Information on US foreign policy in this period can be found on pages 79–84, 88–92 and 95–98.

Task: determine, justify and explain how far US foreign policy between 1919 and 1939 can be seen as isolationist.

Plan: this enables you to brainstorm points on both sides of the argument. Remember that the plan is entirely for your benefit – it's up to you how much detail it includes and, indeed, what format it takes. An example is shown opposite.

Judgement: this type of question is asking you for an *opinion* – there is no 'right' answer and there is no preconceived idea of what a suitable judgement might be. You will not be assessed on what your judgement is but on how well you explain it and support it with valid evidence. A possible judgement might be: 'The USA was isolationist when it came to political intervention in Europe, but it was much more interventionist elsewhere when its own interests, particularly economic ones, were at stake.'

Isolationist	Not isolationist
US reaction against involvement in First World War: USA rejected Paris peace settlement; USA did not join League of Nations	American economic interests meant USA had to be involved in matters of international finance, e.g. Dawes Plan
Government in 1920s was Republican and heavily isolationist; Democrats in 1930s also isolationist because of Great Depression	USA attended Washington Conferences (1921–22) due to concerns about Japanese threats to US economic interests in Far East
US tried to avoid disputes with other countries and signing treaties – e.g. no US representation at Locarno; Kellogg–Briand Pact meaningless	USA signed Kellogg–Briand Pact in 1928
Roosevelt did not take action against aggressive states – e.g. Italy in Abyssinia, Germany in the Rhineland, Spanish Civil War	Roosevelt argued against isolationism; by 1940–41 with lend-lease and the Atlantic Charter he was leading USA out of isolationism
Roosevelt's Good Neighbor policy towards Central America and the Caribbean meant withdrawal of US troops	US involvement in Central America and the Caribbean, especially with various military occupations in the 1920s, e.g. Haiti and Honduras

Argument: there are a number of things to remember when constructing your answer:

- **Focus:** you must make sure that you address the question set. Simply demonstrating that you know a great deal about interwar American foreign policy is not enough.
- **Balance:** it is important that you demonstrate an understanding of both sides of the argument. You need to show how you have compared and weighed the evidence in order to reach your judgement. Therefore, your answer should not be based solely on the evidence that supports your conclusion.
- **Explicit:** in effect, you are aiming to convince the reader to agree with your judgement. It is crucial that your argument is communicated in a clear and obvious way.

- **Evidence:** for your argument to be convincing, it must be supported by evidence. Many examination essays contain *unsupported assertions* – these are statements/opinions for which no factual evidence is provided, and so should be avoided.
- **Consistency:** make sure that your argument remains consistent throughout. Students frequently write essays that are contradictory, the first part seemingly arguing one thing and the second part apparently arguing the exact opposite. The reason for this is that the candidate is trying to show a balanced understanding, but hasn't actually weighed the evidence and come to a judgement. Such essays often conclude with a statement such as 'So it is clear that the USA did follow an isolationist policy between 1919 and 1939.' Since no explanation has been given to justify such a statement, it is invariably an unsupported assertion.

Planning: all these points show just how important the planning stage is. Put simply, you need to know exactly what you are going to say *before* you start writing.

Note:
One of the most difficult skills to master is the ability to demonstrate an understanding of both sides of an argument without appearing to contradict yourself. Most students begin by outlining the evidence that supports their judgement and then refer to evidence that might disagree. This approach can easily undermine the strength of your argument and cause confusion to the reader. It is usually more effective to deal with the evidence that could be seen as disagreeing with your judgement first, and then explain why you find this less convincing than the evidence that supports your argument.

Below is a response to the question on page 172.

> It is clear that the USA did indeed follow a foreign policy between 1919 and 1939 that was largely isolationist. The USA rejected both the Paris peace settlement in 1919 and membership of the League of Nations in 1920. In addition, the USA avoided entering commitments with other countries and kept out of international issues such as the Japanese invasion of Manchuria in 1931. That isolationism was still the preferred policy in the late 1930s is confirmed by the fact that President Roosevelt was ignored when he argued that Japan was becoming dangerous to American interests and should be confronted.

What are the *strengths* of this answer?

- It is clearly focused on the requirements of the question.
- It contains a clear, explicit and consistent argument.
- It provides evidence to support its argument.

What are the answer's *weaknesses*?

- The major weakness is the fact that it lacks balance. It completely ignores evidence that might challenge its argument. In order to demonstrate that the essay is based on a balanced and objective judgement, it is necessary to show understanding of both sides of the argument with an explanation as to why one side is to be preferred.
- The statement that 'the USA avoided entering commitments with other countries' is an unsupported assertion. It needed evidence to back it up. For example, it could have mentioned the fact that the USA did not send a representative to the Locarno Conference.

Here is a similar type of question, although it is written in a rather different way:

Assess the main factors involved in US settlement of the West between 1840 and 1896.

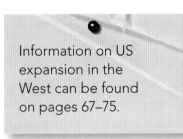

Information on US expansion in the West can be found on pages 67–75.

In this case, you are asked to (a) identify, explain and illustrate main factors in the settlement of the West and (b) assess these factors.

On the following pages is a response to the question, written with a time limit and under examination conditions. As you read through this response, bear in mind its strengths:

- It is well-organised, focused and uses relevant information to build an argument.
- It identifies main factors in the introduction and goes on to explain, illustrate and assess them in the body of the essay.
- It is analytical – it doesn't simply *describe* the relevant facts; it weighs the evidence to reach a *judgement*.
- It reaches a reasoned conclusion.

Paragraph 1
This is a promising start as four relevant factors are clearly identified. However, in terms of knowledge, it is not correct to imply that all Americans had always looked to expand westwards. Also, in terms of technique, there is no explicit link to the question.

Paragraph 2
Strengths of this paragraph include its clear identification of a relevant factor and the explanation of this factor. The final sentence shows some limits to the analysis. It can be argued that manifest destiny was not a reason for the westward expansion, but rather a justification. A really strong answer would make that distinction.

Ever since the birth of the United States, Americans had been looking to expand to fully conquer the entire North American continent. Their expansion westward was made possible by a combination of factors – national spirit, strong foreign policy, legislation, industrial investment and technological advances – that empowered Americans to settle the neighbouring West.

First and foremost, one of the truly key factors that lay behind this migration westward by many people was the concept of manifest destiny. This was a solid belief held by almost all Americans that it was their duty to conquer the North American continent. Such a goal would be accomplished only when the border of the USA touched the Pacific Ocean. American expansion was viewed as a God-given right that was to be executed by any means possible. Much, if not all, of the USA's territorial expansion would occur as a result of this belief.

It was perhaps President Polk who took the first real step to settle the West. His strong foreign policy saw the United States expand territorially by a larger amount than it had ever done so in the past. Beginning in 1846, Polk acquired the Oregon Territory from Great Britain through the use of diplomacy. However, in that same year he provoked and declared war on Mexico in order to obtain California, on the Pacific coast. This was finally won in 1848 by the Treaty of Guadalupe Hidalgo. The significance of such a huge land grab was that the USA now stretched from coast to coast, Atlantic to Pacific.

Paragraph 3
This shows a sound knowledge of the developments of 1846–48 in relation to foreign policy and US expansion. However, the paragraph is descriptive in tone and doesn't explicitly advance the assessment or argument. The only link with the previous paragraph and the impact of national spirit is the coast-to-coast reference, and there is no stated link back to the question.

Although the land might have been there, the people still were not. The West would not be settled without strong incentives to tempt people there. Therefore a series of acts was passed during this period to grant land to US citizens, opening up millions of acres of land for farmers to work. Legislation such as the Homestead Act of 1862 offered up to 160 acres of land to farmers, allowing them to either harvest it for free or to purchase it for very little. Similarly, the Desert Land Act of 1877 gave acres of land to farmers who were able to build proper irrigation on the land. Therefore people not only moved out west, they also settled there and cultivated the land in order to create long-term prospects.

Another factor that contributed to the US settlement of the West was the discovery of gold in California in 1848. Hundreds of thousands of would-be miners made their way across the country in the hope of striking it rich in California. Following the miners came those who set up shops and saloons. The consequent development of small mining towns brought women and non-miners out to the West, people that would otherwise not have come. These towns eventually gave way to large-scale mining operations in the region that set up permanently, bringing business and investments to regions that would not have otherwise been developed.

Paragraph 4
This is a very good paragraph. The Desert Land Act of 1877 is an excellent example that few students are likely to mention, and this shows use of own knowledge. The first sentence provides a neat contrasting link with the previous paragraph, and the second sentence then relates that point to the question. Two detailed examples are used to develop the point before developing it once more and making a new link to the question.

Paragraph 5
The use of 'another factor' to start the paragraph shows that the candidate is focused on the question. However, the paragraph would be better if it finished with a sentence linking the evidence provided with the question. This sentence could be something like 'Thus the discovery of gold and other valuable minerals, and the development of industry surrounding these resources, caused business and finance to play their part in the US settlement of the West.'

Paragraph 6
The answer is still focused on relevant factors. Detailed and valid examples are provided to support the explanation being provided. However, this would be a much better paragraph if the evidence was linked back to the question in a final sentence.

However, the most influential and significant factors in the settlement of the West were the technological advances of the era. These allowed people to take advantage of all the other factors mentioned. Railways, for instance, encouraged many to move out to the West, now that it took days rather than months to travel there. Farming advances such as enhanced irrigation techniques, the McCormick's reaper, the steel plough and barbed wire all allowed the new farmers in the region to work the land. Permanent farming methods would never have established themselves if not for barbed wire to protect the crops, the steel plough to plant them in the rougher ground of the western plains, the reaper to harvest them and the railways to open up more distant markets and give farmers an incentive to produce more.

Paragraph 7
The conclusion starts well, showing that a multi-causal explanation of the settlement of the West is the only valid one. It assesses the evidence and comes to a judgement about the greater importance of one particular factor – technological advances. However, the last sentence does not particularly add anything to the answer.

Ultimately, it was a combination of several principal factors that prompted Americans to move out to the West and settle the land. The technological advances of this time, however, seem to be responsible for bringing together all these factors and making the difficult process of settling the West more achievable. These technological advances were the most significant factor in that they enabled the people of the time to have such a profound effect on American history.

Overview of the response

The response is based on relevant knowledge and good understanding of factors involved in the US settlement of the West. It assesses several different factors and recognises that they are linked and strengthened by the technological advances of the time. The answer is clear, well structured and easy to follow. However, it could benefit from linking more explicitly back to the question at certain points. There are also important factors that have not been mentioned at all, such as the USA's treatment of the Native Americans who already occupied the West. The answer would be more balanced if these were included and assessed alongside the other factors. Overall, however, considering that this has been written as a response to an unseen question in a limited time, it is a good answer.

Note:
Although not included in this response, mentioning the names of historians who hold particular views about an issue can be useful – it can add weight to your argument and suggests that you are widely read. However, this technique should be used with caution. It must be done accurately. You should also not do this too often, as it could imply that you are relying on the opinions of others rather than being able to form your own opinions. Students do not have to reference specific historians, and there is a great danger that memorised quotes are used even when marginal at best, irrelevant at worst, simply because they have been memorised.

Summary

So, what are the key points to remember when answering analysis and evaluation questions?

- Don't simply provide the reader with a series of facts relating to the topic – use your knowledge to make a judgement, form an opinion and develop an argument.
- Communicate your argument in a clear and consistent manner.
- Ensure balance – demonstrate your understanding of both sides of the argument, but do so in a way that does not make your answer seem contradictory. Show, with supporting evidence, why one side of the argument is stronger than the other.
- Remain focused – ensure that each paragraph is making a point directly related to your judgement/argument. Do not drift off into irrelevance.
- Do not make unsupported assertions – ensure that any analytical point you make is backed up by factual evidence.
- Plan carefully *before* you start to write.
- Try to make your answer *flow*, for example by finding ways to link paragraphs together so that one leads logically into the next. This helps to keep the reader's interest and allows them to follow the argument you are making.

Note:
An answer 'flows' when the argument is clear and each paragraph follows in a structured way from the previous one. This makes it easier for the reader to understand and follow your line of reasoning. The reader is not suddenly confronted with something that seems to have no connection to what has gone before. The planning stage is crucial for this – you need to decide what order to put your paragraphs in and how you are going to link them together.

Source-based questions

In order to make judgements and form opinions about past events, historians need to gather as much information/evidence as possible. They use a variety of sources for this – written sources, speeches, photographs, cartoons, posters. Much of the evidence historians use is contradictory, reflecting the different opinions and perspectives of the people who produced the sources. Therefore, historians have to analyse these sources very carefully in order to form their own opinions/judgements about the past.

In much the same way, you will be faced with a variety of different historical sources in examination. You will need to be able to analyse these sources in the light of your own subject knowledge. The key word here is *analyse*. This means going beyond basic comprehension of what a source is saying or showing, and asking yourself questions about how reliable the source is and why it appears to contradict what some other sources seem to suggest.

Historical sources can be categorised under two broad headings: primary and secondary.

Primary sources

A primary source is one that was written/spoken/drawn etc. at or very near the time of the historical event it is describing. It is usually the product of someone who was directly involved in the event or who was, in some sense, an eyewitness to the event.

Advantages of a primary source include:

- It provides a first-hand, contemporary account of the event.
- It provides an insight into the author's perceptions and emotions at the time of the event.
- If the source was created by someone who was directly involved in the event, it might give detailed 'inside' information that other people could not possibly know.

Disadvantages of a primary source include:

- The source only gives us the opinions of the person who created it; these may not be typical of the opinions prevalent at the time.
- If the source was created by someone who was directly involved in the event, it might contain bias, trying to convince the audience to agree with a particular line of argument.

Note:
Primary sources reflect the customs and beliefs of the time and place from which they come. We should not be critical of the contents of a primary source just because they do not share our own values. For example, modern opinions about equal rights are very different from those that were widely accepted even 50 years ago.

Note:
Bias describes an opinion or perception that reflects the prejudices or opinions of the author. Bias can be explicit and conscious, or implicit and unconscious. Propaganda material is an example of explicit, conscious bias, whereas secondary sources, which may appear objective, can often contain implicit, unconscious bias, which expresses the writer's opinion, but is harder to spot.

- Eyewitnesses may not always be completely reliable – they might not have access to the full details of an event or they might be trying to impose their own opinions on the audience.

Secondary sources

A secondary source is one that was written/spoken/drawn etc. significantly after the historical event it describes. It is usually the product of someone who was not directly involved in the event or someone who was not an eyewitness to the event.

Advantages of secondary sources include:

- Because they were created some time after the event they are describing, they can reflect the 'full picture' – they know how the event finally concluded and the impact it had. They have the advantage of hindsight.
- Many secondary sources have been produced by historians and academics. They are often the product of extensive research, including the use of primary sources.
- If the author was not directly involved in the event, there is less potential for bias.

Note:
Hindsight is the ability to look back at an event some time after it has occurred. With hindsight, it is easier to understand the reasons why an event took place, its significance and the impact that it had. It is important to remember that people living at the time of the event did not have the advantage of hindsight.

Disadvantages of secondary sources include:

- The source gives us only the opinions of the person who created it; other people may have totally different interpretations.
- Secondary sources include biographies written years later by people who were directly involved in a particular event. This raises questions of reliability – the author's memory may not always be accurate, or he/she might want to exaggerate or downplay his/her role in an event.
- Secondary sources include accounts by eyewitnesses written years after the event. This also raises issues of reliability – was the author really an eyewitness? How accurate is the author's memory?

Note:
Do not assume that secondary sources are *less* useful than primary sources because they were not created by people who were directly involved in the event they are describing. Do not assume that secondary sources are *more* reliable than primary sources because they were created by people who were not directly involved in the event they are describing.

Assessing a source's reliability

It should be clear from all this information that historians have to be extremely careful when using sources, whether primary or secondary. They cannot afford to accept that everything a source tells them is completely reliable and true. People exaggerate. People tell lies. People have opinions that others may not share. People make mistakes.

Imagine you are out walking – lost in your own thoughts – when you suddenly hear a screeching of brakes and a thud behind you. As you turn in the direction the sound came from, you see a car drive quickly away and a pedestrian lying in the road. Your first priority, surely, would be to tend to the pedestrian, checking for injuries and calling for an ambulance or other assistance. When the police arrive, you would be classed as an 'eyewitness' to the accident, and they would want a statement from you.

But were you *really* an eyewitness? Did you actually *see* the accident or did you just *hear* it? You saw the car drive quickly away, but does that mean it was going too fast when the accident occurred? How far might your sense of pity for the pedestrian affect your idea of what actually happened? Could you be certain that the pedestrian was not to blame for the accident? Would you be able to describe the car in detail and give the police its registration number? How far would your recollection of the event be blurred by your own shock? How and why might the statements of the car driver and the pedestrian differ from your own?

So, what can we, as historians, do to minimise the risk of drawing inaccurate conclusions from sources? There are a number of questions we need to ask in order to determine just how *reliable* a source is and to evaluate its provenance. For example:

- **Who** wrote it?
- **When** was it written?
- What is the **context**?
- Who was the intended **audience**?
- **Why** was it written? What was the author's **motive**?
- **What** does it actually say?
- **How** does what it says compare with our own **subject knowledge** and with **what other sources say**?

Note:
These example questions assume that the source is a written one, but the same principle applies for all sources, whether written, spoken, drawn, photographed etc.

Suppose, for example, that this is the statement given to police later in the day by the driver of the car involved in the accident you 'witnessed':

> *I was driving along the High Street, carefully and well within the speed limit. Suddenly, and without warning, a pedestrian walked out into the road from behind a parked lorry. There was absolutely no way I could have stopped in time to avoid hitting the pedestrian. In a state of panic, I did not stop. I drove away, but later reported to the local police station.*

- **WHO wrote it?** The driver of the car involved in the accident. The driver would clearly not wish to be blamed for causing the accident and therefore might have a reason for being less than honest.
- **WHEN was it written?** Later on the same day as the accident. By this time, the driver would have recovered from the initial shock, realising that there was no option but to report to the police. There would have been time for the driver to reflect on the incident and, possibly, develop an argument to lay blame for the accident on the pedestrian. Would the driver's memory be accurate?
- **What is the CONTEXT?** The driver reporting to the police to admit involvement in the accident.
- **Who was the intended AUDIENCE?** The police, who will make the final decision regarding who was to blame for the accident.
- **WHY was it written? What was the author's MOTIVE?** It is possible that, on reflection, the driver accepted the need to report involvement in the accident. It is also possible that the driver, realising that the police would eventually catch up with them, wanted to report the incident in order to clear their own name by laying blame on the pedestrian.
- **WHAT does it actually say?** The driver argues that they were not driving carelessly and that the accident was the pedestrian's fault (for walking out into the road from behind a lorry, without checking for traffic). They admit to leaving the scene of the accident out of panic.
- **HOW does it compare with what other sources say?** To find out whether the driver was telling the truth or simply lying in order to remove blame from themselves, the police would need to compare the statement with those of other witnesses and with other evidence. Other witnesses might, for example, be able to comment on how fast the car was going at the time of the accident and whether the pedestrian really did walk out into the road without due care and attention. Your own statement does not directly contradict what the driver says, although you did hear a screeching of brakes, which might suggest the car was going too fast. The police would be able to measure the length of any skid marks in order to work out the car's speed. The police might also be able to find out if there really was a lorry parked in the road as the driver suggests.

Now let's take a more specific example. The Gettysburg Address is one of the most famous speeches of modern times, and it was reported in full in the *New York Times* of 20 November 1863.

Source A

The President then delivered the following dedicatory speech:

'Four score and seven years ago our fathers brought forth upon this continent a new nation, conceived in liberty and dedicated to the proposition that all men are created equal. [Applause] Now we are engaged in a great civil war, testing whether this nation, or any nation so conceived and dedicated, can long endure. We are met on a great battlefield of that war. We have come to dedicate a portion of that field as a final resting place for those who here gave their lives that that nation might live. It is altogether fitting and proper that we should do this. But, in a larger sense, we cannot dedicate, we cannot consecrate, we cannot hallow this ground. The brave men, living and dead, who struggled here, have consecrated it, far above our poor power to add or detract. The world will little note, nor long remember what we say here, but it can never forget what they did here. [Applause] It is for us, the living, rather to be dedicated here to the refinished work which they who fought here have thus far so nobly carried on. It is rather for us to be dedicated to the great task remaining before us – that from these honored dead we take increasing devotion to that cause for which they gave the last full measure of devotion – that we here highly resolve that these dead shall not have died in vain – that the nation shall, under God, have a new birth of freedom – and that Governments of the people, by the people, for the people shall not perish from the earth.'

Information on the Battle of Gettysburg can be found on page 42.

- **WHO spoke it?** The address was made by the president of the United States, Abraham Lincoln. It was a very short speech, just over two minutes long.
- **WHEN was it made?** On 19 November 1863, less than a year away from the presidential election of 1864.
- **What is the CONTEXT?** President Lincoln was speaking at the dedication of a national cemetery of war dead on the site of the Battle of Gettysburg fought four months earlier.
- **Who was the intended AUDIENCE?** Certainly the people at the ceremony, a crowd estimated by the *New York Times* to be 15,000. Possibly the entire American people, especially in the North, through wider dissemination e.g. by the *New York Times*.
- **WHY was it written? What was the author's MOTIVE?** To remember those soldiers who had died, to restate the ideological purpose the North was fighting for, to maintain the war effort and maybe to show the importance of Lincoln's leadership.
- **WHAT does the speech actually say?** It remembers the soldiers who died, and states that the purpose of the war is to ensure the survival of democratic government.

- **HOW does it compare with what other sources tell us?** We know from other sources that Lincoln prepared the speech with much care, suggesting that he considered it an important message. Newspaper reports of the time gave varied responses to the speech. We know from our own subject knowledge that at the time the speech was delivered, the end of the war was still a long way off. In fact, the conflict was becoming bloodier and more bitter. Lincoln used the sacrifices of the dead at Gettysburg to sustain the Northern war effort.

In this case, it is hard to assess the impact of the Gettysburg Address at the time. Since the war, the speech has become a fundamental statement of American values. Seen in the context of 1863 and the middle of a fierce conflict, it has a different significance.

'Compare and contrast' questions

In examination, you may be asked to compare and contrast two or more different sources. Again, this will require rather more than basic comprehension of the sources. Below are two sources of the type that might come up in examination.

Information on the US Civil War can be found on pages 38–53.

Source A

The natural manner of living in the Slave States helps to cover up a multitude of Southern shortcomings – tobacco-chewing, brandy-drinking and other excesses of a like character – which would otherwise without doubt render the masses of Southern people as fickle and unstable, as nervous and spasmodic as the masses of the North. God knows dissipation and debauchery are rife enough over the whole land; and our opinion is neither the North nor the South would be justified in casting the first stone at the head of the other. Such irregularities, however, are not so frequently committed by the gentlemen of the South as by a certain class of under-bred snobs, whose money enables them to pretend to the character and standing of gentlemen but whose natural inborn coarseness and vulgarity lead them to disgrace the honourable title they assume to wear.

Daniel R. Hundley, extract from Social Relations in our Southern States, *1860.*

Source B

The state of society in the South and their legislation exhibits a growing tendency to lapse back into barbarism. There are but few schools and the masses are growing up in ignorance and vice. Men resort to violence and bloodshed rather than to calm discussion and courts of justice to settle their disputes and difficulties. All classes are impatient of restraint and indulge in a reckless and lawless disregard and contempt of all institutions of society or religion which obstruct the free exercise of their passions and prejudices …
The Christian world rose up through just such a state of things to its present mild, moral, peaceable, humane Christian and enlightened standpoint. The South has already sunk three centuries back toward the age of barbarism.

An extract from an article in the Milwaukee Sentinel, *5 April 1861.*

In order to look at the similarities and differences between these two speeches, we first of all need to go through the same process of source analysis.

- **Who** wrote them? One is by a little-known Southern writer, the other an anonymous Northern journalist.
- **When** were they published? 1860 and 1861.
  - **Context?** The Southern source was published in 1860, before the Secession crisis of 1861 – when several states seceded from the USA and formed the CSA – got underway. The Northern source was published at the height of this crisis.
  - **Audience?** The readership of the book will have been the literate middle classes of the USA, while the newspaper article probably had a more local, if wider, readership.
  - **Motive?** The Southern writer gives a view of the South that emphasises its good and bad points. The Northern journalist emphasises what he believes to be the bad points of the South. Each is trying to convince the reader that his opinion is correct.
  - **What** do the authors actually say? They are giving their views on life in the Southern states of the USA.
  - **Subject knowledge?** We know that the differences between the North and South were widening at this time, especially as the North became more industrial while the South remained more agrarian. We also know that the crisis of 1860–61, after the election of Abraham Lincoln, caused people on both sides to exaggerate what they believed were the worst features of the other. Emotions were running high by the spring of 1861.

A straightforward way of comparing the views expressed in these two speeches is to devise a plan, such as the one below:

Note:
One of the most important skills that historians must have is the ability to differentiate between *fact* and *opinion*.

Note:
Emotive language is language deliberately designed to play on the emotions of the audience. Emotive techniques can also be use in non-written sources, such as posters and cartoons.

Southern source	Northern source
Argues that slavery helps cover up a number of barbaric practices	No mention of slavery
Argues degeneracy and debauchery are widespread across the USA	Does talk of barbarism in the South but makes no mention of debauched lives in North as well
Argues that debauched practices are carried out by a newly moneyed minority and not by the gentlemen of the South	No mention of any class differences in the South. In fact says all classes are barbaric
No mention of a return to barbarism; the bad behaviour of the newly moneyed suggests that the South is becoming more prosperous	Argues that the South is returning to barbarism
Uses emotive language such as 'fickle' and 'unstable' (about the North)	Uses emotive language such as 'barbarism', 'violence' and 'bloodshed'

From this plan, it is relatively easy to identify the areas over which the two authors disagree:

- The Northern source sees Southern societies as barbaric, whereas the Southern source argues such practices are confined to a small and untypical minority.
- The Southern source says that such practices can be found in both North and South, whereas the Northern source accuses only the South of such behaviour.
- The Northern source sees the North as enlightened, whereas the South refers to it as fickle and unstable.

There is no issue on which the two authors are agreed. The Southern source is more balanced in its description of American society, seeing good and bad behaviour in both North and South. The Northern source uses nothing but opinion and emotion to provide a negative view of the South.

Visual sources: posters

Visual sources should be analysed and evaluated in much the same way. Look at this McKinley campaign poster for the 1900 presidential election.

- **What** is its message? The current McKinley administration has been a success for the USA in terms of economic growth and overseas power.
- **Who** is saying it? Supporters of McKinley.
- **When?** In 1900, a presidential election year.
- **Context?** The presidential election.
- **Readership?** The poster was probably widely circulated across the USA.
- **Motives?** To gain enough support from voters to win the election.
- **Subject knowledge?** Here the detailed content of the poster needs analysing. Is the main assertion of the poster, that 'the American flag has not been planted in foreign soil to gain more territory but for humanity's sake' a valid one?

Information about the Great Depression can be found on pages 137–40.

Visual sources: photographs

You should now be familiar with the process for analysing and evaluating sources. The analysis of photographic sources, however, is slightly different from that for written sources. Look at the photograph below.

- **What** does the source tell us? It shows some shanty buildings within sight of the Capitol in Washington, DC, on fire, and a fire brigade hose trying to douse the fires. The most common website caption to this photograph reads, 'Shacks put up by the Bomus army on the Anacostia Flats burning after the battle with the military.' Another states, 'The US army, led by General Douglas MacArthur, burns the Hooverville encampment put up on the Anacostia flats in Washington, DC in 1932.' Which caption is the more accurate?
- **Who** is providing the information? In the case of photographs, the photographer is often anonymous, as is the case here. Was he – or she – a government employee or an independent photographer? Some photographs are published by newspapers. Was this one?
- **When** was the photograph taken? It must be contemporary with the event, so it dates from 1932.
- **Context?** This was a presidential election year and the destruction of Hoovervilles was controversial.
- **Audience?** This depends on whether it was published or not.
- **Motives** of the photographer? This is impossible to say. They could vary from keeping a record of the event to plans for publishing and helping his photographic career.
- **Subject knowledge?** You can search for sources on Hoovervilles and on what some call the Battle of Anacostia Flats.

Visual sources: cartoons

Cartoons can be the most difficult sources to analyse. In most cases, they are created to achieve two things:

- to amuse and entertain the audience
- to make a point and send the audience a message.

To achieve this, they use symbolism and a subtle form of humour that may have been perfectly understandable to people at the time, but which may be less obvious to us.

PUNCH, OR THE LONDON CHARIVARI.—November 2, 1861.

KING COTTON BOUND;
Or, The Modern Prometheus.

- **Who** is providing the information? The cartoonist hasn't signed this work, but the line at the top of the cartoon tells us that it was published in *Punch*. *Punch* was a well-established, humorous British magazine.
- **When** was the cartoon published? In November 1861, when the Civil War had been ongoing for about six months.
- **Context?** The British cotton industry depended heavily on imports of raw cotton from the Southern states. The South had placed an embargo on exporting cotton in the belief that Britain would have to support the South in order to ensure cotton supplies. The North had imposed a blockade to stop Southern exports.
- **What** is the message? The cartoon aims to highlight the context through symbolism, depicting King Cotton Bound as Prometheus. Prometheus is a figure in ancient Greek mythology, who was punished by the gods for giving fire to humans. His punishment was to have his liver torn out and eaten by an eagle every day for the rest of eternity; as he was immortal, his liver grew back every night.
- **Readership?** *Punch* was a liberal magazine. Its readers were likely to sympathise with liberal causes. In 1861, however, this did not necessarily mean support for the North as it was not yet fighting to emancipate the slaves of the South.
- **Motives** of the cartoonist and the editors of *Punch*? To appeal to its mainly middle-class, liberal readers.
- How far does your **subject knowledge** support or challenge the views represented in the cartoon? You might know that Britain was undecided about which side to support in the early stages of the American Civil War.

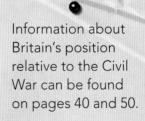

Information about Britain's position relative to the Civil War can be found on pages 40 and 50.

Cross-referencing between sources

A source should never be used in isolation. It needs to be interpreted in the light of information obtained from other sources. There are three main reasons why cross-referencing between sources is so important:

- We can only judge how useful and reliable a source is by comparing it with what we already know and what other sources say.
- Reading several sources can help us to solve mysteries or apparent contradictions.
- By using a combination of sources, we can often deduce things that none of the sources individually say.

For example, look at the three sources below. Analyse and evaluate them as indications of American public opinion on the issue of Cuba in the 1850s.

Source A

It is clear that the annexation of the island of Cuba by the United States is regarded by the great mass of people as certain. If we are to have Cuba, let us buy it because we do not need it at the cost of war. There is no overwhelming necessity for acquiring Cuba. We are rich enough, strong enough, prosperous enough without it.

From the New York Times, *7 October 1851.*

Source B

We are convinced that an immediate effort ought to be made by the government of the United States to purchase Cuba from Spain. It must be clear that, from its geographical position, Cuba is as necessary to the North American republic as any of its present members and that it belongs naturally to the United States.

From the Ostend Manifesto, 18 October 1854.
The Ostend Manifesto was written by three US ambassadors to European states.

Source C

It is said that Cuba naturally belongs to us on account of its position. After we get Cuba, this same claim can be used to acquire Jamaica, which is 90 miles from Cuba, while Cuba is 130 miles from our coast, and so on until we add all the West Indies to our possession and then, when there are no more islands to purchase or conquer, the discovery will be made that Mexico naturally belongs to us, and then when we have acquired Mexico, it will be argued that we have a natural right to all the Central American states. And last of all, Canada will be brought within the operation of this argument and after that, surely, the Russian possession of Alaska.

From a speech by representative H. Royce of Vermont in the US House of Representatives, 15 February 1859.

There is a contradiction between the information provided by Sources A and B. In Source A, the *New York Times* argues that the USA does not need to acquire Cuba. In Source B, the three authors of the Ostend Manifesto argue that it does. How can we explain this contradiction?

- The first thing to note is that Source A is a newspaper source written by journalists in a New York newspaper in 1851, whereas Source B is an official statement written three years later by three American diplomats.
- It is clear from Source C that at least one representative fears that acquiring Cuba will lead to further expansionism. This shows some sympathy with the view expressed in Source A.
- Source C is also worth noting as an example of irony, of someone saying one thing and meaning another. It could be read as Royce being in favour of the expansionism he describes. Nowhere does he explicitly oppose expansionism and yet his use of examples shows that he does oppose it.
- In assessing how representative these sources are, both individually and collectively, it is vital to evaluate each source. Source A is from a newspaper in the most prosperous of Northern cities, Source B from three politicians and Source C from the elected representative of a small Northern state. None is particularly representative.

By linking these three sources with our own subject knowledge, we can also reach another conclusion. From our own knowledge, we know that the USA neither invaded nor purchased Cuba in the 1850s. The Ostend Manifesto, a key document of the time, was initially a private government paper. It was eventually published, causing a huge political row. This supports the view that Sources A and C are more representative, and that Source B was special pleading by three unrepresentative politicians.

Addressing source-based questions: a summary

The key points you need to remember when addressing a source-based question are as follows:

Comprehension: you need to establish what the source is saying.

Reliability: don't simply accept what the source is saying. You need to test how reliable it is by:

- comparing what it says with what other sources say and with your own subject knowledge
- looking carefully at who wrote (drew/said etc.) it, when, why and for what purpose/audience
- establishing if there are any reasons to doubt the reliability of the source.

Interpretation: what can you learn from the source, taking into account your judgement about how reliable it is?

Objectivity: always look at a source objectively and with an open mind.

Do not make assumptions. For example:

- Don't assume that a source must be biased because it was written by a certain person at a certain time. These points might establish a motive for bias, but don't necessarily prove that it is biased.
- Never make unsupported assertions. A statement such as 'Source A is biased' must be accompanied by evidence/examples to demonstrate how it is biased, together with reasons to explain *why* it is biased.

Comparing sources: if you are asked to compare and/or contrast two sources, make sure that you analyse both sources before you start to write your answer. Record your findings in a simple plan.

Draw conclusions: what can you learn from your analysis of the source? How does it enhance your knowledge and understanding of a particular topic or event?

Examination technique

This section offers a few general points about how you should approach examination. Some of them might seem obvious, but it is as well to remember that, under the pressures of an examination, we are all capable of being careless. It is best to be aware of the pitfalls so that we are less likely to make costly mistakes.

Preparation

It is essential that you are fully prepared for examination. In particular, make sure you know:

- what topics the questions will be about
- what form the questions will take
- how many questions you will have to answer
- how long you will have to complete all your answers.

A valuable thing to do is to look carefully at past or sample examination papers and their mark schemes. This will give you a clear insight into the type of questions you will face and, equally importantly, how they may be marked.

Equipment

Make sure that you arrive at an examination with all the equipment you are likely to need. Always ensure that you have more than one pen. Find out exactly what you are allowed and not allowed to take into an examination room. Different centres have their own rules about this, but there are also very clear guidelines issued by examination boards.

Note:
All this information will be freely available on an examination board's website. You will be able to access sample/past exam papers, mark schemes, etc. These things are also available in hard copy.

Rubric

All examination papers contain *rubric* – this provides you with information (such as how long you have to complete an exam) and instructions (such as how many questions you need to answer). Always:

- check the title of an examination paper to ensure you have been given the right one
- check how long an exam lasts
- read *all* the instructions carefully and make sure you follow them.

Question selection

Obviously this is not an issue if you have to answer all of the questions on an examination paper. However, here is some advice if you have the opportunity to select which questions to answer:

- Read *all parts of all questions* carefully *before* making your selection.
- Don't select a question simply because it happens to be about a topic on which you feel confident; just because you know a lot about the topic, this is no guarantee that you understand the question and can answer it effectively. Select by *task* (what the question is asking you to do) rather than by *topic* (basic subject matter).
- If questions consist of more than one part, make sure that you can answer *all parts* of it. For example, do not select a two-part question if you are confident about part (a) but know nothing about (or are confused by) part (b). By doing this you would immediately be reducing the number of marks you could achieve.
- Decide the order in which you are going to address the questions. Do not leave the question you feel most confident about until last – you don't want to run out of time on your best question.
- Make sure that you number your answers correctly (you don't need to waste time writing out the whole question).

Timing

It is a good idea to work out how long you have to complete each question/part of a question. Make a note of it and make every effort to keep to this timing. What should you do if an examination is nearing its end and you realise that you are not going to complete your final answer?

- Write a comment such as 'running out of time – hence notes'.
- Describe, in note form, what you would have written if time had permitted.
- Ensure that these notes make sense and are not just a list of facts – make them relevant to the actual question.

This approach will not get you as many marks as you if you had completed your answer properly. However, you *will* get credit for them provided that they are accurate and relevant.

The best way to avoid the problem of running out of time is to ensure that you have had a great deal of practice of writing answers to examination questions under timed conditions.

Planning

Always ensure that you have planned each answer thoroughly *before* you start to write. When confronted with the time constraints of an examination, too many students assume that it is essential to start writing as quickly as possible. As a result, they are making their judgements and forming their arguments as they write – this invariably leads to confused, unbalanced or unfocused answers. Careful planning is not time wasted, it is time well spent.

Revision

It is widely assumed that the purpose of revision is to get information into your brain in preparation for examination. In fact, if you have followed the course appropriately, all the information you will need for examination is already there. The human brain, rather like a computer, never 'forgets' anything it has experienced. *The key purpose of revision, therefore, is not to put information into your brain, but to ensure that you can retrieve it again when it is required.* Revision should not be something you undertake in the last few days and hours before an examination; effective revision needs to be an ongoing process throughout the course.

How frustrating is it when you need an important document that you know is somewhere on your computer, but you can't access it because you can't remember what file name you gave it? It can take hours of tedious and unproductive searching before you locate it – but, once you do, everything you need is there. All you needed was a simple file name in order to access all the information you required. Revision needs to operate in much the same way; identifying the key points ('file names') that will bring related information flooding back into your memory. The notes you make during the course therefore need to be very carefully planned and structured.

When taking notes from a book, most students simply copy out long passages. They convince themselves that this is essential to ensure that they don't miss anything important. In fact, this is a largely pointless exercise that is invariably undertaken without concentration, comprehension, analysis or discrimination. The outcome is a mass of continuous prose that the student has not really read or understood. This causes problems when it comes to revision.

A more productive way of note-taking and revising is:

- Read a whole section of the book first without making any notes at all, ensuring that you fully understand what the author is trying to say.
- Identify and record the key points being made (just like computer *folders*).
- Under each of the key points, list the arguments/evidence the author uses to support it (like computer *files*).

Here is an example of the type of notes this method produces, using the Ostend Manifesto as a theme.

The Ostend Manifesto (1854)

Description
A document produced by three US diplomats to put forward the case for annexing Cuba.

Purpose
- The Pierce administration in Washington, DC sought ways of acquiring Cuba that would be acceptable in the USA.
- Thus these three ambassadors were asked to meet and draw up the case for annexation.

Context
- Cuban officials had seized a US ship earlier in 1854.
- The row over Kansas–Nebraska was reaching its climax.

Impact
- The Ostend Manifesto became public later in 1854 and caused a huge row as Northern Whigs opposed the extension of slavery.
- The Pierce administration greatly weakened and Pierce was not renominated for president.

Unusual points
One of the signatories of the OM, James Buchanan, became the next president of the USA.

This process takes longer and requires more thought than simply copying out long passages of a book, but it is time well spent. It will ensure that your pre-examination revision becomes far more straightforward, focused and effective.

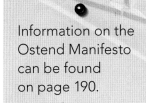

Information on the Ostend Manifesto can be found on page 190.

Practice

The more you practise writing answers, the better you will do. You should practise both writing answers in your own time and writing them against the clock.

In your own time

- Write these answers after you have studied a topic. Use your class notes and handouts and additional reading in order to answer a question taken from a past examination paper. Before you write, you might discuss possible approaches with other people.
- Take care when writing your answer. You might need to write several drafts before you are reasonably satisfied with your efforts.
- Make sure your teacher or tutor gives you detailed feedback. This is vital in ensuring you do that bit better next time, thus gradually improving the quality of your answers.

Against the clock

- There is a world of difference between writing an essay in your own time and doing so against the clock, whether in an examination room or not. Practise writing timed essays at home to get used to it before examination.
- Timed essays do not take long to write. If the first effort is not to the standard you would like, do it again.
- Make sure your school or college gives you the time to do 'mock' exams, especially when it gets close to examination day.

Index

Acknowledgements

The volume editor and publishers acknowledge the following sources of copyright material and are grateful for the permissions granted. While every effort has been made, it has not always been possible to identify the sources of all the material used, or to trace all copyright holders. If any omissions are brought to our notice we will be happy to include the appropriate acknowledgement on reprinting.

Specimen examination questions on pages 168, 171, 172 and 175 are reproduced by permission of Cambridge International Examinations.

Picture credits

Cover Granger Collection/Topfoto; p. 7 Topfoto/The Granger Collection; p. 9 Mary Evans/Illustrated London News Ltd; p. 11 Mary Evans Picture Library; p. 15 Mary Evans/Iberfoto; p. 15 Wikimedia/Library of Congress; p. 16 Wikimedia; p. 19 Mary Evans/Everett Collection; p. 21 Wikimedia; p. 21 Wikimedia/NARA; p. 22 Wikimedia/Library of Congress; p. 25 Library of Congress; p. 26 Wikimedia/Library of Congress; p. 28 Mary Evans/Everett Collection; p. 28 Wikimedia; p. 30 Library of Congress; p. 33 Wikimedia/NARA; p. 39 Mary Evans Picture Library; p. 42 Getty Images; p. 43 Topfoto/The Granger Collection; p. 45 Mary Evans/Classic Stock/H. Armstrong Roberts; p. 50 Mary Evans/Library of Congress; p. 53 Mary Evans Picture Library; p. 54 Wikimedia/Library of Congress; p. 55 Mary Evans/Everett Collection; p. 59 Mary Evans/Everett Collection; p. 62 Getty Images; p. 63 Mary Evans/Everett Collection; p. 67 Mary Evans/Epic/Tallandier; p. 71 Wikimedia; p. 75 Wikimedia/Library of Congress; p. 77 Mary Evans Picture Library; p. 79 Mary Evans/Classic Stock/C. P. Cushing; p. 82 Mary Evans/Epic/Tallandier; p. 87 Wikimedia/Library of Congress; p. 90 Wikimedia; p. 98 Getty Images; p. 101 Mary Evans/Everett Collection; p. 104 Mary Evans/Glasshouse Images; p. 105 Mary Evans/Suedeutsche Zeitung Photo; p. 107 Wikimedia/Library of Congress; p. 107 Wikimedia/Library of Congress; p. 108 Wikimedia/Library of Congress; p. 108 Mary Evans Picture Library; p. 109 Wikimedia; p. 114 Mary Evans/Everett Collection; p. 117 Wikimedia/Library of Congress/J.E Purdy 1904; p. 117 Wikimedia/Library of Congress; pp. 118–19 Mary Evans/Everett Collection; p. 119 Wikimedia/Library of Congress; p. 120 Mary Evans Picture Library/The Women's Library@ LSE; p. 120 Wikimedia/Library of Congress; p. 122 Mary Evans/Glasshouse Images; p. 125 Wikimedia/US Army Signal Corps; p. 127 Mary Evans Picture Library; p. 129 Mary Evans Picture Library/Imagno; p. 132 Mary Evans/Suedeutsche Zeitung Photo; p. 133 Corbis/Bettmann; p. 136 Mary Evans/Sueddeutsche Zeitung Photo; p. 137 Wikimedia; p. 138 Mary Evans Picture Library/Epic; p. 140 Mary Evans Picture Library; p. 142 Mary Evans Picture Library/Epic; p. 144 Mary Evans/Epic/FIA; p. 146 Mary Evans Picture Library/Imagno; p. 146 Wikimedia/NARA; p. 148 Mary Evans/ Suedeutsche Zeitung Photo; p. 156 Mary Evans/Suedeutsche Zeitung Photo; p. 157 Wikimedia/Library of Congress; p. 157 Wikimedia/Library of Congress; p. 161 Mary Evans/Glasshouse Images; p. 187 CORBIS; p. 188 Department of Defense; p. 189 Punch Limited.

Produced for Cambridge University Press by
White-Thomson Publishing
+44 (0)843 208 7460
www.wtpub.co.uk

Project editor: Alice Harman
Designer: Clare Nicholas
Illustrator: Stefan Chabluk

Author **Pete Browning** has over 40 years' teaching and examining experience. This experience has enabled him to lead training courses all over the world, on five different continents.

Author and series editor **Patrick Walsh-Atkins** has an MA and D.Phil in Modern History from Oxford University. He has taught 15- to 18-year-olds history and politics in a number of schools in the UK. He has been an A Level examiner for many years, and is also the author of a variety of textbooks for A Level students.